The Army, James II, and the Glorious Revolution

James II as painted by G. Kneller,
by courtesy of the National Portrait Gallery

JOHN CHILDS

The Army, James II, and the Glorious Revolution

MANCHESTER
UNIVERSITY PRESS

© John Childs 1980

Published by
Manchester University Press
Oxford Road, Manchester M13 9PL

British Library cataloguing in publication data

Childs, John.
    The army, James II and the Glorious Revolution.
    1. Great Britain – History – James II, 1685–1688.
    2. Great Britain – Politics and government –
    Revolution of 1688.
    3. England and Wales. Army – Political activity.
    I. Title.
    942.06'7   DA452

ISBN 0–7190–0688–0

Computerised Phototypesetting
by G.C. Typeset Ltd., Bolton, Greater Manchester

Printed in Great Britain
by
the Alden Press, Oxford

CONTENTS

		page
	Preface	vi
	Abbreviations	vii
	Note on dates, spelling and punctuation	viii
	The regiments of James II, 1685–88	ix
	Introduction	xiii
I	The growth of the army	1
II	Catholic and protestant	18
III	The great purge in Ireland	56
IV	Popularity and politics	83
V	The Anglo-Dutch Brigade	119
VI	The conspiracy in the army	138
VII	The campaign of 1688	168
VIII	Reflections	203
	Appendix A	207
	Appendix B	209
	Appendix C	211
	Index	213

PREFACE

My grateful thanks are extended to the following: the staff of the Brotherton Library, University of Leeds; Leeds City Record Office; Mr Brian Smith of the Gloucestershire County Record Office for assistance with the Blathwayt Papers; Mr Robin Gard of the Northumberland County Record Office for the laborious task of transcribing references from the Guild Book of Berwick-on-Tweed; Mr Austin Whitaker of the Hampshire County Record Office; Miss R. Phillips of Portsmouth City Record Office; Mr A. D. Hill of the Cambridgeshire County Record Office; the staff of the Archives at Churchill College, Cambridge; Mr B. C. Jones of the Cumbria Record Office; Mr P. I. King of the Northamptonshire Record Office; and the staff of the Record Office of Kingston-upon-Hull.

For the fourth time of asking, the History of Parliament Trust has allowed me to make use of their papers and unpublished biographical material relating to members of parliament between 1660 and 1688 and I must record my thanks to the new Secretary of the Trust, Mr Peter Hasler, for this continued indulgence. A grant from the research fund of the University of Leeds enabled me to finish gathering the material for this volume more expeditiously and more thoroughly than would otherwise have been the case. Finally, my greatest debt is to my wife, who not only had to cope with a husband engrossed in writing something which meant little to her but with our baby son, Michael, into the bargain.

J.C.
21 July 1979
University of Leeds

ABBREVIATIONS

Add. MSS.	Additional Manuscript
AHR	*American Historical Review*
BL	British Library
CCSP	*Calendar of Clarendon State Papers*, ed. F. J. Routledge, (Oxford, 1970), v.
CSPD	*Calendar of State Papers Domestic*
EHR	*English Historical Review*
HJ	*Historical Journal*
HMC	*Reports of the Royal Commission on Historical Manuscripts*
HPT	Unpublished research belonging to the History of Parliament Trust
JSAHR	*Journal of the Society for Army Historical Research*
NLI	National Library of Ireland
PC	Registers of the Privy Council, PRO
PRO	Public Record Office, London
RPCS	*Registers of the Privy Council of Scotland*
SO	Signet Office, Irish Letter Books, PRO
SRO	Scottish Record Office, Register House, Edinburgh
SP	State Papers, PRO
TRHS	*Transactions of the Royal Historical Society*
VCH	*Victoria County History*
WO	War Office Papers, PRO

For 'Cesca and Michael

NOTE

Dates

All dates in the text are given in the Old Style (O.S.), which, in the seventeenth century, was ten days behind the continental New Style (N.S.). As in modern usage, the new year has been taken to commence on 1 January and not on 25 March.

Spelling and punctuation

Quotations from original manuscripts or from seventeenth century printed sources which appear in the text do so with their spelling modernised. The punctuation has also been altered in some instances where the meaning of the original was not immediately apparent when it was read for the first time at normal speed.

THE REGIMENTS OF JAMES II, 1685–1688

During the later seventeenth century in England there was no consistent policy in naming regiments: some were called after their colonels, a few rejoiced in official titles, whilst a considerable number were sometimes referred to by one method and sometimes by the other. To reduce this unavoidable confusion to a minimum, the following practice has been adopted throughout the book. Each regiment has been referred to by the name of the colonel who was commanding at the time of its mention in the text. The only exceptions from this rule are those regiments, mostly designated 'Guards', who formed the royal household troops. Unfortunately, the game of 'musical colonels' was a favourite with James II and so the following table has been compiled to assist the reader in tracing and identifying regiments.

If a regiment had an official title this has been shown in capital letters. However, if the official title was rarely employed and the colonel's name used instead, then the proper title appears in capital letters after the name(s) of the relevant colonel(s). The date in brackets after a colonel's name indicates the date when that officer assumed the command of that unit.

England

Cavalry	*Raised*
LIFE GUARD, four troops	
Duke of Albemarle/Earl of Feversham (1 Aug. 1685)	1661
Duke of Northumberland	1661
Earl of Feversham/Baron Churchill (1 Aug. 1685)	1661
Baron Dover (22 May 1686)	1686
ROYAL HORSE GUARDS	
Earl of Oxford/Duke of Berwick (4 Feb. 1688)	1661
Sir John Lanier's/QUEEN'S REGIMENT OF HORSE	1685
Earl of Peterborough's	1685
Earl of Plymouth's/Sir John Fenwick (6 Nov. 1687)	1685

The regiments of James II

Lord Dover's (disbanded in 1686)	1685
Earl of Thanet's/Robert Werden (24 Oct. 1685)	1685
Earl of Arran's	1685
Earl of Shrewsbury's/Baron Langdale (22 Jan. 1687)/Richard Hamilton (15 Feb. 1687)	1685
Earl of Scarsdale's/Duke of St. Albans (1 Dec. 1687)/PRINCESS ANNE OF DENMARK'S REGIMENT OF HORSE	1685
Baron Lumley's/Sir John Talbot (29 Jan. 1687)/QUEEN DOWAGER'S REGIMENT OF HORSE	1685
Marquis de Miremont's (22 Sept. 1688)	1688
Charles, Lord Brandon's (1 Oct. 1688)	1688
Henry Slingsby's (4 Oct. 1688)	1688
George Holman's (10 Oct. 1688)	1688
Earl of Salisbury's (5 Nov. 1688)	1688

Dragoons

ROYAL DRAGOONS	1683
Baron Churchill/Lord Cornbury (1 Aug. 1685)	
QUEEN'S DRAGOONS	1685
Duke of Somerset/Alexander Cannon (2 Aug. 1687)	
John Berkeley's/PRINCESS ANNE'S REGIMENT OF DRAGOONS	1685

Infantry

FIRST FOOT GUARDS	1661
Duke of Grafton	
COLDSTREAM GUARDS	1661
Earl of Craven	
ROYAL REGIMENT OF FOOT/ROYAL SCOTS	1679
Earl of Dumbarton	
Percy Kirke's/QUEEN DOWAGER'S FOOT	1684
Sir Charles Littleton's/PRINCE GEORGE OF DENMARK'S FOOT	1664
Earl of Mulgrave's/Sir Theophilus Oglethorpe (23 Oct. 1685)/ HOLLAND REGIMENT OF FOOT	1665
Charles Trelawney's/QUEEN CONSORT'S FOOT	1684
ROYAL FUSILIERS	1685
Baron Dartmouth	
Baron Ferrers'/Duke of Berwick (1 Nov. 1688)/PRINCESS ANNE OF DENMARK'S FOOT	1685
Henry Cornwall's	1685
Earl of Bath's	1685
Duke of Beaufort's/Marquis of Worcester (26 Oct. 1685)/ Viscount Montgomery (8 May 1687)	1685
Duke of Norfolk's/Earl of Lichfield (15 June 1686)	1685
Earl of Huntingdon's	1685
Sir Edward Hales's	1685

Sir William Clifton's/Arthur Herbert (12 May 1686)/Sackville Tufton
   (12 April 1687)   1685
John Hales's (10 March 1688)   1688
Henry Gage's (27 Sept. 1688)   1688
Solomon Richards' (27 Sept. 1688)   1688
Duke of Newcastle's (29 Sept. 1688)   1688
Archibald Douglas's (9 Oct. 1688)   1688
Bevil Skelton's (9 Oct. 1688)   1688
John Carne's (13 Oct. 1688)   1688
Earl of Stafford's (8 Nov. 1688)   1688

Scotland

Cavalry
LIFE GUARD, one troop   1662
   George, Lord Livingstone
ROYAL REGIMENT OF HORSE   1662
   John Graham of Claverhouse

Dragoons
ROYAL REGIMENT OF DRAGOONS   1681
   Thomas Dalyell/Lord Charles Murray (6 Nov. 1685)

Infantry
ROYAL REGIMENT OF FOOT GUARDS   1662
   James Douglas
Earl of Mar's/Thomas Buchan (29 July 1686)   1674
John Wachop's (11 March 1688)   1688

Ireland

Because of the absence of precise records relating to commissions in Ireland during Tyrconnell's purge it is impossible to give the exact dates of the appointment of new colonels in the Irish army.

Cavalry
LIFE GUARD, one troop (disbanded in 1685)   1664
   Anthony Hungerford
Duke of Ormonde's   1672
Earl of Arran's/Earl of Tyrconnell (1685)   1672
Earl of Ossory's/Earl of Ardglass (1686)/Viscount Galmoy (1687)   1672

Dragoons
Richard Hamilton's/John Butler (1688)   1685

Infantry
REGIMENT OF FOOT GUARDS 1662
    Earl of Arran/Earl of Ossory (1686)
Duke of Ormonde's/Justin Macarty (1685) 1672
Earl of Granard's/Arthur, Lord Forbes (1686) 1672
Viscount Mountjoy's 1672
Sir Thomas Newcommen's 1672
Sir William King's/Theodore Russell (1685)/Anthony Hamilton (1687) 1672
Thomas Fairfax's/Earl of Clancarty (1688) 1672
Roger MacElligott's (12 March 1688) 1688

Anglo-Dutch Brigade

Scottish regiments
Hugh Mackay's — Before 1639
Barthold Balfour's — Before 1639
John Wachop's/George Ramsey (1688, acting colonel) — 1675

English regiments
Sir Henry Bellasise's/Philip Babbington (7 April 1688) — 1674
Thomas Monck's/Thomas Talmash (24 March 1688) — 1674
Alexander Cannon's/Earl of Pembroke (1685)/John Cutts (1688) — 1674

INTRODUCTION

Almost ten years ago the first steps were taken on the long road to the writing of a social and political history of the British standing army between 1660 and 1702. As faltering and shallow beginnings gradually matured into a worthwhile project the work took on the form of a trilogy, with one volume devoted to military affairs under Charles II, the second to the army of James II, and a third covering the reign of William of Orange and the continental wars of the 1690s. The first part appeared in 1976,[1] a rather conservative book which was more descriptive than analytical, and these modest pages represent the second stage. In scope and aim it is very different from its predecessor.

The short reign of James II and the Glorious Revolution have been the subject of numerous modern studies covering the characters of James and William, domestic policies and politics, religion, the role of the Royal Navy in 1688, and the interaction between the planned Dutch invasion and the complicated structure of international relations in Europe. However, apart from the now aged and yellowing leaves of Clifford Walton's *History of the British Standing Army, 1660–1700*, and the always entertaining and elegant, although frequently inaccurate, multi-volume *History of the British Army* by Sir John Fortescue, historical scholarship has only ventured on to the fringes of the military issues in the British Isles between 1685 and 1688. John Carswell in *The Descent on England* has greatly increased our knowledge and understanding of the Dutch military and political role in the downfall of King James, and similar coverage of the British army now seems to be necessary.

A reader who expects a detailed administrative and regimental history of the British army in the relevant three years will be disappointed in the contents of this book. The first section of the trilogy dealt at length with the organisation of the army, its pay, uniform, pensions, staff, tactics and equipment, and as these aspects did not substantially alter under James II they have been omitted.[2] Significant changes in the structure of the British armed forces did not occur until they were forced into existence by the pressures of prolonged foreign war in the last decade of the seventeenth century, a subject which will form the core of the final volume of the trilogy. Similarly, another topic has been left from this work: the joint rebellions of Monmouth and Argyll. So much has been written on these pathetic incursions that yet another repetition of the tragic gavottes around Somerset and the western isles would have proved tiresome, beyond the main themes of this particular survey, and a grievous waste of paper and printer's ink in an age of ever-rising costs. Perhaps, if new evidence about these revolts had come to light, then a different case could have been made but that, alas, has not occurred.

With what, the reader might now legitimately ask, is this small book concerned? Very often a frontal assault fails where an indirect manoeuvre might succeed. Straightforward studies of the personality of James II and the politics of his reign have failed to provide a clear impression of the aims of his monarchy. This book is very much an 'indirect approach' to the kingship of James II, an oblique view from a different angle and through another lens. Controversy about the precise objectives of James II's government is still current – religious toleration for its own sake, some degree of royal absolutism, or a confused amalgam of the two – but as the one major executive instrument at the king's disposal in all three kingdoms was the army it makes logical sense to attempt to discern his political direction by investigating the army, its personnel, and the rôle that it was expected to fulfil. The conceited wish to assist this general debate by employing the new evidence which has been derived from a study of the history of the army between 1685 and 1688 forms the first purpose of this work. In the second place, the Glorious Revolution was achieved following a confrontation between two armies and it belongs as much to military history as it does to political history.[3] William of Orange's virtually bloodless victory was the result of a military campaign, and contemporaries were fully aware that the Dutchman's 'right' to the throne rested upon naked conquest as much as it relied upon his marriage to Mary Stuart and the attitude of parliament.[4] The second preoccupation of this book is accordingly the martial competence and efficiency of James's army and the vital question of its loyalty to the monarch. Last, but by no means least, this is a study of the army and it attempts to provide some illumination upon a hitherto neglected period of British military history.

In pursuit of these aims, much emphasis has been placed upon an almost 'Namierite' historical method – the employment of biographies, as detailed as possible, of 1,250 officers who served in England, Ireland, Scotland, and the Anglo-Dutch Brigade between 1685 and 1688. Through the use of these biographies to ascertain who served in the army and why, how the officer corps changed during the reign, the wealth and social status of the officers, and the course of their careers after the Revolution, a great deal of 'hidden' information has emerged about the allegiance of the officers and the political function of the armed forces. This book is largely devoted to the officers of James II's army, and the reign is seen through their eyes and coloured by their prejudices. A considerable amount of the information available on army officers comes from the tables compiled by Charles Dalton,[5] whose six volumes have received some criticism and have been accused of inaccuracy.[6] Certainly the last four volumes are incomplete and little more than sketches of the extant information about military commissions, but the first two, which cover the period from 1660 to 1688, are in a different category. Whilst, like everything else, they are imperfect, Dalton used all the known official sources that contained records of army commissions and many private papers as well. His commission lists for the reigns of Charles II and James are excellent guides and as nearly complete as it is possible for them to be. Whenever the author has had occasion to check information presented by Dalton in his first two volumes the results have nearly always been most reassuring. Volumes one and two of the commission registers are generally accurate and reliable; any historian with the energy and ambition to improve upon Dalton's labours would probably be dead before he or she could achieve a noticeable revision or improvement. Although the records of military careers inevitably rest on much more than one book, without Dalton's essential groundwork the biographical method which has been adopted in this study would not have been possible.

The standing army of Restoration England was the king's force. Charles II and his brother were able to raise troops as and when they were required and, within reason, they could employ them for whatever purposes they wished. Apart from the vital issue of finance, parliament proved unable to exercise any effective restraint over the sovereign's right to maintain a regular army. By the terms of the Militia Act of 1661, Charles II was given the legal right to command 'all forces by land and sea and all forts and places of strength' – references to the militia, the garrisons of vital strongholds, and soldiers who might be recruited for a foreign war – but no mention was made of a standing army in time of peace. In fact, between 1661 and 1688 parliament gave the army no specific status. The Lords and Commons accepted that armies were necessary for national defence in wartime, and no serious objections were offered when Charles founded a small army in 1661, as England was still politically unstable and the security of the restored monarchy was far from assured. Thereafter, parliament unofficially recognised the new army by mentioning it in debate and pronouncing against its abuses but it did not pass any legislation which declared it to be either legal or illegal. Technically, the peacetime army did not exist in common or statute law. Under Charles and James it occupied an extra-constitutional position and can be regarded as a department of the royal household totally under the authority and patronage of the king and his nominees. Armed with an extra-legal army which relied solely upon the royal prerogative, Charles II enjoyed a free hand in the employment of his soldiers. Fortunately, he generally used his army in the pursuit of national interests: fighting in the colonies and against the Dutch, intervening in riots, patrolling the highways, and supporting the civil magistrates. However, as the army was a loyal instrument of the sovereign it could be employed to execute the king's personal policy and to bolster his position against the more extreme demands of parliament. In this way Charles loaned a number of his regiments to Louis XIV between 1674 and 1678 against the entreaties of the Commons and was able to reserve the army as his ultimate political weapon during the Exclusion Crisis and the Oxford Parliament of 1681.[7]

Although the army was basically apolitical it was very much the king's force and was bound to be employed according to royal rather than parliamentary policies. This emphasis remained uncorrected until the Mutiny Act of 1689 gave parliament control over military discipline and the huge cost of the War of the Grand Alliance ensured that parliament assumed the dominant interest in England's national finances. Apart from the restrictions which were imposed upon him by his perpetual shortage of money, Charles II was his own master in military affairs. Provided that he could raise sufficient cash for their pay and upkeep, Charles could recruit troops when he chose and employ them as he wished. On three occasions during the reign – for the Dutch wars in 1665–7 and 1672–4 and for the projected French war in 1678 – he augmented his army, causing parliament to express fears about the possibility of the king using it to overthrow the constitution and establish an arbitrary government with the support of the military. These worries proved baseless, as Charles always disbanded his additional soldiers and showed no real inclination for adopting so strenuous a form of government as royal absolutism. Even if he had harboured designs of using his increased army in a political fashion, parliament's power over the purse prevented him from being able to retain any of his extra troops after the termination of each war. With the disbandment of these soldiers, Charles was reduced to depending on the core of 6,000 'guards and garrisons' which formed his peacetime army and this, although irritating, was not sufficiently large or threatening to disturb parliament's sense of security. Even during the Exclusion Crisis Charles was financially unable to raise any additional soldiers to protect either himself or his brother. As a result, no legislation concerning the legality of the standing army reached the statute book between 1660 and 1685. There was no necessity for such radical action, as parliament could always emasculate any plans to enlarge the army by refusing to vote additional revenues. Then, in the spring and summer of 1685, by its extravagant grants of income to the new monarch, the tame and inexperienced parliament of 1685 threw away this enormous and decisive advantage. Not only did the 1685 parliament enable James to maintain a large army in peacetime but it also allowed him enough money to avoid having to call frequent sessions. James was in the happy position of being able to increase his armed forces without the prying eyes of the Commons watching his every move. If he did wish to centralise and extend the royal power by using the standing army as both a buttress to the regime and an executive machine, an opportunity for such a policy existed after the summer of 1685, for parliament had destroyed its one effective defence and virtually invited the attacker to enter the citadel.

Notes

1 John Childs, *The Army of Charles II* (London and Toronto, 1976).
2 *Ibid.*, pp. 21–111; John Childs, 'Monmouth and the Army in Flanders', *JSAHR*, lii. (1974), pp. 3–12.
3 Correlli Barnett, *Britain and her Army, 1509–1970* (London, 1970), pp. 121–2.
4 Mark Goldie, 'Edmund Bohun and the *Jus Gentium* in the Revolution Debate, 1689–1693', *HJ*, xx. (1977), pp. 585–6.
5 Charles Dalton, *English Army Lists and Commission Registers, 1661–1714* (London, 1892–1904, reprinted, London, 1960), i–vi.
6 David Allen, in *History*, lxii. (1977), p. 123.
7 C. T. Atkinson, 'Charles II's Regiments in France, 1672–1678', *JSAHR*, xxiv. (1946), pp. 53–65, 129–36 and 161–72; Ruth Clark, *Anthony Hamilton* (London, 1921), pp. 42–71; John Childs, 'The army and the Oxford parliament of 1681', *EHR*, xciv. (1979), pp. 580–7.

I
The growth of the army

Charles II died on 6 February 1685. Despite the political turmoil of the Exclusion Crisis and the subsequent Rye House Plot, his roman catholic brother, James, Duke of York, succeeded to the throne without any serious suggestion of disaffection. During the last week of the old king's life, as the effects of the first stroke became more pronounced, certain precautions were taken to guarantee the peaceful accession of James. The militia in England and Wales was alerted to prevent 'all disorders that may happen' and the regular troops in London and York were held in readiness to suppress any dangerous political demonstrations before or after the announcement of the new sovereign. The principal secretary of state, the Earl of Sunderland, gave orders that incoming passengers at English ports were to be searched and all 'suspected persons' to be arrested. These steps proved unnecessary. On the day following his brother's death, James II issued a proclamation instructing all office-holders to continue in their appointments, a directive which garrison governors were asked to read before their assembled commands. The soldiers then recognised the new monarch by firing volleys of small shot and saluted him with their cannon. The legitimate succession had been peacefully and successfully accomplished.[1]

James II inherited a very modest military establishment. The English army numbered 8,865 men in February 1685, of whom 7,472 were available for service in mobile marching regiments, with the remaining 1,393 being permanently attached to various garrisons.[2] Separate armies existed in Ireland and Scotland but as all three military establishments owed allegiance to the same king there was ample provision for the exchange of personnel and formations between them as occasions demanded. The Irish army possessed 7,500 soldiers in 1685, whilst Scotland could boast of just 2,199.[3] These three national armies were pathetically small for the duties that were demanded of them. As well as the essential military function of securing the country against a foreign invasion, the late seventeenth century army was also responsible for riot control in both the town and the countryside, manning the garrisons and strong-points, providing marines to serve with the fleet, and for executing numerous ceremonial duties connected with the king and the court.[4] When these Lilliputian formations were suddenly faced with the combined threat of the invasions of Argyll and Monmouth in May and June 1685 not only did they have to be rapidly augmented but, in addition, the six regiments of the Anglo-Dutch Brigade had to be summoned from the United Provinces.[5]

At the conclusion of the fighting against the Duke of Monmouth at Sedgemoor on 5–6 July 1685 James possessed a total of 15,710 men in arms in England, and by 31 December 1685 this figure had risen to 19,778.[6] There was nothing remarkable in this continuing increase after the defeat of the Protestant Duke. The campaign against Monmouth was over within four weeks, so that most of the new regiments had not been completed by the time of the Battle of Sedgemoor. It is significant that the king did not order the immediate disbandment of these new troops after his victory but, he argued, given the impotence of the English army before Monmouth had landed at Lyme Regis, the maintenance of some extra military security for England was not an imprudent policy. Until the threat of the Dutch invasion in the later months of 1688 the English establishment hardly altered. A grand total of 242 private gentlemen were added to the three troops of the Life Guard during July 1686 and three staff officers joined the First Foot Guards and the Royal Scots. In the same year James's well known philanthropy caused him to form a fourth troop of the Life Guard composed of roman catholics 'out of charity towards poor country gentlemen of that persuasion charged with children and not able to put them into the world'.[7] This, however, did not result in an increase in the size of the army, as Lord Dover's regiment of horse was disbanded to provide the necessary equipment and funds for the new unit. In relation to the overall size of the English army these augmentations were trifling. Some of the English exiles in the United Provinces reported that James was planning to raise 4,000 new troops in England and to bring over an equal number from Ireland, but these were no more than wild and unfounded rumours.[8] The most that James intended was the formation of a corps of 400 'Musketeers du Roi', a potentially élite band composed of young men of 'unspotted reputation' whose sole duty would have been to attend the royal person.[9] Nothing came of this attempt to imitate the French household troops.

Not until March 1688 was the English army noticeably increased. Following the partially successful recall of the Anglo-Dutch Brigade on 14 March 1688, three new regiments of infantry were formed from those officers and men who obeyed the order to return to England. Each regiment consisted of 700 soldiers, and one was placed on each of the three national establishments: Colonel John Hales commanded the regiment which was added to the English army; Colonel John Wachop headed the regiment sent to Scotland; and Roger MacElligott took his unit to Ireland.[10] Only in late September 1688, when the danger of a naval war against the Dutch had developed into the threat of an actual invasion, was the English army again augmented. Between 22 September and 8 November James added ten men to every troop and company and ordered the creation of five new regiments of horse and seven new corps of foot.[11] This expansion was intended to add a further 12,748 soldiers to the English army. Whether this rapid reinforcement of the English establishment was effectively completed by the time of William's landing at Torbay is open to serious doubt. Early in October the English armed forces numbered 22,364 men, but 'An Abstract of the numbers of all his Majesty's Forces in England' strongly suggests that by the end of the same month all the new units were in being, giving James's English army a paper strength of 34,320. Theoretically this figure was probably correct, but it is most unlikely that it represented the real effective number of English soldiers available to James by the beginning of November.[12] Contemporary estimates considered that a full two months were required to drill, train, clothe, and equip a raw recruit. By this criterion none of the new regiments could have been ready for action by 5 November 1688, and the evidence bears out this conclusion. As late as 27 November, Henry Gage's new regiment of foot possessed no arms, and Colonel John Carne of Ewenny in South Wales was given instructions to stop the recruitment of his regiment soon after Wiliam of Orange's landing, an indication that this corps was not very far advanced either in filling its ranks or in its basic training.[13]

These discrepancies between numbers on paper and effective soldiers in the field make any accurate assessment of James II's actual military might in November 1688 very difficult, but it is possible to offer a rough guide as to how many trained soldiers he had with whom to face his disloyal nephew across windswept Salisbury Plain. On 23 November 1688, the day on which James decided to retreat from Salisbury, his English troops numbered 31,000. Between 4,000 and 5,000 of these men were stationed in various garrisons, leaving the king with about 25,000 soldiers available for duty in the field, with a further 5,000 finishing their training with the new regiments. As James left two infantry corps in London while he concentrated at Salisbury, his actual English field army probably amounted to around 24,000 foot, horse and dragoons.[14] The men of the new regiments were of limited military value to the mobile army, but they were able to relieve more experienced formations from routine garrison duties and thus enable them to deploy in the field; Henry Gage's foot fulfilled this function in Chester. James was able to increase his field army of 24,000 by summoning troops from Ireland and Scotland to join him in the campaign against the Dutch.[15] One regiment of dragoons, one battalion of the Irish Foot Guards, and two regiments of line infantry, a total of 2,820 men, sailed across to Chester from Ireland in September 1688 whilst the whole of the Scottish army of 2,946 soldiers marched south.[16] When James issued the orders for his army to rendezvous upon Salisbury Plain he was able to count on the services of between 29,000 and 30,000 trained soldiers in his field army, some 5,000 in garrison, and another 5,000 readying themselves for service.

Until the addition of John Wachop's 700 infantry in March 1688 the size of the Scottish army had remained constant since 1685. By November 1688 Scotland possessed nearly 3,000 men in marching regiments, with a further 268 elderly veterans or invalids enjoying sinecures in the garrisons at Edinburgh, Stirling, Dumbarton, Blackness Castle, and the dreaded Bass Rock. The entirety of this small force marched into England in October 1688, leaving only the decrepit garrison troops north of the border. This tiny army cost the Scottish treasury £80,000 per annum.[17] Likewise, there was little numerical addition to the Irish army during James's brief reign. A new regiment of dragoons under Colonel Richard Hamilton was raised in June and July 1685 to assist in the reduction of the joint rebellions of Argyll and Monmouth, and this brought the Irish army up to a strength of 8,238 men. Until Roger MacElligott's 700 soldiers joined the Irish establishment in March 1688 the numbers did not alter, although the personnel of the military establishment in Ireland underwent a drastic transformation. In November 1688 the Irish army of 8,938 men was at an annual charge to the crown of £161,590 13s 11d.[18]

Leaving aside the expansion in September and October, which was a direct response to the threat of war, the armies in England, Ireland, and Scotland were not large in comparison with other European peacetime formations. In proportion to her population, which was between five and six million by 1690, England's army was of an average size when judged by the contemporary standards of the late seventeenth century, and even with the addition of the Irish and Scottish establishments it was not regarded as a formidable weapon. The combined kingdom of Denmark and Norway boasted a standing army of 32,000 men in 1690, sufficient to make Denmark resemble 'a monster that is all head and no body, all soldiers and no subjects'.[19] Hesse-Cassel, not one of the largest states in the Holy Roman Empire, possessed an armed force in excess of 10,000 men by 1688, whilst the French army in the 1680s amounted to 100,000 regular soldiers.[20] Apart from the natural reaction to the Dutch build-up in the autumn of 1688, James made no attempt to expand his army after January 1686. Not being an absolute monarch after the manner of Louis XIV of France, Christian V of Denmark, or Landgrave Charles of Hesse-Cassel, his financial resources were finite and this imposed an adequate check upon any military ambitions he might have nurtured.

At the time of the death of Charles II the English military establishment cost £283,000 per annum, a sum which included the pay of all the officers and men, pensions, half-pay, the running of the secretary-at-war's office, the provision of 'fire and candle' for the numerous garrisons, and 'the contingencies'. Arms, ammunition, artillery, tents, and field equipment were provided by the Board of Ordnance and were financed from its own establishments. The additional forces which were raised to deal with Monmouth's Rebellion increased this annual charge to £620,322 17s. 11d. with effect from 1 January 1686. If all the troops which were raised in the autumn of 1688 had remained on foot for a full twelve months, then the whole of the English establishment would have cost the king £900,252 a year, but as the new regiments were in existence for no more than three months the actual cost to the Treasury was substantially lower.[21] Professor Chandaman estimates that, after the first session of the parliament of 1685, James II enjoyed a net disposable annual income of some £1,670,000, a sum which enabled him to maintain his increased army without any hint of fiscal embarrassment. This is an overstatement of the true condition of the royal finances. Clearly, it would have been impossible for James to have supported the number of soldiers which he had raised by the end of October 1688 for any length of time without recourse to a parliament for an extraordinary supply, but there are several indications that even the maintenance of the average peacetime army of approximately 20,000 men caused some strain.[22] The question of the recall of the Anglo-Dutch Brigade in 1688 revolved around whether Louis XIV could be persuaded into paying for them to reside either in France or England, and when those officers and men who did return were formed into three new regiments of infantry the formations were divided between the English, Irish, and Scottish establishments to spread the financial load.[23] Anthony Wood relates how, in June 1686,

any dissenter from the Church of England might now, for money, have a licence to frequent conventicles or a protection from the king to secure him from all oaths' injury – to supply the army .... No French protestant or outlander can trade in England unless he gives so much yearly to the crown for trading – to supply the army.[24]

This was probably no more than malicious gossip of the sort Wood so adored but there was possibly some truth in the allegations. More indicative of the real weight of the cost of the English army was the fact that James began to draw money from the Irish revenues from the very beginning of his reign to help defray this charge. On 10 February 1685 he wrote to the Duke of Ormonde, the lord lieutenant of Ireland, instructing him to transfer £30,000 from the Irish to the English Treasury to assist in the upkeep of the English army, an arrangement which was repeated every year until the Revolution.[25] Initially this scheme was probably an expedient to tide James over the difficult period before his parliament met to settle his ordinary revenue but its extension until 1688 demonstrates the growing financial burden which was created by the English soldiery.

Despite the cost, the invasions of Argyll and Monmouth had shown that an enlarged army was not a luxury but almost a necessity. Such a realistic view was enhanced by the supposedly disappointing performance of the West Country trained bands in the summer of 1685. The major criticism levelled against the amateur soldiers was that they proved unable to face Monmouth's irregulars in battle, but away from the main theatre of war the militia provided useful service. They helped to confine the contagion of Monmouth's Rebellion by arresting his known supporters, interfering with his supplies of arms and recruits, and generally harassing the flanks of his advance. In other parts of the country the trained bands had also undertaken vital tasks with some efficiency. County regiments had done their best 'to apprehend all disaffected and suspicious persons and particularly all nonconformist ministers', as the unfortunate Philip Henry, who was remanded in custody for three weeks in Chester Castle, could testify. After the 'triumph' of Sedgemoor the Norfolk militia was ordered to 'prevent the escape of such of the rebels as are not yet taken . . . and take all possible care by placing guards and otherwise for apprehending and securing all persons whatsoever who shall be found travelling up and down and are not very well known'. On 25 June 1685 four companies of the Norfolk militia took over the routine duty of garrisoning Great Yarmouth, thereby releasing four regular companies of the Royal Scots for service in the field.[26] All these functions were complementary to the work of the standing army, and the militia was indispensable when the army was too weak to fight an invader and simultaneously guarantee internal security. Once the emergency of the summer of 1685 was over, the militia was reassessed in the light of James's personal prejudices and potential policies. He found the trained bands to be inefficient, ill-trained, appallingly equipped and armed, often indifferently commanded, and very expensive. The militia was also inflexible and immobile—at the most it could take the field for one month in every year—and during the western campaign county militias had shown an alarming reluctance to march beyond the boundaries of their own shire. In addition to this catalogue of shortcomings, there had been instances during 1685 when the militias of the western counties had not demonstrated a total loyalty to James II.[27] Much of this criticism was justified but there is the impression that James was determined to 'reform' the militia in any event, as it did not fit in with his plans for domestic government. The failings which became apparent in 1685 merely provided him with a plausible excuse for taking the necessary action. Although the Restoration Militia Acts had placed the provincial forces firmly under the control and direction of the king they were officered and commanded by local gentry and aristocracy. Such a force, composed of members of the local community and commanded by their natural social and political leaders, was not ideal for repression or even for executing the more robust duties of a police force. To James, the militia could not be relied upon either to protect the country against invasion or to assist the central government in the exercise of its authority; it was thoroughly untrustworthy.[28] After the insecurity which had dogged him throughout his life the strengthening of the power of the monarchy was a subject close to his heart, and he could see neither the reason nor the point in continuing to rely on an antiquated system of part-time amateurs when he could afford to depend upon a professional army which would obey him.

With a view to replacing the militia by the standing army, James emphasised the manifest ills of the trained bands. He wrote to the Prince of Orange that the Earl of Pembroke and some militia companies had been forced to quarter in a village behind Sedgemoor, as they had 'no tents to camp with'.[29] The Earl of Ailesbury thought that the militia's 'hearts and inclinations were certainly good, else I lay little stress upon any but regular and well disciplined troops'.[30] If James had been able to read a letter from one John Martin to the Reverend William Moore he might well have been tempted to have its contents published as excellent propaganda.

Immediately after I sent away my last to you we received certain information that the Duke of Monmouth's being at Lyme and presently after that a warrant for our foot soldiers to be that night at Devizes but, I believe, never did such confusion and disorder appear. First the locks being almost eat to pieces with rust. After this there was never a bullet mould to be had neither here nor at Market Lavington and if we had not thought of Laman by chance that possibly he might have one to make bullets for some of his guns, we must needs have sent them away without ammunition. When they were forced by the constable to go in out of town they cried some of them like children going to be whipped. Never, I think, were such fainthearted cowards seen, for they now thought they were leaving their beloved bacon and cale [sic] and were going on to certain destruction. Neither, I think, were some of their commanders more valiant, for Mr. Noys, the lieutenant of our company, appeared amongst them with a white cap and a sad countenance, being taken extremely ill on a sudden. Tis said the king is sending some forces against them and I hope tis true for if I may guess at other militia men by ours 3 valiant rebels may beat 3 score of them.[31]

This image of almost comic inefficiency brought forth some pungent lines from John Dryden:

> The country rings around with loud alarms,
> And raw in fields the rude militia swarms;
> Mouths without hands; maintained at vast expense,
> In peace a charge, in war a weak defence;
> Stout once a month they march, a blustering band,
> And ever, but in times of need, at hand.
> This was the morn when, issuing on the guard,

> Drawn up in rank and file they stood prepared
> Of seeming arms to make a short essay,
> Then hasten to be drunk, the business of the day.[32]

James did not absolutely replace the militia with the standing army but he offered the trained bands no encouragement and ignored them whenever possible, preferring to employ the regular soldiers in local, police duties. For most of each year the engorged army of James II was quartered throughout England except for a brief period during the summer when just over half the regiments assembled on Hounslow Heath for the annual training camp. Whereas the army of Charles II had been concentrated in quarters in London, the Home Counties, and the principal strongholds of Hull, Carlisle, Chester, Plymouth, Berwick, Portsmouth, and York,[33] his brother's troops were spread across England as evenly as possible, leaving few towns and villages far removed from a troop or company of the standing army.[34] In 1686 William Blathwayt, the secretary-at-war, compiled a manuscript volume which recorded 'all the Inns, Ale-Houses, etc., in England with their Stable-Room and Bedding', enabling the War Office to tell at a glance how many soldiers could be accommodated in each town or large village in England and Wales.[35] As a consequence of the variety of quarters and the improved administrative methods the army became more mobile and more flexible, as it had to be if it was successfully to supercede the militia as the provincial police. Although it was not until the middle of the eighteenth century that riot control became the principal occupation of the English army in peacetime,[36] the reign of James II with its wider distribution of troops and the use of the army in place of the militia witnessed the beginnings of the change in rôle. So effective was this policy that, in many parts of the country, the militia was virtually non-existent by 1688. In Staffordshire there was no formed militia, whilst the Lincolnshire trained bands were 'in great disorder by the removal of the chief gentry out of the commission' and they had mustered just once since the coronation.[37] Sir John Bramston informed the Earl of Oxford, the restored lord lieutenant of Essex, on 19 October 1688 that the Essex militia was 'very much out of order, the officers dead or unwilling to act'.

There were some exceptions to this general atrophy. The regiments of Dorset and Norfolk were able to respond to the emergency of November 1688, whilst the Gloucestershire cavalry were sufficiently strong and resolute to engage Lord Lovelace and seventy of his henchmen as they rode through Cirencester towards William's camp at Exeter. The most notable example of a militia which survived James's depredations unscathed was that which belonged to the City of London. The City trained bands had a tradition of military efficiency which put their provincial cousins to shame. At full strength they numbered between 18,000 and 20,000 soldiers who mustered and drilled regularly and their professional edge was constantly whetted by the necessity of having to contain the numerous riots and affrays for which London was justly famous. The City militia had proved its loyalty to the crown during the Exclusion Crisis and this, in conjunction with its undoubted military efficacy, made it as indispensable to James II as it had been to his brother. Even if James had wished to substitute his own army for the London militia, he simply did not possess enough troops for the task of undertaking the routine policing of the largest concentration of population in western Europe. Soldiers were permanently stationed on the fringes of the City to assist in dealing with any exceptional emergencies – in the Tower of London, the Savoy, and Southwark – but their intervention was sporadic and technically dependent upon the request of the City magistrates.[38] That London thus partially thwarted James's attempt to extend royal control through the medium of the army should not be seen as a failure of the royal policy. Louis XIV, with his immensely superior resources in money and troops, could not control Paris but was happy to leave the maintenance of Parisian law and order to a municipal police force and himself chose to live beyond its boundaries. A reform of the country trained bands would have been costly and could not have fulfilled the king's principal purpose: to enforce law and order and the decisions of central government more effectively. The purge of the lords lieutenant, deputy lieutenants, and the commissions of the peace during 1687 and 1688 might have rendered the militia more pliant to his overall aims, but the new order was not in existence long enough to be adequately tested.

Although Charles II had considerably increased his army on three occasions between 1660 and 1685, each expansion had been for the specific purpose of a foreign war.[39] At the termination of each war the additional forces had always been disbanded, leaving the permanent nucleus of the guards and garrisons little larger in 1685 than it had been in 1661, except that the Tangier garrison had returned to England in 1684. In spite of the deficiencies of the militia and the need for an improved system of national defence, contemporaries were very unhappy with the way in which James raised extra forces for Monmouth's Rebellion yet failed to dismiss them after Sedgemoor.

This was sufficient to bring forth the hysterical fears of a standing army which had been so often repeated during the time of Charles II, but whereas Charles had always yielded to parliamentary and financial pressure and reduced his additional forces, James was not financially dependent upon parliamentary supply and did not need to respond to the demands of the Commons.[40] Apart from the matter of the physical increase in the army, James was a roman catholic and there existed the danger that an engorged standing army would become a catholic formation. These fears were exacerbated by his manipulation of the requirements of the Test Acts to commission a certain number of catholics during Monmouth's Rebellion and to continue them in their appointments afterwards. Whether the bogey of arbitrary government by a catholic king commanding a catholic army was ever a serious possibility will be dealt with below[41] but the concern over this issue was well aired and expressed in the second session of James II's only parliament.

The first session of the parliament from 19 May to 2 July 1685 passed without military matters coming into focus and ended on a wave of patriotic loyalty as it voted James substantial supplies to combat the twin menaces of Argyll and Monmouth. When the two houses reassembled to hear the king's speech on 9 November 1685 the mood of the members was very different. Monmouth had been defeated and executed but the increased army was still on foot and the catholic officers had not been relieved of their commands. James's speech began by stressing the inadequacy of the militia:

there is nothing but a good force of well disciplined troops in constant pay that can defend us from such as, either at home or abroad, are disposed to disturb us ... my concern for the peace and quiet of my subjects, as well as for the safety of the government, made me think it necessary to increase the number to the proportion I have done.

The second part of his speech was even more contentious:

Let no man take exception that there are some officers in the army not qualified according to the late Tests for their employments. The gentlemen, I must tell you, are well known to me and, having served with me on several occasions and always approved the loyalty of their principles by their practice, I think them now fit to be employed under me. And I will deal plainly with you that, having had the benefit of their service in such a time of need and danger I will neither expose them to disgrace nor myself to want of them if there should be another rebellion to make them necessary to me.[42]

These words caused 'a great dejection of countenance in very many considering men in the House', and the Commons decided to debate the king's speech on Thursday 12 November.[43]

The Earl of Middleton moved for the king's speech to be considered paragraph by paragraph, and so the first business of the 12 November was whether the army should be expanded at the expense of the militia. Sir Winston Churchill, Lord Preston, and the Earl of Ranelagh showed themselves to be loyal court supporters by decrying the militia and upholding the royal request for a supply to assist with the increased army. Gradually the opposition to the granting of the supply mounted, using the lines of argument which had seen such prominence in the parliamentary sessions of 1678. Edward Seymour summarised many members' opinions when he advocated a remodelling of the militia, to whom he would rather

> pay double ... from whom I fear nothing than half so much to those of whom I must ever be afraid and, say what you will, it is a standing army. The last force preserved the peace and was sufficient to do it in the late king's time and is now ... Supporting an army is maintaining so many idle persons to lord it over the rest of the subjects ... A supply given as moved is a kind of an establishing an army by Act of Parliament.[44]

Sir Richard Temple was even more outspoken in his prophecy of the political potential of a standing army, pointing out that 'it is for kings to come to the House from time to time on extraordinary occasions and if this army be provided for by law they will never come more to this House ... Armies are useful when occasion is for them but if you establish them you can disband them no more'.[45] Members were willing to provide funds for making the militia more 'useful' but they rejected the motion that a supply be granted to the king 'towards the support of additional forces' by 225 votes to 156. The house then agreed to grant a supply to the king without a specific purpose being attached to it and requested the king's leave to introduce a bill to improve the militia.[46]

Two days later, on Saturday 14 November, the Commons debated the next paragraph in the king's speech, that which dealt with the catholic officers. Although 'every man that spake did it with great tenderness and deference to the king' the opinions were firm enough.[47] From a Grand Committee, the Commons resolved to address the king to remove all the recently appointed catholic officers, as they 'cannot by law be capable of their employments'. The pill was magnanimously sugared by the house appointing a committee to bring in a bill to indemnify all those catholics who had taken military commissions in defiance of the Test Acts. Monday 16 November saw the Commons considering how much money to grant the king in the agreed supply. Despite the subject of the debate, Mr. Thomas Coningsby took the opportunity to make another general attack upon the standing army.

Reasons I have heard given against armies, that they debauched the manners of all the people, their wives, daughters, and servants. Men do not go to church where they quarter for fear mischief should be done in their absence . . . The guards I am not against. These showed themselves useful in Venner's business and the late rebellion. I am not against them. I speak only to those that have been raised.[48]

Several sums were mentioned as being suitable for the supply, ranging between £200,000 and £1,200,000. Lord Camden moved for the lowest figure on the grounds that the king still had £400,000 remaining from the moneys voted to him by the first session of parliament and, as the cost of the additional forces was only £300,000 per annum, such a low supply would still give him enough to keep his increased forces in being for two and a half years. Camden's logic was ignored; the house voted to grant James £700,000 and then carried their address on the catholic officers to the king in person.[49]

James's written reply was read to the Commons by the Speaker on Wednesday 18 November. Its petulant and autocratic tone cannot have met with much favour:

I did not expect such an address from the House of Commons having so lately recommended to your consideration the great advantages a good understanding between us had produced in a very short time . . . I had reason to hope that the reputation God hath blessed me with in the world would have created and confirmed a greater confidence in you of me and all that I say to you. But however you proceed on your part I will be steady in all my promises I have made to you and be very just to my word in this and all my other speeches.[50]

Thomas Wharton moved for a debate on this regal rejoinder and was seconded by Thomas Coke, the member for Derby and a captain in Princess Anne of Denmark's regiment of foot. Unfortunately, the house found Coke's remark that 'we are all Englishmen and are not to be frighted out of our duty by a few high words' thoroughly offensive to both the king and themselves and committed him to the Tower of London to reconsider his mode of expression.[51]

On 19 November the Lords assembled to debate the paragraph in the king's speech relating to the catholic officers, and the ensuing discussion was 'very warm'.

The king was present ... and was much concerned at the plainness which they said was used in this debate. The truth is it gave great dissatisfaction to see the laws invaded in that particular and the king's best friends, with his domestic as well as military officers except some few that were popishly affected, were much alarmed at it and were very free in their discourse concerning it.[52]

The combined effect of the effrontery of the Commons' address and the blunt debate in the Lords was too much for James, and he prorogued parliament on 20 November until 10 February 1686, even though this resulted in the loss of the supply of £700,000. Parliament was not to meet again until after the Glorious Revolution.

The mere fact that James continued his enlarged army after the defeat of Monmouth caused parliament to talk of catholic standing armies, the pursuit of absolutist objectives through the political employment of regular troops, and the possible usurpation of parliament's functions in government. Was parliament correct in attributing these policies to James or was its fear unfounded and hysterical?

Notes

1. J. R. Western, *The English Militia in the Eighteenth Century* (London and Toronto, 1965), p. 68; *Norfolk Lieutenancy Journal, 1676–1701*, ed. B. Cozens-Hardy (Norfolk Record Society, 1961), p. 59, 2 Feb. 1685; F. C. Turner, *James II* (London, 1948), p. 243; *CSPD 1685*, Nos. 11–12, 7 Feb. 1685, Sunderland to governors of towns and castles.
2. PRO WO 24/7, Part 1, Establishment for England, 1 Jan. 1684. All the figures in the text relating to the size of the army include only non-commissioned officers and private soldiers. The number of commissioned officers is considered in chapter II.
3. Childs, *Army of Charles II*, p. 204; *HMC, C.S.H. Drummond Moray MSS.*, pp. 135–6, 'Note of the Muster in August 1684'; PRO SP 57/8, Scottish Warrant Book, pp. 420–5, Scottish Establishment on 16 June 1684; *Miscellany of the Maitland Club* (Edinburgh, 1842), iii. Part 1, pp. 72–83; SRO E 100/40/4, April 1687.
4. See Childs, *Army of Charles II*, pp. 66–72.
5. Monmouth's Rebellion has received good attention from: Allan Fea, *King Monmouth* (London, 1902); Bryan Little, *The Monmouth Episode* (London, 1956); Charles Chenevix Trench, *The Western Rising* (London, 1969); Peter Earle, *Monmouth's Rebels* (London, 1977). For the Anglo-Dutch Brigade see chapter V.
6. WO 24/8/Parts 1–6; Nottingham University Library, Portland MSS. PwA 2081, 'King James's Establishments'; BL Add. MSS. 34,516, f. 36; *Memoirs of Thomas, Earl of Ailesbury*, ed. W. E. Buckley (Roxburghe Club,

1890), i. 121; Sir James Mackintosh, *History of the Revolution in England in 1688* (Philadelphia, 1835), p. 707.
7   *Ibid.*, p. 707; *Ailesbury's Memoirs*, i. 130–1.
8   *A Selection from the Papers of the Earls of Marchmont*, ed. Sir G. H. Rose (London, 1831), ii. 72.
9   *HMC, Downshire MSS.*, ii. 283, newsletter of Dec. 1687; Narcissus Luttrell, *A Brief Historical Relation of State Affairs from September 1678 to April 1714* (Oxford, 1857), i. 421, Nov. 1687.
10 Portland MSS. PwA 2081; Dalton, *Army Lists*, ii. 151–6; J.G. Simms, *Jacobite Ireland, 1685–91* (London and Toronto, 1969), pp. 45–8; Luttrell, *Historical Relation*, i. 434; SRO E 100/8/1–12, Muster Rolls of the first muster of Wachop's Foot at Musselburgh on 26 June 1688.
11 Godfrey Davies, 'Letters on the Administration of James II's Army', *JSAHR*, xxxix. (1951), pp. 80–1; BL Add. MSS. 34,512, f. 104, 25 Sept. 1688, Van Citters to States-General.
12 BL Add. MSS. 28,082, ff. 107–18; Portland MSS. PwA 2081; Dalton, *Army Lists*, ii. 165–209; *HMC, Dartmouth MSS.*, i. 171.
13 *Ibid.*, i. 234; *HMC, Kenyon MSS.*, p. 202; A. H. Dodd, *Studies in Stuart Wales* (Cardiff, 1952), pp. 226–7.
14 It is impossible to give accurate figures for the strength of the English army of this period. False musters were a constant problem and, since 1670, official 'dead-pays' had been allowed in all English regiments (see chapter II and Childs, *Army of Charles II*, pp. 107). There is good evidence to suggest that many of James's regimental officers maintained their commands as well below their establishments for most of the year in order to draw the pay of the non-existent soldiers for themselves (BL Add. MSS 38,694, f. 99). The actual effective numbers of the army in this period were almost certainly ten per cent lower than the paper establishments which have been used as the basis for compiling the figures in the text. Ten per cent is probably a very conservative estimate.
15 *HMC, Kenyon MSS.*, pp. 205–6.
16 Luttrell, *Historical Relation*, i. 462; Mackintosh, *History of the Revolution*, p. 509; Portland MSS. PwA 2081; *HMC, Dartmouth MSS.*, i. 171.
17 *HMC, C.S.H. Drummond Moray MSS.*, pp. 136–7; Portland MSS. PwA 2081; *HMC, Dartmouth MSS.*, i. 171; BL Harleian MSS. 7,436, ff. 30–1.
18 PRO SP 63/340, State Papers Ireland, Secretary's Letter Book, ff. 47–8; BL Add. MSS. 9, 762, pp. 1–4; *HMC, Ormonde MSS.*, old series, i. 436–7; WO 9/1, Abstracts of Army Pay in Ireland, 1679–88; PRO PC 2/72, ff. 85–8; Trinity College, Dublin, MSS. 796, Irish Establishment, Jan. 1688.
19 *The Danish Force in Ireland, 1690–1691*, ed. K. Danaher and J. G. Simms (Dublin, 1962), p. 12.
20 F. L. Carsten, *Princes and Parliaments in Germany* (Oxford, 1959), p. 183; *New Cambridge Modern History*, vi. 741–2.
21 WO 24/7/Part 1; BL Harleian MSS. 7,436, ff. 1–16; BL Add. MSS. 15,897, ff. 72–3; WO 24/8/Parts 1–6; Portland MSS. PwA 2081.

22 C. D. Chandaman, *The English Public Revenue, 1660–1688* (Oxford, 1975), pp. 260–1 and 362–3.
23 Sir John Dalrymple, *Memoirs of Great Britain and Ireland* (London and Edinburgh, 1771–88), ii. appendix Part 1, pp. 260–2, 13 Oct.1687, Barillon to Louis XIV.
24 *The Life and Times of Anthony Wood, antiquary of Oxford, 1632–95, described by himself*, ed. Andrew Clark (Oxford Historical Society, 1891–1900), iii. 190.
25 PRO SO 1/11, Signet Office, Irish Letter Book, f. 180; *CSPD 1686–7*, Nos. 109 and 1436; SO 1/12, ff. 130–1.
26 *Norfolk Lieutenancy Journal*, pp. 68, 69–70 and 72; *Diaries and Letters of Philip Henry M.A.*, ed. M. H. Lee (London, 1882), p. 325.
27 *The Autobiography of Sir John Bramston*, ed. Lord Braybrooke (Camden Society, 1845), p. 205.
28 For a fuller discussion of the relations between the army and the militia in the reign of James II see John Miller, 'The Militia and the Army in the Reign of James II', *HJ*, xvi. (1973). A history of the militia between 1685 and 1688 can be found in Western, *English Militia*, pp. 16–59.
29 Dalrymple, *Memoirs of Great Britain and Ireland*, ii. app. Part 1, pp. 133, 7 July 1685, James II to Prince of Orange.
30 *Ailesbury's Memoirs*, i. 118.
31 John Martin to Rev. William Moore, 27 June 1685, ed. Godfrey Davies, in *EHR*, xliii. (1928), pp. 604–5.
32 John Dryden, *Cymon and Iphigenia*, lines 399–408, printed in *English Historical Documents, 1660–1714*, ed. A. Browning (London, 1953), p. 796.
33 PRO SP 29/145, State Papers Domestic, Charles II, f. 94, 1665; SP 29/363, f. 175, 1674; SP 29/415, ff. 156–7, 1681.
34 Luttrell, *Historical Relation*, i. 356; BL Add. MSS. 15,897, ff. 78–81; BL Add. MSS. 38,695, f. 27. During the winter of 1686–7 the units of the English army were quartered in the following stations.

London and the Home Counties: Reading, Newbury, Wallingford, Marlow, High Wycombe, Henley-on-Thames, Canterbury, Maidstone, Sittingbourne, Feversham, Ashford, Thame, Croydon, Epping, Bow, Stratford, Romford, Tooting, Mitcham, Bromley, Carshalton, Streatham, Littlebourne, Ewell, Rochester, Stroud, Chatham, Frinnsbury, Gillingham, Tower of London, Tower Hamlets, Gravesend, Tilbury, Windsor Castle, Upnor Castle, Southwark, Gillingham, Sheerness.

The Midlands: Langham (Rutland), Oxford, Abingdon, Woodstock, Leicester, Ashby-de-la-Zouch, Melton Mowbray, Loughborough, Buckingham, Winslow, Aylesbury, Wendover, Coventry, Warwick.

East Anglia: Cambridge, Huntingdon, Godmanchester, St. Ives (Huntingdonshire), Bishop's Stortford, Hockerell, Dunmow, Stanstead, Saffron Walden, Audley End, Great Yarmouth, Bungay.

The west and south: Shrewsbury, Wrexham, Whitchurch (Shropshire), Oswestry, Ludlow, Bridgnorth, Bridgewater, Gloucester,

Somerton, Bristol, Chepstow, Portsmouth, Exeter, Plymouth, Pendennis, Taunton, Guernsey, Jersey, Scilly Isles, Isle of Wight.

The north: Nantwich, Pontefract, Ferrybridge, Wakefield, Leeds, Halifax, Hull, York, Berwick-on-Tweed, Chester, Carlisle, Tynemouth, Newcastle-on-Tyne.

35 WO 30/48.
36 See Tony Hayter, *The Army and the Crowd in Mid-Georgian England* (London,, 1978).
37 *CSPD 1687–9*, Nos. 1556 and 1566.
38 *Bramston*, p. 325; Miller, 'Militia and the Army', pp. 664–7; David Allen, 'The role of the London trained bands in the Exclusion Crisis, 1678–81', *EHR*, lxxxvii. (1972).
39 The three periods were from 1665–7, 1672–4 and 1677–9.
40 Childs, *Army of Charles II*, pp. 219–32.
41 See Chapter IV.
42 Anchitell Grey, *Debates of the House of Commons, From the Year 1667 to 1694* (London, 1763), viii. 353–4; *The Memoirs of Sir John Reresby*, ed. A. Browning (Glasgow, 1936), p. 394; J. S. Clarke, *The Life of James the Second* (London, 1816), ii. 50–1.
43 *Bramston*, p. 210.
44 Grey, *Debates*, viii. 357–8.
45 *Ibid.*, p. 359.
46 *Ibid.*, p. 360.
47 *Bramston*, p. 214.
48 Grey, *Debates*, viii. 365–6.
49 *Bramston*, pp. 214–15.
50 Grey, *Debates*, viii. 369.
51 HPT; Grey, *Debates*, viii. 369.
52 *Reresby*, p. 398.

II

Catholic and protestant

Charles II had employed roman catholic officers and men in his standing army. The nucleus of his English army – the Life Guard, the Royal Horse Guards, the First Foot Guards, the Coldstream Guards, the Duke of York's Foot, and the Holland regiment – had each possessed a small number of catholic officers, perhaps one or two per cent of the total commissioned into those formations between 1661 and 1685. However, Charles's army really contained more catholics than this figure suggests, but they only occasionally served in England. The garrison of Tangier harboured a considerable number of catholic officers, many of whom were Irish, whilst the regiments that fought for Louis XIV in the Franco-Dutch war of 1672 to 1678 also contained a good proportion of catholic officers. During the mass levies for the second and third Dutch wars and for the projected war with France in 1678 these officers on foreign service, both catholic and protestant, were recalled into England to command the new units. At these specific times there were larger bodies of catholic officers in the English army, but at the conclusion of hostilities the new forces were disbanded and the officers returned to their stations overseas or endured unemployment in England. The number of catholic officers in the permanent regiments of the standing army in England was very small and did not present a problem to the relations between Charles and his parliaments. When the total of catholic officers in England rose appreciably in response to the three national emergencies parliament did express alarm but Charles honoured his pledges to disband his newly raised forces after each war and thus removed the cause of friction. For most of the reign the catholic factor in the English army was of little moment. Roman catholic officers who fought for Charles II did so in Tangier, France, Portugal, the Anglo-Dutch Brigade, and in the colonies where they were far removed from the prying eyes of parliament and the provisions of the two Test Acts. Charles was only able to introduce these officers into the English army when parliament granted him a sufficient supply to augment his English forces for war; parliament was the ultimate arbiter of both the size of the caroline army and of the religious convictions of its officer corps. Parliamentary power over the purse was decisive.[1]

After the first session of his parliament in 1685, James II possessed adequate funds with which to maintain a greatly increased standing army without the necessity of being forced to seek extraordinary supplies from periodic parliaments. The officers who had lingered abroad were presented with opportunities to take commissions in England. They were anxious to do so, as the theatres of war in Europe were unproductive of employment: the French brigade had been recalled in 1678, Tangier had been evacuated in 1684, and France was technically at peace with her many opponents. The conflict in Hungary between the Holy Roman Emperor and the Turk was the sole attractive seat of war for professional soldiers. Being an old soldier, James was well aware of the lean times which a spell of general European peace brought to mercenary officers and troopers. Accordingly, when the English army was expanded to face Monmouth, James took advantage of the occasion to employ a quantity of these unemployed or partially employed professional officers, among whom were some roman catholics. The number, however, was not great. By the end of 1685 there were probably no more catholic officers in the English army than there had been during the three periods of military expansion under Charles II. Both the royal brothers increased the catholic component in their officer corps to meet a sudden need for troops, but whereas Charles disbanded these additional forces after each war James retained his new army in peacetime, thereby continuing his catholic officers in their commissions in open defiance of the Test Acts. Charles bowed before the Test Act of 1678, James did not. It is hard to read any sinister intentions into James's actions. Between 1660 and 1688 the profession of arms was unpopular in England; twenty years of civil war and military government had disillusioned the gentry and aristocracy about the military life. When the Restoration monarchs required troops for war they had to contend with an acute shortage of competent officers and men, and were forced to commission catholics, Irishmen, and itinerant Scotsmen to command their augmented armies. There is little evidence for supposing, as J. R. Western does, that Monmouth's Rebellion gave James his first chance to arm the catholic minority in England.[2] James himself said that his principal reason for employing some catholics in the army in 1685 was the shortage of capable protestant officers.[3] As Charles II had experienced precisely the same difficulties in discovering a sufficient number of good officers to direct his enlarged armies without having recourse to the catholic and protestant officers on foreign service, there is no substantial cause for disbelieving James's claim. Not unreasonably, James wanted an army that was well organised and disciplined, and this demanded the services of professional officers many of whom were in England in 1685 and anxious for employment. As James had made virtually no preparations to resist an invasion before Monmouth landed at Lyme Regis, there was not time for him to cast around for politically acceptable officers; he had to use the material at hand, and some of it, for better or for worse, was roman catholic.

Under the terms of the Test Act of 1673, the king could commission roman catholic officers into the army for a maximum period of three months, after which time they were obliged to swear the oaths of supremacy and allegiance. On 23 November 1685 James dispensed sixty-eight catholic officers from these provisions.[4] In the following January the attorney-general was instructed to prepare a bill to pass the Great Seal to dispense ninety-five officers from the rigours of the Test. This list included all those who had been dispensed in November, except one, with an additional twenty-eight officers[5] – this second dispensation appears to have come into operation on 9 January 1686.[6] A method by which James had either to dispense all his catholic officers every quarter or to issue them with new commissions at similar intervals was unwieldy, inefficient, and expensive, as the officers involved had to pay a fee to the secretary-at-war for each new commission. A more satisfactory solution was required. As soon as he had been guaranteed a docile judiciary, James pushed through the test case of Godden v. Hales, in which it was ruled that he had the right to appoint catholics to civil and military posts regardless of the clauses of the Test Acts.[7] James was now free to commission as many catholic officers as he desired, but he demonstrated very considerable restraint.

Charles Dalton, in editing his lists of Restoration army officers, was able to identify only thirty-seven catholic officers in England by 31 December 1685.[8] This is certainly an under estimate but more accurate are the figures of Mr. Hay, who suggests that in October

1688 the English army contained between five and six thousand catholic soldiers and about one hundred catholic officers. According to a Jacobite pamphlet published immediately after the Glorious Revolution, James 'had scarce one popish officer for thirty or forty protestants and in some entire regiments there were not twenty common soldiers of that persuasion. So that neither from his army nor his priests were we in danger during his reign to have suffered any subversion of our religion.'[9] A reasonably well informed commentator, the Earl of Ailesbury, noted that in 1685 his monarch commissioned 'about eighty persons that were roman catholics and most men of condition and known worth'. Three years later he said 'that the number of roman catholics was not twelve hundred in the whole army and these lurked and hid themselves out of fear and afterwards the officers and soldiers went into the Emperor's service'.[10] Even Gilbert Burnet, intent upon justifying the intervention of William of Orange in 1688, was reduced to the tepid statement that the protestants in the English army 'treated the few papists that were among them with scorn and aversion'.[11] The man in the best possible position to estimate the number of catholic officers was James himself. At Sir Richard Head's house in Rochester, from where he made his second and successful flight, James told Colonel Wycke, the commander of his Dutch gaolers, that 'in his whole army of eighteen thousand men he believed that he had not a thousand roman catholics, "and your army, much inferior, hath two thirds of my religion so cried out against" '.[12] The king was not the only observer of the paradox that William of Orange's invasion force also included a considerable number of roman catholic officers and men. Sir John Reresby recorded:

The Prince declared that he had no design for the crown and yet sought it all he could. He came to settle the protestant religion and yet brought over 4,000 papists in his army which were near as many as the king had English of that religion in his.[13]

A recent study of the catholic officers in the armies of Charles II and James II gives totals of eighty-five in November 1685 and ninety-five in November 1687, with a rider that the real expansion in the number of catholics came with the augmentation of the army to meet the emergency in the autumn of 1688. On this estimate, only about one-eighth of the English army officers followed the romish religion.[14]

It is impossible to present an accurate statement of the number of catholic officers in the English army between 1685 and 1688. Many of the officers have origins too obscure to be traced, some appear in commission lists without their christian names, whilst the difficulties in distinguishing one Thomas Brown from another need hardly be mentioned. Was the Ensign Skinner of Henry Cornwall's regiment of foot related to the catholic gentleman John Skinner of Warwickshire? Without the knowledge of the ensign's christian name it would be imprudent to guess.[15] Although the following figures are based on a wide variety of sources, it must be stressed that they represent only those officers who have been positively identified as roman catholic. There may have been more who owed allegiance to Rome rather than Canterbury but, hopefully, these minimum totals are accurate to within five per cent.[16] By 31 December 1685, 141 catholics had been commissioned into the English army. One year later, only 117 catholic officers have been discovered, a reduction caused by the disbandment of some independent troops and companies during 1686 and the return of Richard Hamilton's dragoons to the Irish establishment. The passage of a further twelve months witnessed the appointment of just two more catholics, but, by the time that James's army concentrated on Salisbury Plain in mid-November 1688, the English army had a total of 209 known catholic officers. When these figures are related to the numbers of commissioned officers in the army at any one time then they appear very moderate. In February 1685 there were 456 commissioned officers, of whom no more than five per cent were of the romish persuasion. At the end of the same year, the total number of commissions had risen to 1,350, ten per cent of which were held by roman catholics. By November 1687 this percentage had fallen slightly to 8·6 but even the expansion of the number of commissions to 1,869 in October 1688 did not significantly raise the proportion of catholics; it increased to just eleven per cent.

These modest and consistent figures do not indicate an army which was being steadily and systematically filled with roman catholic officers. If it was an instrument of potential despotism, then it was a protestant instrument. James showed no intention of trying to 'have in Scotland of Scots papists an army of three thousand men, in England of twenty thousand, without so much as one new convert among them, when he pleases'.[17] William's invasion of 1688 gave James an opportunity to fatten the increased army with his co-religionists, but he seems to have taken no real steps in that direction: the percentage of catholic officers in November 1688 was almost identical to that of three years before. Either James did not want to employ a disproportionately large number of catholics or, more likely, there were not enough available for military employment. If, as Miller suggests, only seven per cent of the English gentry and aristocracy were catholic, then there must have been a dearth of young and able catholic gentlemen ready to take commissions for service in the field.[18] Only by raking in the crippled, the infirm, and the aged could James have attempted to catholicise his officer corps in 1688. To command the engorged forces of that year he had to find an additional 687 officers, and there were insufficient catholics of the requisite social and financial standing to have undertaken this task. The reservoir of professional officers who had helped Charles II to ease his way over the paucity of good officers during his reign had already been received into the English army or had found places in the Irish armed forces. The army which fought both Monmouth and William of Orange was commanded by an officer corps which was ninety per cent protestant. The real question of the reign must be whether James intended to use his protestant army in a political fashion, not whether he had designs to use a catholic army to impose a catholic despotism.[19]

Such catholic officers as the army contained were distributed evenly throughout the regiments. Formations with catholic colonels naturally tended to possess more co-religionists than units commanded by protestants – Sir Edward Hales's regiment of foot had sixteen catholics out of a total of thirty-seven officers. Except for this singular example, the foot regiments of the English army each included an average of three or four roman catholic officers between 1685 and 1688. A similar distribution was found among the dragoon and cavalry regiments. Apart from George Holman's and the Earl of Salisbury's regiments of horse, which were raised in 1688 at the personal expense of their colonels and were almost exclusively officered by catholics, the horse formations each possessed an average of four catholic officers.[20] As every infantry regiment was governed by an officer corps of between thirty and forty, depending on the number of companies within each regiment, and each cavalry unit had between twenty-five and thirty-five officers, the average number of catholics per regiment approximately equates with the overall percentage of catholic officers in the English army. There were no overwhelmingly catholic corps. Catholic officers were in a decided minority and were dispersed among large groups of protestants, a fact which probably made them nervous and unwilling to commit any provocative act. If the English army was not wholly protestant in its composition it was utterly dominated by protestants, although concessions did have to be made to the catholic minority. Catholic chapels were established to serve the army when it encamped on Hounslow Heath in 1686 and 1687, but there is evidence of only one catholic chaplain being appointed to an English regiment: Nicholas Trapps served the considerable body of catholic officers in Sir Edward Hales's foot. The large garrison towns of Chester, Bristol, and Plymouth each received a priest to serve the military catholics.[21] However, these were minor incidents and did not constitute a challenge to the protestant hegemony of either the army or England.

The known catholic officers who served with the English army under James II can be accurately divided into four categories: those who had fought in Europe or the colonies during the reign of Charles II; those who had seen service with the English army at some time between 1660 and 1685; gentlemen who commenced their military careers in 1685; and finally the gentry and aristocracy who became temporary soldiers in the face of the Dutch menace in 1688. From a total of 221 catholic officers about whom we have biographical information, twenty per cent had seen foreign service, 20 per cent had served under Charles II, forty per cent started military life some time between 1685 and mid-1688, and twenty per cent took out commissions during the crisis of 1688.

John Chappell was first commissioned as a lieutenant in the Tangier garrison in 1678, but he had to wait four years to receive a slight promotion into the Tangier troop of horse as a cornet. Following the evacuation of that ill-fated town in 1684, Chappell returned to England and was unemployed until James II expanded his army in the summer of 1685. From then until the Glorious Revolution Chappell served in Sir Edward Hales's regiment of foot as a captain; after the Dutch success he followed James II into Ireland, and was appointed major of Lord Kilmallock's foot in the Jacobite army. His chequered career ended as a prisoner after the battle of Aughrim in 1691.[22] A more unorthodox course was steered by Henry Gage, the fourth son of Sir Edward Gage, fourth baronet. During the 1670s he was the lieutenant-colonel of an English mercenary regiment fighting for Spain in Flanders, and, in 1677, he was raised to command a Scottish regiment in the same service. Gage continued in Flanders until he was summoned to England by James II in September 1688 to take command of a new regiment of foot.[23] Charles Macarty, an Irish catholic, first entered the English army as a lieutenant in the Earl of Mulgrave's foot in 1673. After the disbandment of this formation in 1674 Macarty went to fight in France and there is a record of him as major of Thomas Dongan's foot, an Irish mercenary regiment in the French service, in 1678. Macarty reappeared in England as a captain in the Duke of Norfolk's regiment of foot in June 1685, a rank which he retained until the Revolution when he returned to Ireland to fight in the Jacobite army.[24] Another Irishman, Bartholomew Russell, served with the Anglo-Dutch Brigade until he obeyed the order to return into England on 14 March 1688. He continued in the rank of ensign, which he had enjoyed in the Netherlands, and was posted to Roger MacElligott's foot. Again, after the Revolution he went over to Ireland and became a captain in James II's Irish Foot Guards.[25] The brother of Sir Patrick Trant, Dominic, was a captain in the Royal English regiment, which fought in France during the 1670s, and on its disbandment in 1678 he came over to England and took up an appointment as a captain in the Duke of Monmouth's foot for the projected war with France. Following the dismissal of this regiment in 1679 Trant probably went back to France in search of military employment. On the expansion of the English army in 1685 he became a captain in the Duke of Norfolk's foot and continued in this position until 1 December 1688, when he was temporarily promoted to the majority of the same regiment.[26]

Although those catholic officers who had fought abroad in the previous reign were, without doubt, highly professional and expert in the military art, the officers who had previously served with the army in England under Charles II had some claims to martial efficiency. Thomas Errington, the son of John Errington, a merchant and alderman of Newcastle-upon-Tyne, served briefly as a lieutenant in the Earl of Ogle's foot in 1673. This short military experience, which lasted perhaps twelve months, was sufficient to qualify him for a commission as an ensign in the Duke of Newcastle's new regiment of foot in September 1688.[27] More substantial was the expertise of John Guillims. This catholic was a captain in Lord Wentworth's guards at Dunkirk in 1661 and then became a captain in the First Foot Guards later in the same year. Guillims lost his commission in the anti-catholic purge of 1667 and did not regain his place until the expansion of the army for the third Dutch war in 1672. The restrictions of the Test Act of 1673 again drove him from office, and he did not resume his military exploits until 1687, when he was commissioned lieutenant-governor of Jersey.[28]

Despite the large number of English and Irish military catholics who had either fought abroad or who had served in England under Charles II, the supply was insufficient to fill many of the new commissions available in 1685. Most of the Irish catholics were attracted on to their native establishment as the purge of protestant officers and men gathered pace during the autumn and winter of 1685. Half the commissions granted to catholics between 1685 and 1687 were given to new men without any sort of military experience. Claudius Hamilton, fourth Earl of Abercorn, was created captain of an independent troop of horse in June 1685, and, after the defeat of Monmouth, his troop was transferred into the regiment of Sir John Fenwick. Abercorn surrendered his captaincy to James II at Rochester in December 1688 and then sailed to Ireland to serve his old master as a colonel of horse.[29] At some time during 1687 George Brathwayt was commissioned as an ensign in Sir Edward Hales's foot and in October of the following year he was promoted to a captaincy in Henry Gage's newly raised regiment of foot. The Revolution brought his military progress to a halt.[30] Philip, the fifth son of Sir John Lawson of Brough Hall in Yorkshire, joined the army as a cornet in the Earl of Arran's cavalry regiment in 1685 and, from there, he transferred to the Royal Horse Guards on 1 April 1687.[31] Robert Lowick started army life as an ensign in the Berwick garrison in 1685 and received a number of sideways promotions during the reign until he became a cornet in George Holman's horse in 1688. After the Revolution he fought for the Jacobite army in Ireland and was executed for treason in 1696.[32] Many of the new catholic officers came from impoverished backgrounds. John Trevanion was disinherited by his father for adherence to the romish religion and was thus forced into a military career. He was posted as an ensign in Prince George of Denmark's foot on 3 July 1686 but, without patronage or wealth, was still in the same lowly rank when the regiment was disbanded in February 1689.[33] The aunt of Sir Baptiste Edward Wray, eighth baronet, a private gentleman in the Life Guard 'without one shilling save his pay', implored the Earl of Ailesbury to intercede with the king to obtain a cornetcy in the Guards for her nephew. James referred Ailesbury to Father Petre, who presumably, for some unaccountable reason, controlled this area of army patronage. Unfortunately for Sir Baptiste, Petre was 'pre-engaged', having accepted a bribe of £500 to give the vacant cornetcy to Henry de Foubert, the son of Solomon de Foubert, an exiled Huguenot who established a gentlemen's academy in London in 1686.[34]

The remaining category of catholic officer, the peers and gentlemen who volunteered for service only in the teeth of William of Orange's intended invasion, consisted mostly of provincial catholics who obeyed the call to defend their monarch and country. Their periods of service lasted for no more than three months and must generally have been time-consuming, inconvenient, and very expensive. Few of these officers appear to have possessed any military experience, in contrast to many of the protestant gentry who had a nodding acquaintance with things military through their service with the militia. The new regiments of 1688 in which these officers held commissions were mostly recruited territorially: the Duke of Newcastle's foot drew its officers from amongst the catholic gentry of Newcastle-upon-Tyne and Northumberland – William Clavering, Ralph Brandling, William Jennison, William Radcliffe, Mark Riddell, Thomas Sanderson, Nicholas Tempest, and Edward Widdrington. In order to raise his regiment of foot, John Carne relied heavily upon the support of the catholic gentry of South Wales and the Marches. It is not realistic to regard these catholics as soldiers in the strict sense of the word and in many instances their regiments did not become operational. Militarily ignorant, unpopular in the army in which they fought, they must have found their service to James extremely trying.

The vast majority of the English army under James II was protestant and it was founded upon the structure and personnel which had been bequeathed to him by Charles II, the definition of which has been treated at length elsewhere.[35] However, by 31 December 1685 two-thirds of the officers in the army were newly commissioned, a mixture of veterans with considerable experience and young men just setting forth on their military careers. There was a solid core of professional career officers: Percy Kirke, Charles Trelawney, Sir John Lanier, Sir John Morgan, Thomas Langston, John Beaumont, Sir Charles Littleton, John Churchill, Walter Littleton, Sir John Fenwick, Sir John Talbot, Richard Hamilton, Sir Theophilus Oglethorpe, Henry Cornwall, and Sackville Tufton. All these officers and dozens more like them had gained considerable expertise through service with the English army under Charles II, in Tangier, Portugal, France, the colonies, with the Anglo-Dutch Brigade, and in Spanish Flanders. After the expansion of the army in the summer of 1685 they were able to find permanent senior commissions in England. By the time of the accession of James II the standing army had been in existence for twenty-four years and had become a well established institution, a factor which was of vital importance in developing a sense of professionalism within the officer corps. Commissions were indeed expensive but once the younger son of a peer or a member of the upper gentry had entered the army he increasingly tended to remain in service for most of his active life; by the reign of James II the military was becoming a definite career for the majority of its protestant officers. The old distinctions between 'gentlemen' officers and professionals were fast disappearing. Sir John Hanmer succeeded his father as third baronet in 1678, but even this social and financial elevation was not allowed to interrupt his army career and he progressed from a captaincy in 1678 to a colonelcy in 1689. Apart from the peers and gentlemen who took up temporary commissions during emergencies, the bulk of the officers who entered the army under both Charles II and James II did not leave voluntarily even if they had the good fortune to inherit titles and estates. The fact that James II was personally attracted to martial affairs and held soldiers in high regard added to the status of military commissions, whilst the expansion of the armed forces clearly indicated that the army had become a stable and secure institution. This was enhanced under William III and Anne when England's almost perpetual engagement in European warfare gave ample encouragement to young men to buy commissions with every prospect of advancement and profit, very different circumstances to those which were current under Charles II, when the army was small, fought rarely, and offered scant hope of promotion. By enlarging his army James created a flourishing institution and concentrated English military talent into the national armed forces.

Scotland was unable to offer similar opportunities to either protestant or catholic officers. Unlike its English equivalent, the standing army neither expanded nor contracted between 1685 and 1688[36] and thus new blood could join only by purchasing such vacancies as arose in the five regiments. These three formations of cavalry and two of infantry could offer only 141 commissions, although a further thirty-four posts were attached to the various garrisons. Without an overall increase in its physical size the Scottish army did not benefit from an influx of experienced professional officers, and the military efficacy of James's northern force was suspect. However, the restriction which prevented experienced officers from joining the Scottish forces also prevented an influx of roman catholics. The Scottish high command was solidly protestant, and the procession of commanders-in-chief – Thomas Dalyell, John Graham of Claverhouse, William Drummond, and James Douglas – presented a firm bulwark against the catholicising tendencies of the Earls of Perth and Melfort. The only catholic patron to whom papist aspirants for Scottish commissions could turn was the Earl of Dumbarton, but he spent much of the reign in England with his own regiment and appears to have exercised little influence over Scottish military appointments. Some catholics did acquire commissions. The Duke of Gordon was quietly ushered into the government of Edinburgh Castle in February 1686 and Captain William Oliphant, his son, Lawrence, Captain Charles Carney, and Ensign James Henderson gained places in the Scottish Foot Guards. Of the 175 commissions available in the Scottish armed forces, only sixty-seven changed hands between 1685 and 1688, and very few of these were granted to catholics, to the chagrin of the Earl of Perth.

> Others here would have us believe they are our friends who are really our more dangerous enemies, especially some in the army, the hundredth man in which is not a catholic, and we have scarce any officers of that persuasion; not that they are not to be had but, with all the art imaginable, the king is diverted from any such design as might bring in the army to us.[37]

Whereas we are relatively well informed about the social background and religion of the officers of James II's army, we are not in the same happy position when we come to consider the nature of the rank and file. Information about the number of catholic non-commissioned officers and soldiers is scant. An anonymous letter to the king in 1687 noted that Major Hugh O'Connor of the Earl of Peterborough's regiment of horse had introduced some forty catholic troopers into that formation, about sixteen per cent of the establishment. However, during the camp on Hounslow Heath in the summer of 1688 the Duke of St. Albans's regiment of cavalry was listed as containing only thirteen catholic troopers. Clearly much depended on the officers in each regiment. O'Connor was an Irish catholic whose father had been reasonably wealthy, but he was prevented by the Act of Settlement from enjoying his inheritance. Instead he turned to a military career and fought in France between 1671 and 1678, when his regiment was disbanded. Although he remained in France and tried to acquire a commission in the French army, O'Connor did not receive any employment until the expansion of the English army in 1685, when he was commissioned as the captain-lieutenant of Peterborough's horse. On 1 March 1687 he was promoted to the majority of the same regiment. Such an officer was a professional who, as a roman catholic and an Irishman, was likely to use the considerable power which his rank conferred on him to introduce some catholics into his unit.[38] St. Albans's regiment was officered almost entirely by protestants and, as a consequence, few catholics were recruited. It is most unlikely that the bulk of the protestant officers would willingly have tolerated catholics in their commands, although more pliant protestants like the Dukes of Beaufort and Norfolk were sometimes inclined to turn a blind eye. As approximately ten per cent of the English officer corps bowed towards Rome rather than towards Canterbury, an uninspired guess might assume that a similar proportion of the men were of a like mind. Translating this into actual numbers, the army possibly contained some two thousand catholic soldiers between the autumn of 1685 and the summer of 1688, rising to three thousand in the autumn and early winter of the latter year. Almost certainly these represent the maximum numbers of catholic soldiers in the English army, as only a small minority of the catholic officers were field officers or troop and company commanders, leaving the majority of the catholic officers as subalterns who would not have been able to directly influence the choice of recruits. The only statement that can be made with any certainty is that the dramatically high figure of five or six thousand catholic soldiers in the English army which is presented by Mr. Hay is wrong. Probably he has included in his calculations the 2,820 catholic troops who were imported from Ireland in 1688, but these were never a part of the English establishment and formed no more than a temporary reinforcement during the emergency. In the English army catholic soldiers were in a decided minority, probably constituting considerably less than ten per cent of the whole.

When the army was increased in 1685 and 1688 substantial demands were made upon the manpower available in England. James wrote to William of Orange on 19 June 1685, 'I am raising great store of horse and foot and men come in very fast and the nobility and gentry are very zealous for my service and offer ... to raise me men enough, they being very sensible that they [the rebels] design nothing less than their destruction as well as that of the monarchy',[39] but the reality of recruiting was not always as straightforward as the king maintained. In the loyal city of Oxford 'an officer with drums, who came overnight ..., beat up for volunteers to supply the places of the king's foot guards at Whitehall who were drawn out of London toward the rebels in Dorsetshire. The lustiest and tallest they took and others they put aside.' However, in Abingdon, a few miles to the south, 'a most factious town, they could get ... but four volunteers'.[40] Men seem to have been willing to come forward in 1685, as the demand for troops was in direct response to an armed invasion and rebellion. There was no suggestion of being tempted into taking the king's shilling only to be hustled abroad or into the hated colonies. In the summer of 1685 James was able to profit from the flood of loyalty which flowed towards him. The council of the city of Oxford raised two independent companies of foot to demonstrate its allegiance, an expensive operation,[41] but once the threat of rebellion and civil war had been quashed the recruitment of suitable men became more difficult. The governor of Chester Castle, Peter Shakerley, moaned to William Blathwayt, the secretary-at-war, in 1687 that his own company 'were all either very little or old men, so that I have been and still am at hard labour to get better and indeed 'tis now difficult enough to persuade good men to come into the service and no less to instruct 'em to do well when they are come in'.[42] Again, in 1688 the immediate danger of invasion appears to have produced a positive reaction which expressed itself through the recruiting figures. James was able to report to Lord Dartmouth on 5 October 1688 that recruits 'come in apace and the new levies will soon be completed. Both officers and soldiers are very hearty.' Narcissus Luttrell observed that the volunteers 'come in very well' from both town and country, but as in 1685 there were areas which proved less than productive. For ten days the recruiting parties beat their drums in the city of Durham 'but got none',[43] despite the common loathing of the Dutch.

The new regiments of 1685 and 1688 were raised through a heavy reliance upon the territorial influence of the leading nobility and dominant country families. Of the nine new regiments of horse created in 1685, only one was raised by a commoner, Sir John Lanier, and he was a seasoned professional soldier with great experience in all aspects of military affairs. The Earls of Peterborough, Plymouth, Thanet, Arran, Shrewsbury, Scarsdale, Baron Lumley and Baron Dover raised the remainder of the cavalry. Of the two new regiments of dragoons one was recruited by the Duke of Somerset and the other by John Berkeley, another hardened career officer. The same principle of depending upon the landed interest to create new formations was followed in the infantry. The Dukes of Norfolk and Beaufort, the Earls of Bath and Huntingdon, Barons Dartmouth and Ferrers, Sir Edward Hales, and Sir William Clifton were all charged with the task of raising foot soldiers. The only new colonel who was untitled was Henry Cornwall, but he was a substantial landowner in Herefordshire and a professional officer. As a result of this method of recruiting, most of the infantry regiments tended to be composed of men from very distinct regions, reflecting the location of the estates of their captains and colonels. Lord Ferrers's foot was drawn from Leicestershire and the Midlands; Lord Bath had a considerable interest in Nottinghamshire and Derbyshire, whilst Henry Cornwall was able to exploit his influence in Herefordshire and Gloucestershire. The Earl of Huntingdon concentrated his attention on Buckinghamshire, the Duke of Beaufort was strong in Somerset and Wales, and the Duke of Norfolk attracted men of the county from which he took his title. Sir Edward Hales, a leading gentleman of Kent, naturally raised his forces from within that county, and Sir William Clifton caused his drums to beat in Nottinghamshire. Amongst the new cavalry regiments the attachment to specific areas of the country was not so marked, as they were largely formed from the independent troops of horse which had been created initially to deal with Monmouth's rebellion. Lord Plymouth's six troops came from Worcestershire, Oxfordshire, St. Albans, Dunstable, Huntingdon, and Dorking, diverse origins indeed, but some of the cavalry units did have a more regional flavour. The Earl of Shrewsbury's regiment contained three troops from the Welsh borders, one from Bristol, one from Kingston-upon-Thames, and another from London, whilst Lord Scarsdale's six troops were principally recruited in the Peak district of Derbyshire.[44]

After being granted a commission to raise a regiment of foot, the Earl of Huntingdon announced his intention of recruiting his own company in Leicestershire. He sent his ensign, Henry Anderson, and two sergeants to 'beat up' for soldiers actually within the city of Leicester and requested the assistance of the corporation. The city fathers were assured that there would be no trouble or disorder during this operation and the recruits 'need not doubt of good usage and all the care that a captain ought to take of his soldiers'.[45] In East Anglia, the Duke of Norfolk took advantage of his authority as Lord Lieutenant of the shire of his title to raise his regular infantry formation from among the militias of both Norfolk and Suffolk. He wrote to his deputy lieutenants:

His Majesty has given me the command of a regiment of foot with directions to raise them in Norfolk and Suffolk. Therefore I desire your assistance and countenance that when my respective officers shall cause drums to be beaten for volunteers to be listed to receive his Majesty's pay, that they may complete their companies as soon as may be.[46]

Colonel Thomas Strangways was specifically instructed to take the personnel for his new regiment of foot from the reservoir of the Dorsetshire trained bands, although the scheme was later abandoned and the regiment never came into being.[47]

The methods of recruiting for the expansion of the English army in 1688 were necessarily different. So many of the aristocracy and principal gentry had been alienated by James's domestic policies and personally affronted by 'closeting' and the 'regulations' that the king was unable to trade upon the same aristocratic goodwill which had been evident in 1685. Compliant protestants like the Duke of Newcastle and the catholic Earls of Stafford and Salisbury were willing to co-operate, but the majority of the new regiments had to be entrusted to professional soldiers and middling gentlemen who could not claim the same territorial interests as the colonels of 1685. This was probably one of the factors which led to so many of the new formations of 1688 not being completed in sufficient time to be effective in the campaign against the invaders: Henry Gage, the Marquis de Miremont, Lord Brandon, Henry Slingsby, Archibald Douglas, Bevil Skelton, George Holman, John Carne, and Solomon Richards did not belong to the same social league as the grandees who had raised troops three years earlier. Richards indeed was a most bizarre choice of colonel by a catholic monarch. He was an Irish nonconformist who had been the lieutenant-colonel of Cromwell's own regiment of foot and later, in 1659, had become the governor of Wexford. After the Restoration he endured a short term of imprisonment before he was allowed to retain the estate of 3,000 acres in County Wexford which he had acquired during his military service for the Protectorate. For twenty-seven years he lived peacefully on his Irish domain, raising a large family, until James II suddenly called upon his services on 27 September 1688. Presumably, Richards owed his appointment to one of the final attempts by the king to woo the Dissenters and give his army a broader religious base. Faced with an invasion, and anxious for popular support, the last thing that James could have afforded was the permanent addition of an Irish regiment to the English establishment; as a consequence, Richards raised his infantrymen from London and the home counties, thereby negating any territorial influence that he might have exercised on his own estates. There were also some indications that the willingness to volunteer was less in 1688 than it had been in 1685. No levy money had been issued in the first year of the reign, captains and colonels having been seemingly content to meet the expenses of recruitment from their own pocket, but in 1688 a colonel was allowed £20 for each horseman and £12 for every dragoon in an effort to both ease and hasten the flow of men. Perhaps the levy money was also designed to lengthen the purses of the new colonels.[48]

It is impossible to come close to the common soldier of James's army. Information is exceedingly scarce. The nucleus of the standing army of Charles II continued in service, but the identity of the new soldiers who joined the ranks between 1685 and 1688 remains a mystery. All the seven privates who were tried before the Middlesex Quarter Sessions for having run from their colours were described as having been 'labourers' before they took the king's shilling but it is not clear whether they were from the town or the countryside.[49] Some of the new men were less than desirable additions to the army and James was obliged to write in a circular letter to all his colonels that 'the taking into our forces persons unknown or of ill fame is found very prejudicial to our service'. The king gave orders that all new private soldiers must render to their officers 'a good account' of themselves and of 'their past behaviour'; even a statement that a man had previously served a foreign power was an insufficient testimonial. If a recruit had fought for an overseas army within the last two years he had to produce 'proper references from the officer under whom he last served'.[50] Some very considerable difficulties must have arisen if a recruit had recently returned from fighting for the Venetians in the Morea. In the haste of creating new regiments to meet Monmouth such a complicated and precise procedure represented an impossible ideal, and there is every suggestion that officers cared little about the character of the men they recruited provided they achieved their quotas. Even the ranks of the hallowed Life Guard were invaded by the 'wrong sorts'.

Any bankrupt merchant, a virulent French Huguenot, a valet de chambre or any little broken tradesman that can advance but £60 gets in to be a life guard man, which makes that a scandal now that was formerly counted and courted as an honour. The Guards ought to be a nursery where none should be planted but known honest gentlemen and the sons of persons of quality that might grow up, improve, and be there ripened and fitted for military employs but many that would otherwise reckon it a great honour to guard their prince's person do not covet being ranked with a company of scandalous fellows.[51]

This anonymous writer went on to regret that a former squire of Titus Oates had enlisted in the Life Guard. Any candidate was suitable for the catholic Lord Dover's fourth troop of the Life Guard provided he could cross his lordship's palm with fifty guineas; 'above half the troop were French Huguenots . . . if a Turk had come the fifty guineas had been acceptable to that lord the captain'.[52] Among the scant evidence that does survive about the soldiers of James's army there is no indication of any deliberate policy to recruit catholics – filling the ranks was the principal objective, with religious affiliations a minor consideration. Captain Dalton's company in Henry Gage's foot, a regiment which was raised in October 1688 and officered mainly by catholics, consisted of an incongruous mixture of old men and young boys, many of the latter so immature that the muster-master felt bound to release them from their engagements. This company's personnel was summarised as 'very shabby fellows and childer'.[53] As with the officers, there were probably too few catholics in England to provide more than a handful of soldiers for the army.

Most of the common soldiers were poor and entirely dependent on the service for their livelihood. Unfortunates who had been forced from the army by reason of serious wounds received during active service under Charles II in Tangiers, Portugal, and the colonies periodically applied for county pensions between 1685 and 1688. On 15 April 1686 the Buckinghamshire Quarter Sessions generously awarded Edmund Serch the sum of £1 'for having been an old soldier in his Majesty's service'. The magistrates must have been smitten with conscience after this parsimonious performance, for the same Edmund Serch was later admitted to a county pension of 40s per annum, 'having faithfully served his Majesty four years at Tangier and being burst in the said service'.[54] With an army which increased permanently in size, and in the absence of foreign war, James's military administration did not have to face the problems caused by numerous disabled veterans or hordes of disbanded soldiers. However, the king's army policy did create a complication. He was determined to improve the quality of his troops by removing the ancient, the sick, and the disabled and replacing them with young, well trained, and healthy men.[55] It would have taken considerably longer than three and three-quarter years to effect a substantial alteration in the rank and file, but some small beginnings were made. Sir Theophilus Oglethorpe, the colonel of the Holland regiment of foot, was given permission on 14 January 1688 to exchange fifty of his soldiers for an equivalent number of 'better men', the displaced troops being dismissed rather than put into some remote garrison to live out their lives in ease at the king's expense.[56] Some soldiers who were disbanded in this way were probably delighted at the chance to escape but the majority must have faced financial ruin and severe deprivation. A lucky few, like Edmund Serch, may have gained county pensions; Hamond Thornton was granted the sum of 15s per quarter by the Nottinghamshire Quarter Sessions in 1688 'for his service done to the king',[57] but such cases were the exception rather than the rule. The official army establishments during the reign included some provision for soldiers who were injured during their engagements but little allowance was made for men who lost their place through age, illness, or under pressure from 'better men'. The Royal Hospital at Chelsea was designed to cater for these individuals, but when it was first able to receive its full complement of 472 pensioners in 1687 it was already far too small for the number of qualified veterans. As a temporary expedient James introduced on 21 July 1685 a scheme of official pensions for private soldiers and non-commissioned officers. All those eligible who had been either disabled in the course of their duty on active service for the crown or who had served for a minimum period of twenty years were to receive monetary pensions until the Royal Hospital was able to accommodate them. These gratuities ranged from 5*d* a day for a private foot soldier to 1*s* 6*d* a day for an ex-trooper of the Life Guards. This scheme was continued after the completion of the hospital in order to offer some relief for those who could not be housed within its walls. Apart from those fortunate enough to find places at Chelsea the outlook for private soldiers was very bleak if they fell ill or were dismissed.[58]

Whereas the financial status of the rank and file was uniformly low, that of the officers varied considerably. Often the professional officers were men of limited means who relied heavily upon their army pay and emoluments to make a living. Captain Edmund Barry, Lieutenant Terence O'Brien, and Lieutenant James Barrett petitioned the Lord Treasurer on 17 February 1685, 'praying for half pay'. All three had fought in France during the 1670s but had left their employments in response to Charles II's recall order in 1678. They were granted their request but, more significantly, they each received commissions in the expanded English army within the year. Barry became a lieutenant in Henry Cornwall's foot, O'Brien entered the Duke of Norfolk's foot as an ensign, and Barrett was commissioned as an ensign in Sir William Clifton's infantry regiment.[59] Two officers whose only services appear to have been in independent troops of horse in 1685 petitioned the Lord Treasurer on 7 September 1685, seeking some assistance, as they had exhausted their 'small fortunes' in buying horses for their troops and in maintaining them at their own expense. The cost of loyalty was obviously high.[60] In raising an independent troop of horse in the summer of 1685 the Earl of Ailesbury spent £32 1*s* 8*d* on uniforms for his sixty troopers.[61] When the Duke of Newcastle recruited an infantry regiment in 1688 his own company within that formation cost him a total of £141 7s 6d for pay, quarters, clothes, and equipment, and there is no record that His Grace was ever repaid.[62] Commissions in the Guards and the standing regiments were expensive, although it is unlikely that commissions in the new regiments of 1688 were bought or sold. Regardless of the heavy initial charge, army life could represent a considerable financial burden. The annual camp on Hounslow Heath meant for the officers involved, from the highest to the lowest, a sizeable outlay. 'Every commission officer has his tent, which is a very great charge ... this last year has been an unprofitable one for the officers.'[63] Reresby, noting that with few exceptions, all the officers in the army were at a double expense through 'rouleing' and encamping at Hounslow, was secretly delighted that as he was a garrison governor his own company did not have to attend the rendezvous, thus sparing him this expense.[64] John Evelyn visited the camp in 1686 and recorded the sight of the 'commanders profusely vying in the expense and magnificence of [their] tents'.[65] Even the Earl of Dumbarton, James's trusted military adviser, seemed less than enthusiastic about Hounslow Camp:

Tomorrow I go to the camp and the king dines with me. This camp will cost me a good deal of money therefore I must draw upon your bills for what moneys you have of mine in your hands.[66]

Although an officer required some capital to purchase a commission and an income sufficient to maintain his dignity, the military duties were not onerous. The Earl of Ailesbury, whose independent troop of horse was regimented into the Earl of Peterborough's cavalry in August 1685, took part in a review before the king the same year but his overall contribution to regimental life was extremely limited.

I was one week in quarters at Reading with the said Earl [Peterborough] in order to prepare to pass before the king in review at Maidenhead Common, near Windsor, and our regiment did not camp that summer after the review. I retired to my father's in the country until after his death.[67]

Officers were able to obtain leave very easily. Captain Lenthall Warcup of the First Foot Guards was granted a furlough to go abroad to recover his health on 10 February 1688, and Major Hugh O'Connor was given leave of absence for the same purpose in August the same year.[68] However, these two sought official permission to pass overseas for specific purposes. If an officer required leave from his command and merely wished to remain in England, then, very often, he absented himself without seeking the approval of either his immediate commander or of the secretary-at-war. Charles Hatton was obviously somewhat hurt that his colonel, the Earl of Huntingdon, 'obliged me to go some part of the way with our regiment' when it left Hounslow Camp on its march to winter quarters in Plymouth. Fortunately, Huntingdon only insisted on Hatton travelling 'part of the way' and then 'was so favourable as to give me leave to be absent for some months'.[69] Occasionally the secretary-at-war heard a very sad tale.

> I received the king's orders for all governors to repair to their governments. Since I came from Windsor I have had two fits of an ague and do expect another tomorrow and I do intend to take the Jesuits' Powder for it. And my doctor tells me [that] if I take the Jesuits' Powder and should not put it off and go to Tilbury . . . my ague will return again and then I am afraid I shall have it all this winter. So I desire the favour of you to get me the king's leave for two or three months, three months if you can.

Two days later the writer, Colonel Sackville Tufton, asked to be recalled if the Dutch should attack.[70] Some officers seeking a respite from their arduous military careers did not bother to offer excuses and simply ignored their duties altogether, with or without permission. On 19 August 1686 Ralph Widdrington, the lieutenant-governor of Berwick-on-Tweed, reported to William Blathwayt that all the captains in Lord Ferrers's regiment of foot whose companies were in garrison were absent without leave. Blathwayt could do no more than order them back to their duties 'upon pain of displeasure'.[71] One of Sir John Reresby's lieutenants, Ralph Flood, was absent in London from the time of the disbandment of the Hounslow Camp early in August 1687 until the end of September. Reresby wrote to him repeatedly at his lodgings in the 'Naked Boy' in Fleet Street but received no reply. As a final resort he asked the commissary-general of the musters, David Crawford, to respite Flood's name from the last muster roll. This had the desired effect, and the errant lieutenant was back at his post by December 1687.[72] In the following year the governor of Chester Castle, Peter Shakerley, asked that similar treatment be given to three officers, Sir John Jacob, Thomas Condon, and John Tidcomb, all captains in the Earl of Huntingdon's foot, for taking 'longer absence than they had leave'.[73] By 7 October 1688 Sackville Tufton had managed to shake off his ague, but when he returned to his command at Tilbury Fort he discovered an abysmal state of affairs. Of the companies of the Earl of Bath's foot on duty in the garrison only the major and the captain-lieutenant were present, and the latter was 'sick, like to die'. Upon investigation, Tufton found that Ensign Thomas Carew had been absent since March; Captain Bernard Strode had been out of the garrison for some time; and Lieutenant Dering Bradshaw had requested a furlough of three days but had still not returned after three weeks. Tufton concluded that 'if the king does not make examples of some officers that are absent without leave it will be impossible for any governor to keep them in garrison'. Most of these unofficial leaves took place in regiments which were always quartered outside London. The Life Guards, the Royal Horse Guards, the First Foot Guards, and the Coldstream Guards spent most, or a good part of their time in and around the capital, enabling the young officers to remain in contact with fashionable society and with their patrons. Not only was garrison life in Chester or Chepstow Castle extremely dull and monotonous but the officers involved were denied the opportunity to lobby possible patrons or to lead the civilised existence of a gentleman. Lieutenant Talbot Lascelles, the adjutant of Lord Huntingdon's foot, had the misfortune to be quartered in Carlisle during the winter of 1686. He could find 'not a man fit for conversation' nor a woman who could be described as 'diverting; a nasty town which cannot produce a sheet of gilt paper'.[74] Carlisle was bad enough, but for those with a commission in the Scottish army the position was clearly intolerable. Any Scotsman wishing for patronage and promotion needed to be within the orbit of Whitehall and, as a result, large numbers of Scottish officers were frequently away from their commands. Out of the 175 officers in the Scottish regiments and garrisons, forty-five were either officially or unofficially absent from their posts during April 1687.[75] If the taking of unofficial leave seemed the only solution, the only possible reply from the government was to stop their pay.

Not until 1 May 1711 was it illegal to commission an army officer who was below the age of sixteen. Certainly under James a number of officers were distinctly juvenile. Sir John Reresby commissioned his fourteen-year-old son, Tamworth, as the cornet of his independent troop of horse in 1685, and Captain Thomas Norgate of the Anglo-Dutch Brigade secured an ensign's place for his son, Mathew, when the boy was just ten years of age.[76] However, despite these exceptions, the quality of the English officers was rapidly improving. The solid core of catholic and protestant officers who had fought overseas or served with the English army under Charles II was substantial and formed the backbone of the forces. Officers who could prove their military experience and aptitude were able to acquire commissions in

England under James II, and the army was treated as a serious career. The lack of professionalism which had characterised the Restoration army up to 1685 was quickly evaporating.[77] Many colonelcies and governorships were still awarded to courtiers and peers, but beneath this veneer most of the English regiments and garrisons were effectively commanded by lieutenant-colonels, majors, and captains who were increasingly professional in their outlook. Lord Dover might have been more interested in using his captaincy of the fourth troop of the Life Guard to line his own pocket but the executive command of his troop rested upon seasoned veterans – Patrick Sarsfield, James Griffin, and Henry Morgan. The field officers and captains of the Royal Horse Guards were efficient technical soldiers, and the regiments of Percy Kirke, Charles Trelawney, and Lord Cornbury were full of experienced officers from France and Tangier. The Earl of Scarsdale ranked as a military amateur but his lieutenant-colonel, Thomas Langston, and his major, Ambrose Norton, were present to advise and direct their colonel. Naturally, the transition from an army of courtiers to a modern army took time and there remained a number of very poor officers. Several gentlemen resigned their commissions rather than endure the 'fatigue and inconvenience' of the Hounslow Camp.[78] Sir John Reresby's two lieutenants were thoroughly inadequate: George Butler was 'a bad officer and infirm' as well as having committed a number of military offences, while Ralph Flood, as we have seen, was rarely at his post.[79] Lord Cornbury, the colonel of the Royal Dragoons, had the reputation of maintaining every troop in his regiment below its establishment strength through the persistent use of false musters. When he deserted to William he was very coldly received by the Duke of Schomberg, who was of the opinion that Cornbury had done James a service by defecting.[80] Since James's army did not fight but was ruined by internal conspiracy it is difficult to assess exactly its military competence. The Dutch sought to ridicule the English forces by picturing 'King James at the head of them shooting at butterflies in the air' but, although it was untested by battle, the army made great strides forward under James II. By 1688 it was more than capable of giving a good account of itself.[81]

Despite the lack of formal provision for military education in England, there was ample opportunity for young officers to gain experience by taking temporary service overseas. Although the theatres of war in France, Iberia, and the Spanish Netherlands which had proved so convenient for professional soldiers under Charles II were dormant in the 1680s, the war against the Turk in Hungary provided a chance to witness large-scale warfare and modern techniques. James was well aware of the educational potential of this seat of war for his English and Irish officers. Edward Clark was dispatched to Europe in 1686 to observe continental military methods. His first task was 'to take a view of and represent to us a design of the French king's camp at present drawn up in the plain between St. Germains and Paris'. After this he journeyed into the United Provinces to survey 'the Prince of Orange's army at the general rendezvous and to take notice of the method of their encamping, embattling, exercising ... and thereof to make us a true and exact representation'.[82] It is difficult to resist the conclusion that the experience of his own army's camp on Hounslow Heath during the summer of 1686 encouraged James to investigate the procedures of his European neighbours. Late in 1685 he ordered Jacob Richards, a son of Solomon Richards and a young engineer attached to the Ordnance Office, to travel into Hungary to visit the Imperial army and to record his findings and observations in a journal which was published on his return to England in 1687. Accompanied by Francis Negus, an ensign in the Holland regiment, Richards served at the siege of Buda and took note of the fortifications in Venice, northern Italy, and the Morea before sailing for England in order to employ some of his ideas in the rebuilding of the defences of Hull.[83] Another junior officer, Ensign Richard Burton of the Princess Anne's regiment of foot, went over to Hungary in February 1688 charged with the study of the 'art military, modern fortification, and modern artillery, and all aspects of military science'.[84] Apart from these official missions, a number of serving officers travelled across Europe to fight with the Imperial armies in 1686 and 1687, attracted by the magnet of the famous siege of Buda. James's illegitimate son, the Duke of Berwick, was present at Buda in 1686 in the company of Edward Vaudrey, who was to be knighted and appointed lieutenant-colonel of Sir John Talbot's regiment of horse in December 1687 after he and Berwick had made another excursion into Hungary.[85] William Steward and his father, the Viscount Mountjoy, as well as 'other noblemen of Ireland' reached Ratisbon on 9 May 1686 on their way to Hungary. Captain Frederick Fife of the Scottish army and Edward Rupert, a lieutenant in the Duke of Norfolk's foot, made the pilgrimage in 1686.[86] Perhaps as many as twenty British officers were present during the siege, among them Captain Sir Oliver St. George of the Queen's Dragoons; Captain Thomas Bellasise of the Irish Foot Guards, who was wounded before Buda and allowed to transfer into the Coldstream Guards on his recovery in 1687; Captain Mark Talbot, a catholic in Sir Edward Hales's foot; and Lieutenant-Colonel Robert Forbes of the Irish army.[87] William Herbert, the only son of the catholic Marquis of Powis, received a colonelcy in the English army in 1687 on the strength of his experience in Hungary during the previous year.[88]

Once the great siege was over only the really committed military men returned to Hungary the following year. Edward Vaudrey and the Duke of Berwick were again in attendance, as were Lord Charles Hamilton, a major in the Life Guard; Lord Walter Dongan, another Life Guard officer; Ensign Peter Atcherley of Sir Edward Hales's regiment; John Cutts, at this time an unattached mercenary; and Thomas Brown from the Anglo-Dutch Brigade.[89] The majority of these expeditions were probably made on the individual initiative of the officers concerned but they undoubtedly had the approval and encouragement of the king. He even allowed private soldiers to fight in the Imperial armies, Edward King, a trooper in Richard Hamilton's Irish dragoons, being granted such permission in 1687.[90] Hungary was not the sole theatre for foreign service. Two officers, Lieutenant Thomas Legard of the Earl of Plymouth's garrison company in Plymouth and Cornet Richard Foliott of the Queen's Dragoons, were given leave to fight for the Venetians in the Morea during the campaigning season of 1687.[91] Disease and the generally unhealthy conditions in the tropics meant that the East India Company was perpetually short of officers and soldiers, and in 1687 the company was offering a bounty of 40s for every private soldier who could be persuaded to volunteer.[92] A more ambitious scheme for foreign service was proposed by James Porter in 1686. Porter suggested that Carlos II, king of Spain, pay and equip a brigade of 4,000 English, Scottish, and Irish soldiers in the Spanish Netherlands. Such a force would always be at the disposal of the governor of the Spanish Netherlands, the Marquis de Castanaga, but would be available for service in England should an occasion arise. This design came to nothing, as Carlos II did 'not wish to take any decided attitude', but it does indicate that James might have been interested in establishing a reserve of trained troops overseas in a catholic country, possibly to act as a counterbalance to the Anglo-Dutch Brigade in the United Provinces. James had seen the six regiments of the Anglo-Dutch Brigade in England during the summer of 1685 and although impressed by their soldierly appearance he had been less enthusiastic about their political and religious attitudes. Although the proposal had been put to Castanaga and Carlos II through the offices of James

Porter it seems likely that the idea had James's support, since Porter was catholic, a groom of the bedchamber, and a confidant of the king. Perhaps the failure of this plan led to the decision later in 1687 to recall the Anglo-Dutch Brigade from the United Provinces and place it either in France or England, away from the harmful political and religious atmostphere of the Netherlands. There was little point in possessing an overseas reserve if it was politically unreliable.[93]

As James tried to improve the standard of his officer corps he was beset by the indiscipline which seriously affected most European armies in the later seventeenth century. There was an understandably cool relationship between the protestant and the catholic officers. 'There is great dissensions amongst them,' wrote Abraham de la Pryme, 'for the papist Irish and the protestant officers are commonly striving for superiority.' Narcissus Luttrell recorded rumours of 'some difference in the army between some protestant and some of the popish soldiers', whilst the officers themselves spent a good deal of time abusing each other's religion.[94]

A cornet of horse coming into his Majesty's chapel tent while some service was performing and making irreverent postures and gestures which, his Majesty perceiving, immediately sent for his commission and bestowed it on another.[95]

A Venetian newsletter of the same year reported how

An officer, a catholic, entered Bury church in Suffolk whilst the clergyman was preaching and, having drawn his sword, picked up some dirt and threw it at the preacher whom he compelled to desist and made his congregation depart. The church sent deputies to the king to acquaint him with the insolence and his Majesty had the goodness to suspend the said officer from his charge.[96]

One Morphew, a catholic house painter of York, drank confusion to all who did not read James's second declaration of indulgence. For this he was attacked and beaten by an army officer quartered in that part of the city. A complaint was naturally made to the king, who summoned the offending officer to London.[97] It was not in James's interest to have his English army internally divided between catholic and protestant but there was little he could do to prevent rivalry.

Religious differences were only a minor cause of indiscipline among the officers compared with the curse of the age, duelling. The great pastime of the gentry and aristocracy, it was as prevalent in the army as in civilian life. The Duke of Grafton killed Jack Talbot, the brother of the Earl of Shrewsbury, after a contest in Chelsea Fields on 2

February 1686, and on the same day Captain Henry Wharton of the Duke of Norfolk's foot, who came from a family with a reputation for forcibly preserving its honour, killed Lieutenant Robert Moxon, an Irish catholic from his own regiment.[98] Cornet Henry Gasshion crossed swords with Sir John Guise in January 1687, but both parties escaped with only slight wounds.[99] On the afternoon of Saturday 19 March 1688 two catholic ensigns, Henry Tern and William Delaval, slipped unnoticed into a private garden in Chester: a short while later Tern was dead and Delaval had hurried from the scene. The offender was tried under the common law but the jury returned a verdict of manslaughter and Delaval was granted a royal pardon.[100] Captain Charles Adderley, a protestant officer of the Royal Horse Guards, cut down his catholic major, Walter Littleton, in a duel in the streets of London on 19 December 1688.[101] When the army officers came into close contact with one another during the camps on Hounslow Heath their inflammatory tendencies overflowed. In the course of the camp of 1686 Colonel John Culpepper, a man with an abominable temper, shot a gentleman of the Life Guard with a blunderbuss. At his subsequent trial at the Old Bailey 'Mr. Culpepper owned he might have done the act but says he did it in his sleep and produced half a hundred witnesses to prove how he often committed those extravagancies in his sleep which he much abhorred when awake.' Captain Richard Cooke of the Earl of Huntingdon's regiment killed 'one Mr. Ash ... being a small officer in the camp', and Captain Simon Pack fought with Captain Allan Bellingham in Leicester Fields.[102] Whilst drinking together in Carlisle a lieutenant of Huntingdon's foot stabbed his major, Charles Morgan.[103] The Earl of Peterborough's horse lost two of its subalterns after Cornet Samuel Yeates and Lieutenant John Scott had settled an affair in the New Parks in Oxford.[104] These gentlemanly and fashionable pursuits often involved clashes between the civil and the military. Archibald Clinkard of the Duke of St. Albans's horse killed Mr. Nutt, a gentleman of Kent, in a duel in September 1688, whilst Captain William Freeman 'had the misfortune lately to wound a gentleman of his own name in a duel which happened upon some slight occasion at Epsom as they were in company'. Captain Freeman was also wounded in this affray and forced to retire temporarily until a pardon could be procured, as his adversary, Ralph Freeman, died from his injuries. The haughty and arrogant manner of some of the officers is well illustrated by one of Percy Kirke's captains who 'killed a waterman as he landed in Southwark ... upon a very slight occasion which was flashing a little water casually with an oar on the officer's coat.'[105]

The ill discipline of army officers was not restricted to physical violence among themselves or against civilians. A large number falsified the muster rolls of their troops and companies in order to enlarge their financial perquisites. Information placed before the Portsmouth Quarter Sessions in May 1685 related how 'this little rascal, Lieutenant William Games, took a false oath for the soldier . . . the officers were all rogues and . . . they cheated both the king and country and had not above sixteen men in a company'.[106] Even when the First Foot and the Coldstream Guards mustered in Hyde Park to be reviewed by the king the officers did not bother to fill up their companies and James demanded 'to know the reason for their being so defective, for he was exact in these things'.[107] During the reign a mere five cases involving false musters were tried before the general court-martial, but, undoubtedly, these represent only the tip of an iceberg: how many men James II actually had in his army is a matter for conjecture.[108] A novel variation on false musters was the practice of 'selling soldiers'. Lieutenant George Butler of Sir John Reresby's independent company in York, a man 'not very easy in his fortune and extravagant in his expenses', sold some of Reresby's soldiers while the company was in garrison in Hull – he accepted bribes from some men in order to secure them their discharge. When faced with this malpractice by his captain, Butler shrugged and replied that 'other lieutenants had done the same thing'. This was most unsatisfactory to Sir John, who clearly saw the quality of his company deteriorating as his lieutenant released 'old, disciplined men for money and took novices and unexperienced [sic] in their stead'.[109]

Perhaps the greatest problem within the army was the impossibility of imposing a code of discipline upon the officers which was effective enough to overcome the traditional allegiances of class and social status. How could a duke be forced to take orders from an untitled, catholic Irishman? Immediately after the successful reduction of Monmouth's Rebellion, the Duke of Albemarle, the colonel of the first troop of the Life Guard, resigned all his military offices in a fit of pique. The substance of his tantrum was that the Earl of Feversham and Lord Churchill had been promoted to major-generalships over his head.[110] The Duke of Beaufort became very worried in 1685 about the seniority of his new regiment in case the regiment of Henry Cornwall, a commoner, should have received precedence.[111] A similar question of social prestige caused the Duke of Norfolk and Lord Brudenall to resign their commissions in June 1686, the former 'considering it to be against his honour to be obliged to receive the commands of him of less dignity than himself'.[112] With these very unmilitary attitudes prevalent among some of the senior officers it took little for the subalterns to frequently disobey orders.[113] Despite the high incidence of duelling and physical violence among the officers, despite their sensitivity about matters of social status, and despite frequent disobedience, punishments were weak or non-existent. Cases involving officers which did come before either regimental or general courts-martial were tried by bodies of officers of the same social background and outlook as the offenders, a pleasant arrangement which resulted in sentences of such leniency that they were totally ineffective. Even a conviction for murder did not automatically result in the loss of a commission; the majority of wrongdoers were gently reprimanded and allowed back into their commission. As each commission represented a sizeable financial outlay for each officer, however lowly, it did not lie within the commonly accepted power of the king or the army to deprive the holder in such a material way. An offence had to be heinous before a man could be parted from a property which often represented the major investment of a lifetime. Murderers, duellers, perpetrators of false musters, all continued in the commissions they had purchased. In the Stuart army a commission offered a certain security of tenure, unless it was in a temporary formation raised solely for a specific and finite purpose. Across St. George's Channel this comfortable state of affairs where property counted for more than civil or military discipline or political affiliation was being systematically attacked and destroyed; protestant officers were being forcibly evicted from their appointments with little or no monetary compensation. Any rumours or portents that a similar policy might be introduced into England were bound to be met with the fiercest resistance. The removal of a commission in which an officer might have invested between £1,000 and £2,000 without any guarantee of adequate recompense was sufficient to undermine the most ardent loyalty to the crown.[114]

From the later months of 1685 James II gave sufficient indication that he was prepared to use the power of dismissal in England over political and religious issues. An officer could behave disgracefully, disobey orders, and cheat the Treasury by false musters but if he displayed overt political dissent he apparently stood in grave danger of forfeiting his place. Most of the government officials and military men who voted in favour of the parliamentary address of 14 November

1685 to remove catholic officers lost their appointments. The first casualty was John Coke, the member for Derby, whose provocative words had ended in his being committed to the Tower of London. In addition he was deprived of his captaincy in Princess Anne's regiment of foot.[115] According to Van Citters, the ambassador from the States-General, James was resolved to dismiss a great number of officers, perhaps as many as thirty, 'most of whom are members of parliament and who on some occasions have not acted so much according to his Majesty's wishes as he would have liked to do and will supply their places with others'.[116] Those who suffered included the paymaster-general, Charles Fox, Lieutenant-Colonel John Darcy, Major Edmund Webb, Captain Ambrose Brown, and four members of the Bertie clan – Henry, Richard, Peregrine, and Lord Willoughby. Charles Bertie moaned that

> my nephew Willoughby, my brother Dick, and brother Harry – the three battering rams of our family – are all turned out of their employment as captains and new commissions drawing for others to command their troops and I am further told that my nephew Peregrine Bertie – who is cornet to his brother Willoughby – is also dismissed, so that they have cleared the army of our whole family, which proving so unlucky a trade I would not have us bend our heads much to it for the future.[117]

By the end of December 1685 sixteen army officers had lost their commissions because of political opposition in parliament, among them Captain Charles Fitzwilliam of the Royal Fusiliers, the member for Peterborough.[118] James replaced these men with a wide variety of individuals, very few of whom were catholic. John Darcy's place in the Life Guard was assumed by a Scottish catholic, William Constable, but Ambrose Browne's captaincy in the Earl of Plymouth's foot passed to Sir Thomas Bludworth, a protestant and a gentleman pensioner. Henry, Richard, and Peregrine Bertie had all held commissions in independent troops of horse which were regimented in the autumn of 1685 but there are insufficient lists extant to discern their successors. Robert Bertie, Lord Willoughby d'Eresby, was a captain in the Earl of Peterborough's horse but forfeited his place to Allan Bellingham, a protestant. Charles Fitzwilliam made way for Edmund Wilson, a protestant career officer who was promoted from a lieutenant's place in Prince George of Denmark's foot.[119]

Early in the summer of 1686 James began to 'closet' individual peers, members of parliament, and men in public positions to ascertain their attitude to the proposed repeal of the Test Acts and Penal Laws. The Earl of Shrewsbury and Lord Lumley both refused to commit themselves and were removed from their colonelcies. Shrewsbury, himself a recent convert from catholicism, saw his commission pass to Richard Hamilton, an Irish papist, but Lumley's appointment went to Sir John Talbot, a seasoned and well respected professional soldier.[120] Sir John Egerton's troop in the Earl of Peterborough's horse was given to Henry Lawson in 1687, presumably because of Egerton's failure to comply with his monarch's political requests.[121] For not declaring against the Tests and Penal Laws the Earl of Scarsdale was forced to hand over his colonelcy of horse to the more pliant Duke of St. Albans, and the Earl of Gainsborough was similarly dismissed from the government of the important garrison of Portsmouth. Aubrey de Vere, the last Earl of Oxford, saw the command of the prestigious Royal Horse Guards, which he had held since 1661, pass to the catholic Duke of Berwick, James's bastard son. Another aristocratic casualty was Lord Worcester, the eldest son of the Duke of Beaufort, a more brittle protestant than his father: his colonelcy of foot was given to the Welsh catholic William Herbert, Viscount Montgomery.[122] The largest number of military changes seem to have occurred in February and March 1687, when 'every post brought fresh news of gentlemen losing their employments both military and civil'. Sir Michael Wentworth of Peterborough's horse lost his commission after he himself had been appointed to the vacancy created by the removal of Richard Bertie on 16 December 1685. Captain Robert Beverley and Captain Allan Bellingham were faced with unemployment in 1687, along with Captain Charles Fairfax and Major Sir Walter Clarges.[123] Sir Francis Edwardes, the second baronet, was forced to surrender his captaincy in Henry Cornwall's foot on 1 April 1687, as was the lieutenant-colonel of the same regiment, Sir John Morgan, a seasoned veteran who had seen service in the Anglo-Dutch Brigade, Flanders, and the English army under Charles II.[124] James was obliged to recall Morgan in October 1688 because of the acute shortage of trained officers to instruct the numerous recruits. Unless some private arrangements were made between the dismissed incumbents and the new officers the former incurred considerable financial deprivation, as no recompense was forthcoming from the crown. Sir Richard Temple's remark that James did much during his brief reign 'to disoblige the army' was a very restrained description of the true state of affairs. The fact that the king was able to turn out 'Chief Justice Herbert's elder brother ... from a company bought for eight hundred guineas for refusing to repeal the Test' was a very serious matter for the officer corps and a naked assault upon the rights of property.[125] By attempting to purge the English army of all those who did not agree to comply with his political and religious wishes, James created a degree of ill-will and suspicion. The cashiered officers were not exclusively replaced with catholics – the majority of the new men were protestant careerists – and the English officer corps contained the same proportion of papists in 1688 as it had in 1685, but the king succeeded in 'disobliging' some forty or fifty of his English officers. In order to create a reliable and professional army he disrespected investment and property and treated both gentlemen and peers in a manner to which they were not accustomed. No doubt the king hoped that the developing professionalism of his English officers would bind them to him whatever policies he pursued, but he undermined this fount of potential loyalty by attacking the sanctity of property and by acting without tact. In the unforeseen and unforseeable combination of circumstances in 1688 a small section of the officer corps, with the support of some of those who had already lost their commissions, defied James and greatly assisted in his fall. Instead of donning the velvet glove he blundered through his reign with an amazing lack of circumspection; the dismissals of politically unacceptable officers took place against a backcloth of the purge of almost all of the protestant officers from the Irish army.

James's policy of removing politically suspect officers had another important effect. Whereas during the reign of his brother, and again in the crisis of 1685, men of national and local political worth had been prepared to accept commissions – the Dukes of Beaufort, Norfolk, and Somerset and the Earls of Shrewsbury and Scarsdale – there were very few of these still in possession of their commands by the summer of 1688 and their replacements were not of the same social or political standing. Throughout the reign there was a tendency for commissions to be bought by or given to men who were usually without great political pretensions and who regarded military service as a career. This rendered the army more remote from the mainstream of national and provincial politics and helped to separate it from everyday society, making it increasingly dependent on the will of the sovereign.

Through the defeat of Monmouth, James had acquired a large and loyal army. Within the short space of three and three-quarter years he had greatly improved its technical efficiency and its political allegiance but, in 'disobliging' a small section of the protestant officers by threatening their pockets, careers, and dignities, he unwittingly planted the seeds of his own destruction. The protestant career officers were grateful to him in 1685 for providing them with opportunities in England, but three years later some of these same gentlemen were in the van of an army conspiracy which helped William of Orange in bringing down the monarch. When faced with an invasion by the hated Dutch in 1688 the huge majority of the officers and men remained loyal to their king, but enough officers considered themselves to have been sufficiently intimidated and unsettled as to make this asset worthless.

Notes

1. Childs, *Army of Charles II*, pp. 25–9, 133, 175–9, 218–32 and 244–50.
2. J. R. Western, *Monarchy and Revolution* (London, 1972), p. 190.
3. H. C. Foxcroft, *The Life and Letters of Sir George Savile, Bart., First Marquis of Halifax* (London, 1898), i. 448.
4. *CSPD 1685*, No. 1936; J. R. Jones, *The Revolution of 1688 in England* (London, 1972), p. 65; *HMC, Downshire MSS.*, i. 59.
5. *CSPD 1686–7*, No. 101.
6. *The Ellis Correspondence*, ed. George Agar Ellis (London, 1829), i. 6–7; BL Add. MSS. 34,508, ff. 102 and 105, 11 and 22 Jan. 1686, Van Citters to the States-General.
7. Turner, *James II*, pp. 319–20; BL Add. MSS. 29,561, ff. 110–11; Portland MSS. PwA 2242.
8. Dalton, *Army Lists*, ii. 1–64.
9. M. V. Hay, *The Enigma of James II* (London, 1938), pp. 127–9.
10. *Ailesbury's Memoirs*, i. 126 and 220.
11. Gilbert Burnet, *History of His Own Time* (Oxford, 1833), iii. 261.
12. *Ailesbury's Memoirs*, i. 220–21.
13. *Reresby*, p. 553.
14. John Miller, 'Catholic officers in the later Stuart army', *EHR*, lxxxviii. (1973), pp. 39–40; John Miller, *Popery and Politics in England, 1660–1688* (Cambridge, 1973), p. 199.
15. Dalton, *Army Lists*, ii. 176.
16. These figures are based wholly upon biographies of catholic and protestant officers compiled by the author and which he hopes to publish separately at some time in the future. The biographies, to the number of approximately one thousand, are derived from a wide variety of sources of which the following are the most important: unpublished materials of the History of Parliament Trust; Dalton, *Army Lists*, i–vi.; G. E. C(okayne), *The Complete Peerage of England, Scotland, Ireland, Great Britain, and the United Kingdom* (London, 1910–59), i–xii.; G.E.C., *The Complete Baronetage* (*Exeter, 1900–06*), *i–vi.*; *DNB*; *Le Neve's Pedigree of the Knights*, ed. G. W. Marshall (London, Harleian Society, 1873); John Kirk, *Biographies of English Catholics in the Eighteenth*

Century, ed. John Hungerford Pollen and Edwin Burton (London, 1909); *CSPD 1685*; *CSPD 1686–7*; *CSPD 1687–9*; WO 25/1–2; SP 44/69; SP 44/64; SP 44/165

17 *Correspondentie van Willem III en van Hans Willem Bentinck, eersten Graaf van Portland*, ed. N. Japikse (The Hague, 1928), p. 18, 'Memorial upon the Edict in Scotland of 12th February 1687', drawn up by Scottish exiles in the United Provinces.
18 Miller, *Popery and Politics*, pp. 9–12.
19 See chapter IV.
20 Clarke, *Life*, ii. 235.
21 *CSPD 1686–7*, No. 619; William King, *The State of the Protestants of Ireland under the late King James's Government* (London, 1692), p. 368; Dalton, *Army Lists*, ii. 87, 144 and 155; Miller, *Popery and Politics*, pp. 243–4.
22 Dalton, *Army Lists*, i. 240 and 295, ii. 35 and 144; *CSPD 1687–9*, p. 270.
23 Sir G. F. Duckett, *Penal Laws and Test Act* (London, 1882–3), i. 188, ii. 260; Dalton, *Army Lists*, ii. 171; *Wild Geese in Spanish Flanders, 1582–1700*, ed. Brendan Jennings (Irish Manuscripts Commission, Dublin, 1964), Nos. 2820, 2827–8, and 2837; *HMC, Portland MSS.*, iii. 417.
24 BL Add. MSS. 41,822, ff. 215–18; Dalton, *Army Lists*, i. 158, ii. 33 and 142.
25 John D'Alton, *Illustrations Historical and Genealogical of King James's Irish Army List* (Dublin, 1860), ii. 4 and 27–31; BL Add. MSS. 41,822, ff. 215–18; *HMC, Laing MSS.*, i. 460.
26 Dalton, *Army Lists*, i. 207, ii. 33, 142 and 206; *CSPD 1685*, No. 1936; *CSPD 1686–7*, No. 101; Childs, *Army of Charles II*, p. 246.
27 'Mark Browell's Diary', ed. J. C. Hodgson, *Surtees Society*, cxxiv. (1915), pp. 182 and 186; Miller, 'Catholic Officers', p. 49n.; Dalton, *Army Lists*, i. 134, ii. 175.
28 *The Life of Marmaduke Rawdon of York*, ed. Godfrey Davies (Camden Society, 1863), p. 144n., Childs, *Army of Charles II*, p. 26.
29 Dalton, *Army Lists*, ii. 15 and 122; King, *State of the Protestants*, p. 367; *CSPD 1685*, No. 1936.
30 Dalton, *Army Lists*, ii. 144; *HMC, Le Fleming MSS.*, p. 231.
31 Kirk, *Biographies*, p. 148; Dalton, *Army Lists*, ii. 15, 101 and 120; *CSPD 1685*, No. 1936; *CSPD 1686–7*, No. 101.
32 D'Alton, i. 255; Dalton, *Army Lists*, ii. 39, 61, 137 and 191.
33 *HMC, Laing MSS.*, i. 449–50; Dalton, *Army Lists*, ii. 81 and 133.
34 *Ailesbury's Memoirs*, i. 128–9; Childs, *Army of Charles II*, pp. 65–6.
35 *Ibid.*, pp 30–42.
36 John Wachop's foot, which was raised in Scotland in March 1688 from returning officers of the Anglo-Dutch Brigade, formed part of the Scottish establishment but as it spent nearly all its time in England it has been treated as a corps of the English army in the discussions of this chapter.
37 PRO SP 57/5–13, Scottish Warrant Books; Charles Dalton, *The Scots Army, 1661–1688* (Edinburgh, 1909), pp. 60–168; *HMC, Stuart MSS.*, i. 31,

3 Feb. 1688, Lord Perth to the Cardinal of Norfolk.
38 'A Series of Eight Anonymous and Confidential Letters to James II about the State of Ireland', ed. William Frazer, *Notes and Queries*, 6th series, vi. 62. Because of the curious history of these letters their political tone and factual content have been treated with caution; James Macpherson, *Original Letters containing the Secret History of Great Britain, from the Restoration to the Accession of the House of Hanover* (London, 1775), i. 228; *HMC, 7th Report*, App. pp. 268, 275 and 409.
39 Dalrymple, *Memoirs of Great Britain and Ireland*, ii. app. Part 1, p. 130.
40 Wood, *Life and Times*, iii. 145.
41 *Oxford Council Acts, 1665–1701*, ed. M. G. Hobson (Oxford Historical Society, 1939), p. 173, 26 June 1685.
42 BL Add. MSS. 38,694, f. 87, 12 Feb. 1687.
43 *HMC, Dartmouth MSS.*, i. 144; Luttrell, *Historical Relation*, i. 463, 23 Sept. 1688; *HMC, Le Fleming MSS.*, p. 215, 12 Oct. 1688, E. Wilson to Sir Daniel Fleming.
44 C. T. Atkinson, 'Two Hundred and Fifty Years Ago: James II and his army', *JSAHR*, xiv. (1935), pp. 4–6; Bodleian Library, Rawlinson MSS. D. 148.
45 *Records of the Borough of Leicester, 1603–1688*, ed. Helen Stocks and W. H. Stevenson (Cambridge, 1923), p. 582, 25 June 1685, Earl of Huntingdon to Mayor of Leicester.
46 *Norfolk Lieutenancy Journal*, pp. 68–9.
47 *CSPD 1685*, Nos. 935 and 940.
48 BL Add. MSS. 5,752, f. 223; Luttrell, *Historical Relation*, i. 463; F. J. Hebbert, 'The Richards Brothers', *Irish Sword*, xii. (1975), pp. 200–1.
49 Childs, *Army of Charles II*, pp. 21–5 and 123–4; *Middlesex County Records* (Middlesex County Records Society, London, 1892), iv. 290, 310, 311–12, 315 and 327–8.
50 BL Add. MSS. 38,694, f. 54, 2 June 1685.
51 Frazer, 'Anonymous Letters', v. 62, 14 Feb. 1687.
52 *Ailesbury's Memoirs*, i. 130–1.
53 *HMC, Le Fleming MSS.*, pp. 221–2, 24 Nov. 1688, William to Sir Daniel Fleming.
54 *County of Buckingham, Calendar to the Sessions Records* (Aylesbury, 1933), i. 202 and 205, 15 April 1686 and 15–16 July 1686.
55 Dalrymple, *Memoirs of Great Britain and Ireland*, ii. app. Part 1, p. 132; Clifford Walton, *History of the British Standing Army, 1660–1700* (London, 1894), p. 488.
56 Davies, 'Letters on the Administration of James II's Army', p. 76, William Blathwayt to Sir Thomas Haggerston.
57 *Records of the Borough of Nottingham*, ed. W. T. Baker, (Nottingham and London, 1900), v. 96, 25 April 1688.
58 WO 24/8/Parts 1–6; Christopher Clay, *Public Finance and Private Wealth: The Career of Sir Stephen Fox, 1627–1716* (Oxford, 1978), pp. 137–9; *HMC, Montague of Beaulieu MSS., p. 191.*

59 *CSPD 1685*, No. 395.
60 *Ibid.*, No. 1589.
61 Earl of Cardigan, *The Life and Loyalties of Thomas Bruce* (London, 1951), pp. 98–9.
62 Portland MSS. PwA 332.
63 *A Young Squire of the Seventeenth Century*, ed. J. C. Jeaffreson (London, 1878), ii. 287, 1686, Christopher Jeaffreson to Colonel Thomas Hill, lieutenant-governor of St. Kitts.
64 *Reresby*, p. 429, 17 June 1686.
65 *The Diary of John Evelyn*, ed. E. S. de Beer (Oxford, 1955), iv. 553, 12 June 1687.
66 *HMC, Hamilton MSS. (Supplementary Report)*, pp. 110–11, 14 June 1687, Earl of Dumbarton to Duke of Hamilton; *Letters of Philip, Second Earl of Chesterfield* (London, 1829), pp. 323–4, 20 July 1686.
67 *Ailesbury's Memoirs*, i. 121.
68 PRO SP 44/165, pp. 16 and 62.
69 *Correspondence of the Family of Hatton*, ed. E. M. Thompson (Camden Society, 1878), ii. 89–90, 9 Aug. 1688, Charles to Lord Hatton.
70 BL Add. MSS. 33,924, ff. 68 and 70, 23 and 25 Aug. 1688, Sackville Tufton to William Blathwayt.
71 WO 4/1, pp. 33–4.
72 BL Add. MSS. 9,735, f. 22.
73 BL Add. MSS. 38,694, f. 113, 21 Jan. 1688.
74 Archives Department of Leeds' City Libraries, Letters of Sir John Reresby, 45/31, 23 Dec. 1686, Talbot Lascelles to Reresby; BL Add. MSS. 33,924, f. 72, 2 Oct. 1688, Tufton to Blathwayt.
75 SRO E 100/46/3, 'List of the Commissioned Officers who were absent from the Muster by furlough and otherways'.
76 I. F. Burton, 'The Committee of Council at the War Office: an Experiment in Cabinet Government under Anne', *HJ*, iv. (1961), p. 80; *CSPD 1687–9*, No. 1980; Dalton, *Army Lists*, ii. 15; *Reresby*, pp. 381–2.
77 Childs, *Army of Charles II*, pp. 30–46 and 65–6.
78 *HMC, Downshire MSS.*, i. 165–6, 10 May 1686, Dr. Owen Wynne to Sir William Trumbull.
79 *Reresby*, p. 480.
80 Frazer, 'Anonymous Letters', vi. 62, 14 Feb. 1687; *HMC, Leeds MSS.*, p. 26, 20 Nov. 1688, Richard Hast to Sir Walter Vavasour.
81 *The Diary of Abraham de la Pryme*, ed. Charles Jackson (Surtees Society, 1870), p. 8, referring to the Hounslow camp of 1686; see chapters IV and VII.
82 SP 44/164, pp. 345–6, 17 July 1686.
83 BL Stowe MSS. 447; *The Letters of Sir George Etherege*, ed. F. Bracher (London, 1974), pp. 24–5; *Journal of the Siege and Taking of Buda by the Imperial Army* (London, 1687); Hebbert, 'The Richards Brothers', pp. 201–3.
84 SP 44/165, p. 22, 24 Feb. 1688.

85 *Etherege's Letters*, pp. 44 and 123; Dalton, *Army Lists*, ii. 113 and 125.
86 *CSPD 1686–7*, No. 1849; *Ellis Correspondence*, i. 74–5; *Memoirs of Mary, Queen of England, 1689–1693*, ed. E. Doebner (London, 1886), p. 67, 6 May 1686; *HMC, 2nd Report*, p. 215.
87 *HMC, Downshire MSS.*, i. 166, 10 May 1686, Ratisbon, Hugo Hughes to Sir William Trumbull's secretary; *Etherege's Letters*, pp. 31, 37, 49–50 and 56; *HMC, Ormonde MSS.*, old series, i. 414; Richards, *Journal of the Siege . . . of Buda*, pp. 18–32; *CSPD 1685* No. 1248; *CSPD 1686–7*, No. 739; BL Stowe MSS. 447; *CCSP*, v. 668.
88 *Etherege's Letters*, p. 31.
89 *Ibid*, pp. 123, 125n., 128 and 211.
90 SP 44/69, p. 210, 6 May 1687.
91 *CSPD 1686–7*, Nos. 1597 and 1610.
92 *HMC, Downshire MSS.*, i. 253.
93 *Wild Geese*, No. 2844, 1 Aug. 1686; *CSPD 1686–7*, No. 1545; E. and M. S. Grew, *The English Court in Exile: James II at Saint-Germain* (London, 1911), pp. 96 and 129.
94 *Pryme's Diary*, p. 8; Luttrell, *Historical Relation*, i. 381, 18 June 1686.
95 *HMC, Downshire MSS.*, i. 251, 30 June 1687.
96 Quoted in Hay, *Enigma of James II*, p. 100, 21 March 1687.
97 *HMC, Portland MSS.*, iii. 411, 19 June 1688, letter to Robert Harley.
98 *Ellis Correspondence*, i. 36–41; *HMC, Downshire MSS.*, i. 115–16; *HMC, Rutland MSS.*, ii. 103.
99 Gloucester Record Office, Blathwayt Papers. D.1799/Accession 3328, 8 Jan. 1687, Anthony Ovington to William Blathwayt.
100 BL Add. MSS. 38,694, f. 119, 19 March 1688, Peter Shakerley to Blathwayt; BL Add. MSS. 38,695, f. 11, 25 April 1688, same to same.
101 *Ellis Correspondence*, ii. 368.
102 *Memoirs of the Verney Family during the Seventeenth Century*, ed. M. M. Verney (London, 1907), ii. 448–9; *Ellis Correspondence*, i. 204.
103 *Reresby*, p. 441.
104 Wood, *Life and Times*, iii. 220.
105 BL Add. MSS. 34,152, f. 21, 16 Sept. 1688; Jeaffreson, ii. 304, 3 Aug. 1686, Christopher Jeaffreson to Thomas Hill; *The Portledge Papers*, ed. R. J. Kerr and Ida Coffin Duncan (London, 1928), p. 43, 19 Aug. 1688, Richard Lapthorne to Richard Coffin; *Ellis Correspondnece*, ii. 132.
106 *Portsmouth Record Series: Borough Sessions Papers, 1653–1688*, ed. A. J. Willis and M. J. Hoad (Portsmouth, 1971), p. 120, 15 May 1685.
107 *Reresby*, p. 413.
108 WO 89/1, pp. 94–104; WO 92/1, fragment.
109 *Reresby*, pp. 435–6, 27 Sept. 1686.
110 Bramston, pp. 205–6; *Verney Memoirs*, ii. 447; *Reresby*, p. 390; *The Correspndence of Henry Hyde, Earl of Clarendon, and of his brother, Lawrence Hyde, Earl of Rochester*, ed. S. W. Singer (London, 1828), i. 149.
111 *Ibid.*, i. 156–7, 4 Sept. 1685, Duke of Beaufort to Clarendon.
112 BL Add. MSS. 34,508, f. 122, 28 June 1686, Van Citters to the States-

General.
113 WO 89/1, pp. 92–3 and 105–11; *Reresby*, pp. 442–3; WO 92/1; WO 4/1, pp. 89–90; *Hatton Correspondence*, ii. 106 and 108.
114 John Carsell, *The Old Cause* (London, 1954), pp. 6 and 64.
115 Wood, *Life and Times*, iii. 170.
116 BL Add. MSS. 34,508, ff. 99, 28 Dec. 1685; *Reresby*, p. 395.
117 *HMC, Rutland MSS.*, ii. 97, 17 Dec. 1685, Charles Bertie to Countess of Rutland.
118 Luttrell, *Historical Relation*, i. 367; *Hatton Correspondence*, ii. 61; *HMC, Downshire MSS.*, i. 75–9; Wood, *Life and Times*, iii. 131 and 171; Clay, *Public Finance and Private Wealth*, pp. 270 and 297–8; *Reresby*, pp. 399 and 402–3.
119 Dalton, *Army Lists*, ii. 5, 26, 60 and 63; HPT.
120 D. H. Hosford, *Nottingham, Nobles and the North* (Hamden, Connecticut, 1976), pp. 14–15; *Etherege's Letters*, p. 275; J. P. Kenyon, *Robert Spencer, Earl of Sunderland, 1641–1702* (London, 1958), p. 138; HPT.
121 Duckett, *Penal Laws*, ii. 88; Dalton, *Army Lists*, ii. 78 and 122.
122 Hosford, *Nottingham*, pp. 20–1; *Reresby*, p. 487; BL Add. MSS. 34,510, ff. 65 and 85; *HMC, Portland MSS.*, iii. 398.
123 *Reresby*, pp. 444–5; Luttrell, *Historical Relation*, i. 396–8; Reresby's Letters, 4/12, 8 Feb. 1687, Blathwayt to Reresby.
124 Reresby's Letters, 48/27, 21 June 1687, Captain Edmund Reresby of the First Foot Guards to Sir John Reresby; HPT; Childs, *Army of Charles II*, p. 243.
125 Charles Herbert of Aston was the brother of Admiral Arthur Herbert and the son of Sir Edward, the attorney-general of Charles I. Before his dismissal from the army Charles Herbert had been at Whitehall, where 'some questions were asked to which he did not give satisfactory answer, as is supposed' (*Herbert Correspondence*, ed. W. J. Smith (Cardiff and Dublin, 1963), p. 328, 7 May 1687, John Oliver to Humphrey Owen; Dodd, *Stuart Wales*, pp. 218–19); *Verney Memoirs*, ii. 461.

III

The great purge in Ireland

Numerically the Irish army of February 1685 was almost as large as its sister formation in England, but in quality it was decidedly inferior. During the first twelve years of the restored monarchy the armed forces in Ireland had consisted of thirty independent troops of horse and sixty-six separate companies of foot without any organised structure of command and with little sense of corporate identity. Although these disparate elements were welded into three regiments of cavalry and seven of infantry in 1672, this did not really contribute towards creating a unified army, as the new corps rarely came together in formed units but continued to be scattered around the countryside in small groups. The officers were drawn exclusively from the protestant gentry and aristocracy. In the earlier part of the reign of Charles II there were many officers who had seen service in the Great Rebellion or under Cromwell, but by 1684 only ten of these veterans remained on the active list and their old comrades had been replaced by protestant peers and gentlemen who, usually, spent as short a time as possible at their posts. Even the soldiers were frequently allowed to leave their martial duties for much of the year and follow their trades in towns or work as agricultural day labourers, with the result that, for ten out of every twelve months, the Irish forces resembled a territorial rather than a regular army. The equipment and arms of this miserable and half-hearted part-time army were entirely appropriate to its physical condition – defective, rusty, and out-of-date. James inherited an Irish army that was thoroughly demoralised and disorganised; just about capable of hunting catholic bandits, it was inadequate for serious military operations.

It was inconceivable that he would have permitted this state of affairs to continue. Despite such an unpromising legacy, the new monarch adopted a policy of remodelling the military in Ireland, yet in attempting to improve the army he actually succeeded in making it even worse through emphasising political and religious loyalty rather than martial efficiency. By removing the majority of the protestant officers and men and replacing them with catholics James erased the small reservoir of military expertise that the army possessed and substituted inexperience and ignorance in its place. When he was obliged to rely upon his Irish armed forces in 1689 as the sole means of regaining his throne he found them to be virtually useless against the trained troops of Williams III. That ultimate defeat was staved off for two years was due to a combination of French assistance, the distraction of the war in Flanders, and the dogged loyalty of many Jacobite officers from England and Scotland who tried, in the short time available, to undo much of the harm which had befallen the Irish army between 1685 and 1688.[1] Not only did James ruin the army by purging its personnel but he failed to make any determined effort to modernise its antiquated equipment. In January 1686 most of the officers were agreed that the muskets and pikes were in a deplorable state. The firearms which had been issued to the soldiers were described as 'very bad' and lacked any standardisation, whilst the armaments in the ordnance stores were rusted and rotten. Ireland's fixed fortifications and military installations had been surveyed in 1674, and the subsequent report had suggested an outlay of £554,116 19s to repair and modernise the most important works. Talk of such sums was a certain method of turning Charles's attention away from the subject, and nothing was done until another survey was ordered in 1684. The task was entrusted to an engineer from the Ordnance Office in London, Thomas Phillips, but Charles was dead by the time his findings were ready. Phillips considered that only Kinsale, Passage, Limerick, Londonderry, and Culmore were potentially capable of resisting serious attack provided that £144,316 was expended, a sum of money well beyond the resources of the Irish treasury unless it received funds from England. These were not forthcoming, as James's ordnance budget in England was fully committed to improving the defences of Plymouth, Portsmouth, Hull, and the Medway towns.[2]

Although James undermined the military efficacy of his Irish corps he did succeed in converting it into a religiously subservient force and ensured that its political aims and allegiance were in tune with his own. Under both Cromwell and Charles II the Irish army had reflected the dominance of the protestant minority over the huge catholic majority of the island's population. Between 1685 and 1688 James II's government in Ireland made considerable progress in its attempt to reverse this political and religious structure by raising a catholic army from among the catholic Irish. Hypothetically, James probably visualised Ireland as the great bastion of religious support that was denied to him in England, yet the exact degree of his personal involvement both in the decision to catholicise the Irish army and the civil administration and in the execution of that policy was ambivalent. There is no evidence whatever that he intended to use the reformed Irish army in England, nor is there any support for the idea that, initially, he himself wished to employ the catholic army to overawe the protestant minority in Ireland, although this was the probable direction of Tyrconnell's thoughts from the very commencement of the reign. Contemporaries feared that the dramatic events which were taking place across St. George's Channel would eventually lead to Irish military intervention in England and to the ruin of the protestant interest in Ireland. These anxieties were ably expressed by Gilbert Burnet in his statement that 'the king resolved also to model Ireland so as to make that kingdom a nursery for his army in England and to be sure at least of an army there while his designs were to go on more slowly in the isle of Britain'. Charles O'Kelly indirectly supported Burnet's opinion when he said that it was to James's advantage to 'preserve' the Irish nation and to secure its 'loyalty and assistance', but he failed to elaborate upon why and where the king might require this 'assistance'. Tyrconnell stressed the same point by telling his master that he could never be 'secure' against another rebellion unless he removed the ex-Cromwellian and 'disaffected' officers from his army and put loyal catholics in their stead. Naturally, the Jacobite biography of the sovereign was more sympathetic in its suggestion that the reform of the Irish army was undertaken

to mitigate the cruel oppression the catholics had so long groaned under in that kingdom. He [James] thought it no injury to others that the roman catholics, who had tasted so deeply of his sufferings, should now, in his prosperity, have a share at least of his protection.[3]

Apart from the worries about the future employment of a remodelled Irish army, it was recognised by both protestant and catholic alike that the standing regiments of Ireland were in need of drastic reform. They had not drilled for a dozen years and the private soldiers were often quartered on the estates of their captains, where they were used as cheap labour.[4] James was determined to have an effective and loyal military establishment in his third kingdom, and this recognition of the necessity for change made him listen with interest to the suggestions of Tyrconnell. In effect, the Irishman was able to preach to a monarch who was already converted: James and Tyrconnell agreed on the immediate objective even if they differed over the means and the ultimate end.

The reasons behind the purge of the Irish army should be seen solely in terms of the domestic politics of that country. Apart from the concern that such a large cleansing operation created, the purge did not materially affect either the English or the Scottish forces – in the military history of the Glorious Revolution the importance of events in Ireland was emotional and suggestive rather than actual. James knew little of Ireland, he had never set foot on its soil, and he was utterly dependent for advice upon a few so-called 'experts'. The principal of these was Richard Talbot, later the Earl of Tyrconnell, a roman catholic of 'old English' extraction with a domineering, blustering, and abrasive manner, who had been one of the gang of violent rakes with whom James had surrounded himself whilst Duke of York. Indubitably, James's policy towards Ireland was the result of Tyrconnell's persuasion and highly partial information. His main aim was to make the maximum possible use of the golden opportunity which was suddenly presented by the reign of a catholic monarch to overthrow the pro-protestant land settlement in Ireland in order to improve the lot of his own class. This involved disarming the protestant militia, removing all the protestant officers and men from the regular army and replacing the former with catholic 'old English' and the latter with native Irishmen, and giving the majority of places in the civil administration and in municipal government to the same group. To achieve these specific aims Tyrconnell played upon James's 'duty' to assist the 'poor catholics'. Tyrconnell's policy was not concerned with England, and he certainly did not envisage building Ireland into a religious and military base from which to interfere in English affairs. On the contrary, he seems to have desired a separation of the two states rather than closer ties. There was a distinct possibility that, after the death of James II, he might have declared Ireland an independent state and it is conceivable that James actually agreed to this scheme during his meeting with the Lord Deputy at Chester in 1687. However, early in his reign, James as king of England and Ireland could not be so radical or precise in his own policy. Somehow he had to reconcile his personal obligation to ameliorate the conditions under which the catholic Irish suffered with the political necessity of retaining English control over Ireland through the auspices of the protestant minority. There was a great deal of English investment in Irish land and offices, Irish revenues derived wholly from the trade and commerce of the protestants, family connections between the two islands were strong and numerous, and Englishmen regarded the defence of Ireland as a necessary pillar against the increasing might of France. James was thus torn between his religious convictions and the demands of his regal position. By 1687 Tyrconnell had forced his hand. In purging the Irish army and government with remarkable speed and effectiveness, Tyrconnell was able to present his sovereign with the essential foundation for a catholic Ireland; whether James had really wished it or not, protestant control of the Irish government and army had been eroded and the protestant position, with which James had been concerned in 1685, was no longer a reality by the autumn of 1687. Accordingly, during their conference at Chester James acquiesced in Tyrconnell's plans for establishing a catholic state which was to be relatively independent of England. The key to Tyrconnell's success in outmanoeuvring his king had been his reform of the Irish army, the instrument of the protestant minority.[5]

The Exclusion Crisis and the rebellions of Argyle and Monmouth affected James deeply. Tyrconnell, who knew the king well, exploited these fears when he stressed the potential disloyalty of the Irish officer corps, with its supposedly high proportion of ex-Cromwellians and disguised republicans. This was a wicked misrepresentation of the true picture, for by 1685 the Irish officers were protestant and Anglican, far removed from the doctrines of social upheaval. Between 1682 and his accession James appears to have been the driving force behind the English government, and it was during this period that Tyrconnell persuaded him to introduce a few catholics into the Irish army and to recall the solidly protestant lord lieutenant, the Duke of Ormonde. This was the merest hint of the later policy, for before the purge could begin in earnest it was thought necessary to disarm the protestant militia. All militia captains were instructed to store the arms of their troops and companies in their own houses, an operation that was to be completed by 14 July 1685. Ostensibly this measure was designed to ensure that the weapons were better protected against theft but, in reality, it made the later collection of all the militia armaments a great deal easier.[6] In the summer of 1685 Tyrconnell assumed almost total control over the military in Ireland and was in a position to begin his reform of the armed forces: all the protestant officers were to be removed from their commissions and replaced by 'old English' catholics, whilst the protestant rank and file were to be dismissed in favour of the native Irish. Publicly, the earl did not admit that this was the real purpose of the reform, saying that he made 'no distinction between man and man provided he were qualified to serve the king', and insisted that he was altering the Irish army in order to improve the quality of its officers and men. Privately, he was intent upon catholicisation. Although contemporaries in Ireland were not blind to his real objectives, Tyrconnell was unable to reveal his intentions, as he was acting without specific instructions from James; catholicisation was his own personal policy, to which the king turned a blind eye. During the summer of 1685 Tyrconnell was forced into giving secret orders to his officers which he then denied in public. The Earl of Roscommon, lieutenant-colonel of the Duke of Ormonde's regiment of horse, was given private orders not to admit 'any into the regiment ... but only such as were roman catholics'. When challenged by Clarendon, Tyrconnell cursed and swore that he had never given this order. Even so young and inexperienced an observer as Robert Parker was able to summarise Tyrconnell's military policy as the ejection of all the officers and soldiers who had fought for Cromwell and putting 'none but Irish papists in the room of them'. Lieutenant Robert Stearne of the Earl of Granard's foot also observed how all the officers and men who were superannuated or who had fought for Cromwell were disbanded and replaced by catholics.[7]

The purge of the Irish army was both rapid and thorough. With the addition of the new regiment of dragoons under Richard Hamilton in June 1685 the Irish army amounted to 8,238 other ranks and 406 commissioned officers. During the last quarter of 1685 the purge gathered speed, 1,150 men having lost their places by 2 December.[8] Two hundred blank commissions were sent to Tyrconnell by William Bridgeman, one of the clerks of the English privy council, in March 1686, to be followed by a further 140 in June of the same year.[9] James had clearly resigned the details of the remodelling of the Irish military into the hands of his lieutenant-general. By 30 September 1686 5,394 private soldiers and non-commissioned officers and 155 officers followed the romish faith.[10] The majority of the alterations appear to have taken place when individual companies and troops were reviewed or mustered, so that the soldiers were disbanded in large numbers and not individually. Three hundred and fifty men were dismissed from the Irish Foot Guards on one day in July 1686, and

117 were forced to leave the Duke of Ormonde's horse after a muster in the same month. On 17 August a regiment was exercised on the Artillery Ground in Dublin and at the conclusion of the proceedings 195 'old soldiers' lost their places. The muster-master-general of the Irish army, Abraham Yarner, wrote to Ormonde on 8 September 1686 proffering the opinion that about two-thirds of the army had been remodelled, the corollary of which had been the appointment of catholic chaplains to three of the seven regiments of foot.[11]

Among the first casualties were the sons of three protestant earls, Lord Shannon, Captain Robert Fitzgerald, and Captain Richard Coote, in company with Captain Sir Oliver St. George, who had been active in the restoration of Charles II. They were replaced by Captain René de Carnes, 'one of the ruffians'; Captain John Anderson, 'a person of no fortune'; Captain Dominick Sheldon, 'a professed papist'; and Captain Ronald Graham, who had fought in the Royal English Regiment in France between 1675 and 1678.[12] Once Tyrconnell had taken command in Ireland the purge began to take on a more regular and organised form. The Lords Justices ordered every colonel and governor to send in 'the names of their commission[ed] officers with an account of how long every one has served in the present army, whether he served the usurpers, and by what means he came to his employment'. The instructions reached the regiments during July and August.[13] Upon the basis of the information contained in these confidential summaries the purge began in earnest. To begin with, any catholic officer who was brought into employment had to be dispensed from the necessity of swearing the oaths of supremacy and allegiance, and on 12 May 1685 eight catholics were slid into their commissions by the operation of the dispensing power.[14] However, if the entire officer corps was to be composed of followers of the Bishop of Rome, then each individual would have required a separate dispensation, an administrative task that would have been expensive and time-consuming. The English Test Act of 1673 was unknown in Ireland, where the governing legislation was contained in the Elizabethan Act of Supremacy, exemption from which had many precedents. The obstacle erected by the oaths was cleared away on 21 July 1685 when Sunderland wrote to the Lords Justices ordering them not to administer the oaths to garrison governors, officers, and soldiers in Ireland. Instead, all new military personnel were to take a general oath of fidelity to James II. The gates were open.[15]

At first, every effort was made to conceal the real objective of the purge. Circumspection was vital for Tyrconnell, as he was acting without official orders from his monarch, but he was able to bluff and lie his way through a series of interviews with Clarendon and senior officers to such good effect that Lord Granard, the Marshal of the Irish army, was convinced that Tyrconnell was executing the royal policy.[16] Despite being no more than a colonel during 1685, although powerfully armed with the authority of an executive inspector-general, Tyrconnell seems to have experienced little difficulty in carrying out his reforms, especially as the dismissal of officers was at first camouflaged. Justin Macarty, a new popish colonel, recommended that Captain John Bingham be cashiered, as he had been away from his command without leave for some time 'though he had strict charge not to be absent'. In his stead Macarty put forward Thomas Nugent, a catholic professional soldier with a record of service in France and Flanders, who was duly commissioned in Bingham's place in 1686.[17] Natural vacancies also provided an excellent opportunity for introducing papists. Sir Nicholas Armourer expressed a desire to resign his captaincy in Thomas Fairfax's foot, 'being very aged and infirm'. Another catholic careerist, Walter Butler who was well known to both Fairfax and Tyrconnell, was subsequently given Armourer's company.[18] It would scarcely have proved possible to accuse all the protestant officers in Ireland of breaches of discipline, although their lax behaviour during the previous twenty-five years laid many open to such charges, or to wait for them all to retire. Anxious to speed the alterations, Tyrconnell took the bull firmly by the horns. On 17 September 1685 he dismissed all the officers in his own regiment who had originally received their commissions from the Duke of Ormonde. When he was informed that this had ruined the duke's patronage as well as many of his friends and relatives, Tyrconnell feigned great surprise and said that he had not realised that all the disbanded officers had been clients of the hated duke.[19] The main weight of the purge fell in the following year. Once the two parcels of blank commissions had been dispatched from London, James instructed the lord lieutenant, the Earl of Clarendon, to direct Tyrconnell, now promoted to lieutenant-general, to hasten the passage of the reform, to inspect all the Irish regiments 'from time to time' and to dismiss all 'unfit persons' and to supply their places with others fitly qualified'. Armed with these delightfully vague instructions, Tyrconnell reviewed Lord Blessington's troop of horse on 19 June and seemed to be well enough pleased with their appearance. However, it had not escaped Blessington's notice that he had been presented with a new lieutenant on the day before the parade, a catholic named John Taafe. As Tyrconnell rode away from the ceremony he spoke to Taafe and through him ordered Blessington to remove eleven men from his troop and to replace them with catholics to be nominated by Taafe. Similar mass evictions took place throughout the army.[20] Brigadier Anthony Hamilton took the salute of several regiments at Mullingar and used the occasion to disband numbers of protestant soldiers.[21]

Yesterday your troop mustered under the command of one Captain James Hamilton. Your lieutenant and cornet have both lost [their commissions]. Tyrconnell is resolved to make none capable to serve the king but romish Irish.[22]

Clarendon, who was powerless to intervene, was extremely annoyed with the high-handed actions of Tyrconnell and his catholic senior officers. As he watched the Irish Foot Guards being put through their paces he noticed that 'there are as proper men put out, and as seemingly lusty, as those who are taken in'.[23] Some of the new officers went about reforming their commands in the most open and blatant fashion, declaring that they would tolerate none in their troops and companies but Irish catholics, and hinted that they would soon regain their lands from the protestants.

Mr. Nicholas Darcy, who has the company late Captain [John] Mutlowe's, called his company together and asked them if they went to mass, to which forty of them said, 'no'. Whereupon he immediately dismissed them and said he kept as many above a week at his own house upon his own charge who, the next morning, were all admitted.

Not all the colonels and captains undertook their alterations in this tactless and offensive manner. Clarendon actually commended Sir John Fitzgerald, Lawrence Dempsey, Dominick Sheldon, and Robert Lacey for 'their proper manner' of proceeding in these delicate operations.[24] From his elevated but impossibly weak position Clarendon did his best to retard and moderate the progress of the purge, accusing Lieutenant-Colonel William Dorrington of the Irish Foot Guards of going 'too fast' and advising him 'to do the king's business with less noise'.[25] There are a few faint indications that Clarendon occasionally steeled himself to try and interrupt the headlong charge of the reformers. He personally reviewed the regiments of Ormonde and the Earl of Ardglass before Tyrconnell was due to inspect them as if he was noting their condition with a view to lodging a protest at a later date. Nothing positive resulted from this or from any of Clarendon's repeated objections to Sunderland and the king, as he was never sure whether he was attacking just Tyrconnell or the hallowed person of the monarch. When it came to personal complaints, Tyrconnell with his roughness and deceit was more than equal to the rather gentle lord lieutenant.[26]

Despite the acceleration of the purge in the summer of 1686, the aims of the exercise were still concealed in orders pregnant with imprecision and *doubles entendres*. Major Alexander MacDonnell ordered his lieutenant, Christopher Nugent, to dismiss all those from Captain Ambrose Aungier's troop 'who are not fit and to receive into their places such as are good men and well mounted and otherwise well qualified for his Majesty's service'.[27] By the summer of 1687 the day of the euphemism was past. Robert Parker, then a young man of twenty-one, recalled how Tyrconnell made a 'strict review' of all the regiments in the Irish army at the camp at the Curragh in order to assess the numbers of protestant officers and men who were still with the forces. Immediately after the camp had broken up most of the remaining protestants were removed, except for a few who were retained 'to countenance the matter'. The new catholic officers brought with them 'parcel[s] of raps' who were put into the ranks vacated by the protestant soldiers, although a few veterans continued in the service to drill the new recruits. Himself a protestant, Parker was dismissed at this time and went home in disgust.[28] According to some sources, the purge of officers was virtually complete by the autumn of 1687 but, in at least one regiment, a number of protestant officers and men survived in their positions until the Glorious Revolution.[29] Sensing the direction of the wind, the Earl of Granard resigned the colonelcy of his regiment of foot to his eldest son, Lord Forbes, in 1686. Forbes was a firm protestant and 'a bold and daring man' who had, 'in spite of Tyrconnell, kept in a great many protestant officers and soldiers'. This resolute and determined soldier was a thorough professional who had served his military apprenticeship under Turenne in Alsace between 1672 and 1675. He acquired more experience in 1686 when he fought at the siege of Buda in the company of his brother, Lieutenant-Colonel Sir Robert Forbes, who was killed in the trenches. So successfully did Forbes resist the catholicising tendencies of Tyrconnell that when his formation was summoned into England in 1688 as part of the Irish reinforcement for the royal field army, out of a total of 780 privates, seventy-eight non-commissioned officers, and forty-one commissioned officers, he could boast of 130 protestant soldiers, 'several captains and subalterns ... besides several sergeants, corporals, and drum[mer]s'. As Forbes was one of only two protestant colonels to retain their command beyond March 1688 it is probable that no other regiment in Ireland contained so many non-catholics, although even the most rabidly papist of the new colonels were in the habit of keeping a few protestant officers and senior non-commissioned officers to train their raw recruits. The second protestant colonel who was continued in office throughout the reign, the Ulsterman Lord Mountjoy, was made of different stuff. During the winter of 1685 he crossed to England to meet his sons, who were about to return from a tour in France. At Whitehall he was buttonholed by James II, who

> questioned me very particular about the officers of my regiment of whom I could give no ill character, though I found he wished and expected I would. By that ... and many other things, I saw I should meet great mortifications in Ireland to avoid which, and at the same time to preserve my integrity and my employment, I could see no better way than to spend the summer with my son in Hungary.

Accordingly, Mountjoy spent most of 1686 and 1687 fighting for the Emperor rather than on behalf of the protestant interest in Ireland; he did indeed keep the nominal command of his regiment but it was heavily infiltrated by catholic officers and men.[30] After the winter of 1687 very little evidence exists about the progress of the alterations, indicating that the work was substantially complete. One or two weak pockets of resistance still held out, as in Forbes's regiment, but over 90 per cent of the strength of the Irish army must have owed allegiance to Rome by the final year of the reign of the catholic king.

In a country that was both poor and overwhelmingly catholic there was no shortage of volunteers to fill the vacancies in the ranks. Although Tyrconnell was only interested in bringing 'old English' catholics into the officer corps, he was quite prepared to pour any available catholic material into the lower positions in the army, whether native Irish or 'old English'. Among the favourite recruiting grounds were the numerous shrines and places of devotion which were liberally scattered around the island. St. John's Well near Dublin was haunted by Lieutenant-Colonel William Dorrington, whilst other officers caused their drums to be beaten at various fairs and religious festivals.[31] The quality of these new recruits was uniformly low. Clarendon observed how 'fourscore new men are come to town today to be admitted in the rooms of some of the others and [are] little and look very shabbily. I wish there may be no stealers amongst them.'[32]

All this while the protestants are under great discontents that so many soldiers were dismissed without a cause and the very scum of the people put in, culled by priests and sent to the officers, which was looked on as done for some bloody end.[33]

To replenish the regiments the new officers took in 'silly cowkeepers and wretched creatures out of the country who will give the officers trouble sufficient before they learn their right hand from their left'.[34] The religious bigotry of the native Irish was 'scarce possible' for the lord lieutenant to understand, 'for the generality of them do believe ... that this kingdom is the pope's and the inheritance of St. Peter's chair'.[35] Much of this violently anti-catholic language emanated from the protestant clique about the lord lieutenant, to whom the sight of a deeply catholic country was both novel and frightening. A considerable amount of the scathing criticism of the new recruits must be tempered by the fact that the critics were often dispossessed officers, or their close friends or relatives, who were in no mood to make balanced judgements. Certainly the new soldiers were financially very poor and unable 'to provide themselves with what is proper or necessary', and, to begin with, they were often without uniforms because of the rapidity of the purge and so appeared 'very piebald'.[36] Probably, when drilled and professionally trained, the men made passable soldiers, and less biased commentators were able to detect some potential in the native soldiery. Clarendon exercised Justin Macarty's regiment and found that they performed 'as well as can be expected from new men who have been no longer in service', whilst a review of Richard Hamilton's dragoons convinced him that they were 'as adroit as is possible for new men to be'.[37] These two examples should not be taken as representative of the entirety of the new army, as Clarendon made no claims to military expertise, Hamilton's was the oldest of the new regiments, and both Hamilton and Macarty were amongst the very best and most experienced of the catholic officers. Reviled and mocked by the protestants though they may have been, there was a stream of men anxious to enlist, as a place in the army was a sought-after commodity. Crowds of fortune-hunters travelled to Dublin from the countryside, hoping 'to get a vacancy', only to be jeered at by the more sophisticated protestants.[38] There was probably little difference between the quality of the catholic recruits in Ireland and the new men who filled the English army in 1685 and 1688 except that in England these volunteers joined a solid trained and professional cadre. In Ireland ignorant and inexperienced soldiers came under the command of officers who mostly suffered from the same disabilities.

Between 1685 and 1688 more than 7,000 protestant soldiers were dismissed from the Irish army. Many of the disbanded men had spent a lifetime bearing arms and knew no other way of life, and in a country which was quickly turning against the protestants their opportunities for finding alternative employment were severely restricted. A minimum of seven years' service with the colours was required before an old soldier became eligible for a place in Kilmainham military hospital, and although many of those dismissed were fully qualified the hospital was in debt and could not hope to accommodate the considerable numbers clamouring for admission.[39] Clarendon asked Sunderland to discover whether James had any plans for giving compensation to the deprived soldiery but nothing constructive was forthcoming. Most of the unemployed men made their way to Dublin in expectation of a pension from Kilmainham, some offer of work, or possibly some material assistance, so that by July 1686 the capital was 'full of poor soldiers'. There was a regulation in the Irish army that if a man was disbanded through no fault of his own then his officers were legally bound to grant him an allowance for any money which had previously been deducted from his pay for clothing which had not yet been worn. This generally amounted to half the sum of money which had originally been stopped from his pay: £2 8s to a private in the Guards and £1 6s to all others. Cavalry troopers were forced to surrender their horses, arms, and equipment to the incoming recruits in return for which they received promissory notes worth barely a quarter of the value of the forfeited property.[40] With large numbers of hopeful catholics crowding into Dublin and equally sizeable bodies of deprived protestants searching desperately for employment or help, clashes were bound to occur. At the height of the purge in July 1686 there were frequent disorders between the two groups in the streets which resulted in a number of fatalities.[41] The eventual fate of the old soldiers is unknown. Possibly, some came across to England, others may have taken service in the Anglo-Dutch Brigade or with the Imperial armies in Hungary, whilst a not inconsiderable proportion remained in their homeland and turned to brigandage.

'All the scum and rascality of the kingdom were made officers. The better sort of their captains and inferior officers had been footmen or servants to protestants. One gentleman's cowherd was made a lieutenant,' thundered one protestant source, adding, for good measure, that most of the new officers were descended from the rebels of 1641. Typical of the protestant reaction to the catholic officers was the remark made about a certain Murtagh McGennis who had murdered a Captain Hamilton in Dublin – 'it is said that as soon as he is acquitted he is to be a captain of horse to which his valour entitles him having dared to kill a man that two men held'.[42] These biased accounts were probably not far removed from the truth of the matter. The huge majority of the new incumbents were catholics from 'old English' families who had lost much, or all, of their land during the Irish Rebellion and who had failed to recover their property at the Restoration. The material deprivation and the political and religious domination of the protestants resulted in many of the 'old English' ranking as 'decayed gentry', and, as a consequence, the new officers were often so poor that they were unable to afford the proper fees which were payable upon the receipt of a commission, a mere two guineas in the case of a captain of horse.[43] This widespread poverty meant that it was impossible for the new officers to pay compensation to the outgoing incumbents; purchase of the commissions at their full market value was out of the question. Impecuniousness among the officer corps on this scale adversely affected the quality of the army's organisation, as the smooth running of the military administration depended upon an officer's personal credit for obtaining clothing, horses, and advances on pay. Without financial assistance from its officers the army was utterly dependent on the inefficient Irish treasury and the chaotic army pay office.[44]

Greed was a complement to hardship. Put into positions from which they could make money by withholding pay, falsifying musters, or manipulating clothing contracts, many of the new officers fell into temptation, to the detriment of the efficiency and unity of the army. Clarendon found the officers 'very gripping and sell their quartermaster's, adjutant's, and clerk's places for whatever they can get which, with some other things, must undo an army'. Some of the new officers confidently expected their commands to yield up to £400 per annum in addition to their official pay and were very disappointed when they discovered that the reality was not so profitable. Without any experience of the operation of the pay system the novice captains were inclined to leave such detailed matters in the hands of their regimental agents, which, moaned Clarendon, 'will be the ruin of the army here'. The officers milked their men unmercifully, often leaving them with as little as $2\frac{1}{4}d$ a day for their basic subsistence, seizing the remainder of their full daily remittance of $6d$ in official and unofficial deductions. Clothing contractors rapidly appreciated the naivety of the new officers and charged very high prices to dress the regiments, sums which had to be hauled back from the soldiers themselves through punitive off-reckonings. The lord lieutenant attempted to impose some discipline upon this free-for-all and actually succeeded in securing an agreement with the senior officers whereby every soldier was guaranteed at least 4d per diem for his subsistence. It is most unlikely that this paper commitment had any practical effect in limiting the abuses, especially as some of the highest officers were among the very worst of the offenders; Sir Thomas Newcommen 'does shark most abominably upon his men'.[45] A proclamation of 29 April 1687 laid down the correct amount of subsistence money and off-reckonings for each soldier and insisted that the army be reclothed every eighteen months. These rules were reiterated in a further proclamation on 20 July in the following year, a strong suggestion that the officers were continuing in their bad habits despite orders to the contrary.[46] Irish officers enjoyed the right to dismiss soldiers from their command whenever they chose without having to account for their action. As a result, once a muster had been completed, an officer often disbanded half his troop or company and did not bother to refill the ranks until just before the next parade. In all probability, for over nine months in every twelve, the Irish army was at half-strength and the officers were able to pocket the pay of the non-existent men.[47]

According to the reports of Clarendon and Sir Paul Rycaut, most of the officers who were brought into the Irish army during 1686 and 1687 were totally inexperienced, yet there were a number of professionals who were thoroughly acquainted with military business. Disqualified by their religion from serving in either the English or the Irish armies of Charles II, large catholic Irish contingents had fought in Tangier, in Portugal, for Louis XIV, and in the Spanish service in the Netherlands. Since European hostilities were largely in abeyance in the 1680s, many of these catholic officers found themselves unengaged and were thankful to have the opportunity of taking commissions in both the English and the Irish establishments of James II. Out of eighty-seven officers who had manned Thomas Dongan's mercenary regiment in France in 1678, thirty-six reappeared in James's Irish army as holders of new commissions.[48] Gerald Ferrall was a veteran who had fought in the Duke of Gloucester's regiment in Flanders in 1657 but had stayed abroad after the Restoration and entered the Spanish service. In the next decade Ferrall took his sword to the French flag and there he continued until the peace in 1678. Without employment, Ferrall returned to his native Ireland and served as a private trooper until the death of Charles II, when the dawning of the catholic era allowed him to take a commission as captain-lieutenant in Sir Thomas Newcommen's foot.[49] Terence O'Brien was an ensign in Thomas Dongan's foot in 1678 but he obeyed Charles II's recall order of the same year and found himself without work. Following his successful petition to the English treasury for half-pay in 1685, O'Brien became an ensign in the Duke of Norfolk's foot in England and then transferred to the Irish establishment as a lieutenant in Lord Forbes's foot.[50] A much-travelled Irish catholic was Lawrence Dempsey. His first position after the Restoration was the majority of Henry Pearson's foot in the British Brigade which fought in Portugal between 1662 and 1668, and from there he transferred into the French service, rising to be the lieutenant-colonel of Thomas Dongan's foot in 1678. By September 1686 Dempsey had acquired a similar rank in the Earl of Ardglass's regiment of horse in Ireland.[51] The curiously named Tege Regan was a lieutenant in the Earl of Dumbarton's regiment of foot in France in 1666 but he lost his commission when this formation finally returned to England in 1678 because of the restrictions of the Test Act. Regan was the major of Theodore Russell's regiment of foot in Ireland in September 1686 and ended his military career three years later when fighting in the Jacobite army.[52] For over twenty years James Dempsey served under Spanish colours in the Low Countries before retiring to Ireland to take up an appointment as a captain in Richard Hamilton's dragoons in 1686.[53] Beginning his military career as a captain in the Royal English Regiment in France in 1675, William Dorrington later became a soldier of great distinction. Of an English family, he served as a captain in Monmouth's foot in England in 1678 and transferred to the Irish establishment as lieutenant-colonel of the Irish Foot Guards in 1686. He adhered to James at the Revolution and fought for his master at the Boyne and Aughrim, where he was captured and suffered a subsequent short period of incarceration in the Tower of London. On his release he sailed to France and joined the Irish Brigade, ending his days in 1718 in the uniform of a French lieutenant-general. Another professional catholic officer with a history of service in France was Ulick Burke, and he was a living witness to the fact that a military life could be moderately profitable; by 1684 he rented 1,566 acres from the Earl of Clanrickard at a cost of £156 12s per annum.[54] There were, however, too few of these professional officers in the new Irish army, probably less than fifty out of a total officer corps of 406, and these were spread thinly throughout the twelve regiments. The bulk of the officers were novices and were 'guided by what is done in England'.[55] Because of the ease with which catholics could be commissioned in Ireland, James was able to make use of the Irish army as an area of patronage for deserving catholic officers. In 1688 a Lieutenant Butler was recommended to Tyrconnell for a place after he had served in Hungary for several years.[56] Not all the new officers were Irish. Dominick Sheldon was a catholic gentleman from Warwickshire and a brother of James II's equerry, Ralph Sheldon. He had fought in France during the 1670s and was captain-lieutenant to the Duke of Monmouth in 1678, but this successful phase in his career was followed by seven years of unemployment before he was made a captain in the Irish Foot Guards. Rapid promotion followed, until he achieved a colonelcy in 1688. During the Irish wars he rose to the rank of major-general in the Jacobite army and finished a distinguished career as a lieutenant-general in the French armed forces.[57] Just as there were insufficient professional officers, either catholic or protestant to fill all the new commissions in England after 1685, so there were not enough catholic careerists to remodel the Irish regiments in 1686 and 1687. Raw and untrained men had to be employed, much to the detriment of the army.

Amongst the old protestant officer corps, the curse of the duel was as prevalent in Dublin as it was in London. There were reports of a challenge involving six officers on 27 June 1685, and so common did duels become that, one month later, the Lords Justices were empowered to dismiss any officer who took part in an affair of honour, with the additional sanction that any officer thus cashiered would not be re-employed. As no noticeable improvement resulted from this legislation, a proclamation was issued on 11 August condemning the practice. Again the effect was negligible, and Cornets Ambrose and Henry Jones both died after a fight in October. Four officers from the Irish Foot Guards fought in two separate quarrels within the space of three days in Dublin in August 1685 but, suddenly, the problem faded away. Duelling disappeared with the removal of the protestant officers. Fighting to retrieve injured honour was clearly a prerogative of the protestant landed classes, and the landless and impoverished catholics seem not to have indulged in this vice to any great extent.[58]

The protestant officers dismissed by Tyrconnell had nearly all purchased their commissions. 'Many of them had laid out whole fortunes and contracted debts to purchase a command yet no sooner was King James settled in his throne but he began to turn out some of the officers' without any financial compensation.[59] Captain George Brooke had paid £1,600 for his troop of horse in Lord Ardglass's regiment and Henry Pargiter's lieutenancy had cost £800 but both were dismissed from their commissions without any recompense. In order to become a lieutenant in the Earl of Arran's regiment of cavalry John Phillips had paid £1,100, the whole of his younger brother's patrimony, but he was forced to accept a mere £600 for this commission from Anthony Townley, who replaced him in 1686. Yet Phillips was one of the lucky few. Although 140 officers had been ousted from their commands by 12 June 1686, hardly any of them had received even a small payment either from their successors or from the Irish government.

But whilst these poor officers are provided for [i.e. the catholics] we have sad outcries and complaints from many gentlemen who are displaced who having perhaps laid out all their patrimony to purchase a command are now, by this disappointment, reduced to want and perhaps to beggary.[60]

Clarendon and the Irish administration were powerless to alleviate the financial sufferings of these officers. By ensuring that the new officers received their pay only from the date when they actually assumed their full duties and that the old officers continued to draw their remuneration until the precise moment of their departure something was achieved, but it could only make a shallow impression upon the overall situation.[61] So grave was the condition of many officers that eighty-six were glad to accept temporary places as reformadoes in the Irish army at the magnificent salary of £9 2s 6d per annum.[62]

Financially ruined, deprived of place, torn from their property and investments without adequate compensation, those protestant officers who did not own sufficient land upon which to support themselves sought military employment overseas. The most obvious source of engagement was the army of the United Provinces, where 'perhaps their clamours and sufferings did contribute to move the compassion of the Prince of Orange . . . and forward his designs'.[63] 'Perhaps' is the operative word, for it is highly improbable that William of Orange allowed his political judgement to be swayed by such emotional considerations, although he did permit some of the 'discarded officers' into the Netherlands and 'entertained them'.[64] D'Avaux, the French ambassador at The Hague, reported that William offered employment to all the protestant officers who had been dismissed by Tyrconnell, whilst Thomas Sheridan was of the opinion that the 'greatest part' of the disbanded officers 'went into Holland and instigated the Prince of Orange to the invasion which, the year afterwards, was made'.⁶⁵ Tyrconnell's purge resulted in over 350 officers losing their place, but there is no extant evidence to suggest that many of these gentlemen found niches on the Dutch establishment. Judging from the biographical details of 213 out of the approximate total of three hundred officers who served with the six regiments of the Anglo-Dutch Brigade between 1685 and 1688, only seventeen can be positively identified as Irish officers who had been removed by Tyrconnell and his acolytes. However, in March 1688 the brigade was recalled into England and over 100 officers obeyed the loyal summons; it is more than likely that a small number of unemployed Irish protestant officers were drafted into some of these vacant commissions. No doubt some more of these wandering Irishmen received commissions in the regular Dutch army, but a report on the 'officers and others coming with the Prince of Orange' in 1688 gives the very clear impression that the 'abundance of officers turned out of Ireland' held no official positions in the Dutch armed forces but formed yet one more element among the hordes of political and religious exiles who infested the principal Dutch cities.⁶⁶ At the most, no more than 100 Irish ex-officers spent their time in frustration and idleness pacing the streets of The Hague and Amsterdam. Others, like Sir Oliver St. George, sailed to England and took commissions in the enlarged English army; many used their enforced retirement to seek experience and profit with the Imperial forces in Hungary; eighty-six were content to remain in Ireland as reformadoes; a further thirty-two sought military places in Scotland, whilst some of the more financially buoyant threw in the martial sponge and returned to their estates.⁶⁷

Captain Henry Boyle was dismissed from his command to make room for one of Tyrconnell's 'creatures' and his uncle, Lord Burlington, gave him permission to leave Ireland and seek military employment in England or 'elsewhere'.⁶⁸ He was unsuccessful in his quest in England and in the United Provinces but was able to resume army life in 1689 when he was commissioned as the major of Lord Cavendish's cavalry regiment. Another unlucky aspirant was Thomas Flower, one of the last protestants to be dismissed in 1687, who was also unable to find any position either in England or abroad.⁶⁹ Eighty-nine officers who had been removed from the Irish army during James's reign were 'in and about London' in March 1689 petitioning 'to be entertained in his Majesty's service'; they had almost certainly been without work since the time of their dismissal.⁷⁰ The rapid expansion of the British army in 1689 and 1690 allowed most of these officers to continue their interrupted military progress. Lord Coote's captaincy in the Duke of Ormonde's horse was sequestered in March 1685 and he was forced to leave Ireland in his search for a flag. Eventually he settled in the Dutch Republic and was granted a temporary commission by William for the period of the invasion, and thereafter his fortunes considerably improved.[71] Henry Cunningham lost his lieutenancy of foot only to be compensated with a captaincy in the Anglo-Dutch Brigade.[72] Although he was one of the few remaining protestants in the Irish army in May 1688, Captain John Cunningham resolved to resign his commission, as he had no wish to be instrumental in overthrowing the protestant church. Accordingly, he successfully sought an appointment under William of Orange, 'upon whom, at this time, all protestant eyes are fixed'.[73] Despite the fact that the majority of the dismissed protestant officers had to endure two or three years of unemployment, the Revolution and England's entry into continental war in 1689 proved singularly fortunate. In most cases it was not the act of disbandment that was so damaging to the officers but the failure of their replacements to purchase their positions. Officers who had initially invested one or even two thousand pounds in an army commission found their capital suddenly wiped out, and all but the wealthiest of the officers had difficulty in raising sufficient money to be able to buy a place in another establishment. This financial aspect made foreign service especially attractive, as an officer could serve as a volunteer and even acquire a commission on merit rather than by the weight of his purse. Similarly, the augmentation of the English, Irish, and Scottish establishments in 1689 created a large number of vacancies for trained officers, commissions which could be gained for little or no capital outlay. Although the benefits were illusory, the length of the War of the Grand Alliance and its rapid sequel, the War of the Spanish Succession, cushioned these officers. The majority of them were able to secure commissions in 1689, but mostly in regiments which were raised solely for the duration of war, and in 1697 those officers who survived were disbanded, still out of pocket and still unable to purchase a commission in a permanent formation. The onset of the War of the Spanish Succession shelved the problem for a further twelve years, long enough to outlast the active careers of most of the Irish protestant officers. However, two decades of ample military employment and foreign war did not compensate for the initial financial loss which these officers had suffered when they were evicted from their commissions during the reign of James II.

Irish protestants greeted the new army with a mixture of fear and derision, but suspicion was mutual to both sides. Some catholic soldiers who were quartered in Dublin so distrusted their protestant landlords that they refused to eat or drink until their hosts had first tasted the victuals. The capital city witnessed numerous scuffles between the catholic soldiery and the 'rabble', but these were usually contained by the lord lieutenant and the civil magistrates. Naturally, during these troubled and insecure times Ireland was a prey to rumour and baseless stories about supposed conspiracies and dastardly designs. A 'plot' was uncovered in Longford, Westmeath, and Roscommon which possessed all the hallmarks of contemporary religious hysteria. Thousands of protestants were reported to be meeting at night and distributing arms and ammunition 'with the intention to cut the throats of the Irish': so scared were the natives that they took to camping out at night in the woods and ditches for fear of being murdered in their houses. 'The alarm was so warm that the town and garrison of Athlone have put themselves in continual watches and wards, both of soldiers and townsmen, all of which is grounded upon a letter of Father Ambrose Fitzgerald who relates this matter without place, time, or persons.' Rycaut thought the whole affair akin to the Popish Plot. Apart from the farcical there were some real demonstrations of discontent. Serious riots occurred on the holy days of 23 October and 5 November 1686, when the catholic soldiers found themselves unable to endure such vividly protestant occasions and 'extinguished bonfires and broke the glass windows of the mayor's house, giving them most opprobrious terms, which . . . ended in murders and other disorders.'[74]

Whereas the old protestant army had been gentle and ineffective the reformed institution was thoroughly ill-mannered. The poverty of the officers and men led to irregular payment for quarters, whilst the sheer ignorance of military affairs of many of the subalterns ruined discipline. A sign of the future came when Lieutenant-Colonel Anthony Hamilton, a man trained in the French army, had the temerity to billet four soldiers upon the Anglican Bishop of Limerick, an intolerable insult to the English.[75] Many of the new officers were either too poor or too domineering to pay for their own lodgings, and the council of Waterford was compelled to devise a method of raising voluntary contributions from the townsmen to meet the cost of the quarters of the officers of the regular garrison.[76] A proclamation of 24 February 1687 instructed all officers to ensure that their men obeyed proper discipline upon the march and paid for their billets, but fair words could not rectify the real problem, the low standard of the officers.[77] Dragoons quartered in Limerick were in the habit of boarding all ships that entered the harbour and beating up the king's customs officials. Complaints were made to the officers in command but 'received little satisfaction'.[78]

They everywhere insulted over the English and had their mouths continually full of oaths, curses, and imprecations against them ... They might kill whom they pleased without fear of law as appeared from Captain [Robert] Nangle's murdering his disbanded officer in the streets of Dublin ... They immediately ruined all the protestant inns in Ireland partly by oppressing them with quarters, partly by paying nothing for what they had in their quarters, and partly by driving away other guests by their rudeness.[79]

Even Clarendon, intent as he was upon representing his government in the best possible light, was forced to admit that some 'excesses' had been committed by the new army, a fact which he partially explained by drawing attention to the number of known thieves and robbers among the new recruits. Much of the irregularity and indiscipline might have been prevented if the officers had known how to control their men, but some of them were 'a little backward' in attending to these matters. Robert Parker's parents, both protestants, were 'much abused and plundered' by a party of dragoons, whilst Richard Power and seven or eight soldiers 'robbed perpetually' for over six months in the area around Burton.[80] Apart from the understandable desire of an oppressed majority to take revenge on the minority who had held them in check for so long and the inexperience and poverty of the new officers, the basic trouble with the remodelled Irish army was that it drew its officers from the wrong sectors of society. Seventeenth century European armies depended for their discipline and internal cohesion upon social distinctions between officers and men. By drawing officers exclusively from the ranks of the land-owning gentry and the peerage, social deference was made the basis of military order, but the reforms in Ireland removed the natural officer class and replaced it with a socially inferior breed who had neither rank, wealth, nor extensive landed estates. Unable to inspire proper respect, the catholic officers could not prevent their men from taking free quarter and stealing—indeed they were frequently the instigators of unruly behaviour.[81] However, they were not the sole fount of military disorder in Ireland.

You had need to keep good watch and guard about your house for they have lately turned ... a company of Irishmen out of the Guards that people are afraid will do much hurt. Parson Barry of Termonfecklin was robbed last night and as good as £200 taken from him. They bound him and all the rest of the house. There were six robbers with black faces. I think it is good for us that have many servants to let them watch their turns about every night.[82]

The Irish army of 1685 was undertrained, ill-paid, but commanded by officers of social respectability and considerable martial experience. Tyrconnell overturned this entire establishment by changing the officers and men, thus removing the military expertise that the army had accumulated over twenty-five years. Not only did he have to train an army of raw recruits but he was faced with the mammoth task of instructing the officers as well. Such an operation was bound to be protracted and depended heavily upon the small caucus of professional career soldiers who were introduced into Ireland during the purge: Justin Macarty, Patrick Sarsfield, Richard and Anthony Hamilton, and Lawrence Dempsey. For the first time since the Restoration the Irish army came together in a camp on the Curragh in the summer of 1686 and drilled and exercised as one formation. This valuable practice was repeated the following year, when one of the training sessions involved a re-enactment of the siege of Buda 'and a great many other feats at arms'. These general rendezvous, which were continued up to the time of the Revolution, were clearly based upon the examples of the French army camps and the Dutch assembly at Mockerhide as well as the Hounslow camps of the English armed forces.[83] Despite these concentrated attempts to improve the Irish army, the continuation of the purge into the winter of 1687 meant that the force was not in a settled condition before the spring of 1688; Tyrconnell's purge was too rapid and thorough for the resulting catholic corps to be able to establish itself before it was summoned into action. An even greater disadvantage was that this inexpert force had to be used as a training cadre for the vastly expanded Jacobite army of 1689 and 1690. Throughout the Irish wars, although the individual soldiers fought well for their king, the Irish army was found to be wanting in leadership, discipline and simple adminstration.

Neither James nor Tyrconnell had any intention of using the Irish army to intervene in English affairs. A brigade was dispatched into England late in 1688 but this was a specifically military operation to assist in opposing the Dutch invasion. However, the impressions of contemporaries were necessarily different. Within the space of two years the army in Ireland was transformed from an institution which tolerated no catholics into one which included but a handful of protestants. Disbanded protestant soldiers were ignored and allowed to drift into penury and brigandage whilst their officers, who had paid large sums of money for their commissions, were ejected with little or no financial compensation. The events in Tyrconnell's Ireland must have been prominent in the minds of Englishmen and have given enormous credence to rumours that James had plans to remodel the English army. Although there is no extant evidence of any sinister designs upon England by an Irish catholic army, excepting the trivial incident of the 'Portsmouth Captains', Englishmen outside the governing circle could only judge the policies of their monarch by precedent and inference.[84] To them, the presence of a catholic army just across the Irish Sea must have seemed a grave threat to their liberties and religion.

Notes

1. Childs, *Army of Charles II*, pp. 203–9; J. C. Beckett, 'The Irish Armed Forces, 1660–1685', in *Essays presented to Michael Roberts*, ed. John Bossy and Peter Jupp (Belfast, 1976), pp. 41–53; Charles Dalton, *Irish Army Lists, 1661–1685* (London, 1907), Introduction; *CCSP*, v. 655.
2. *Clarendon Correspondence*, i. 212, 16 Jan. 1686, Clarendon to Sunderland; *Ibid.*, i. 546–8; *HMC, Ormonde MSS.*, new series, ii. 309–35; 'Sir Paul Rycaut's Memoranda and Letters from Ireland, 1686–1687', *Analecta Hibernica*, xxvii. (1972), pp. 131 ff.; C. Costello, 'Irish Military Surveys of the Seventeenth Century', *An Costantóir*, xxi. (1961), pp. 433–42; for Thomas Phillips see *DNB*; Howard Tomlinson, 'The Ordnance Office and the King's Forts, 1660–1714', *Architectural History*, xvi. (1973), pp. 5–25.
3. Charles O'Kelly, 'Macariae Excidium, or the Destruction of Cyprus', in *Narratives Illustrative of the Contests in Ireland in 1641 and 1690*, ed. T. C. Croker (Camden Society, 1841), pp. 35–6; *HMC, Stuart MSS.*, vi. 5, Thomas Sheridan's, 'Historical Account'; Burnet, *History of His Own Time*, iii. 72; Clarke, *Life*, ii. 59–68.
4. *Clarendon Correspondence*, i. 440–5, 12 June 1686, Clarendon to Rochester.
5. John Miller, 'The Earl of Tyrconnell and James II's Irish Policy, 1685–1688', *HJ*, xx. (1977); John Miller, 'Thomas Sheridan (1646–1712) and his "Narrative"', *Irish Historical Studies*, xx. (1976), pp. 117–18; J. P. Kenyon, *Stuart England* (London, 1978), pp. 222–4.
6. *A Full and Impartial Account of all the Secret Consults, Negotiations, Stratagems, and Intrigues of the Romish Party in Ireland, from 1660 to this Present Year 1689* (London, 1689), pp. 52–3; *HMC, Egmont MSS.*, ii. 154, 20 June 1685, Proclamation by the Lords Justices.
7. Rycaut, pp. 129–30 and 157; *HMC, Ormonde MSS.*, n.s., vii. 430; Robert Parker, *Memoirs of the most Remarkable Military Transactions from the Year*

    1683 to 1718 etc. (London, 1747), p. 5; *Secret Consults*, pp. 53–4; Simms, *Jacobite Ireland*, pp. 20–1; Bodleian Library, Oxford, Clarendon State Papers, vol. 88, f. 90; NLI MSS. 4166, Robert Sterne's Diary, 1686.

8 Simms, *Jacobite Ireland*, p. 25; Miller, 'Tyrconnell', p. 818; *HMC, Ormonde MSS.*, n.s., vii. 397–8.
9 *HMC, Ormonde MSS.*, n.s. viii. 345; Rycaut, pp. 146–7.
10 *HMC, Ormonde MSS.*, o.s., i. 431–5.
11 *HMC, Ormonde MSS.*, n.s., vii. 433 and 454–5; Rycaut, p. 155.
12 King, *State of the Protestants*, pp. 58–9; *CSPD 1673–5*, p. 530.
13 PRO SP 63/340, f. 47, 30 June 1685; *HMC, Ormonde MSS.*, n.s., vii. 347, 2 Aug. 1685; *HMC, 2nd Report*, p. 214.
14 SP 63/340, ff. 28–32 and 42, Colonels Richard Talbot, Justin Macarty, and Anthony Hamilton; Majors William Dorrington and Patrick Lawless; Captains Dominick Sheldon, Francis Carroll, and Réné de Carnes.
15 Simms, *Jacobite Ireland*, p. 20; SP 63/340, f. 51.
16 Richard Bagwell, *Ireland under the Stuarts and during the Interregnum* (London, 1909–16), iii. 149–50.
17 SP 63/351, ff. 32–3, 13 Sept. 1685.
18 *Ibid.*, f. 93, 18 Dec. 1685.
19 *HMC, Ormonde MSS.*, n.s., vii. 360 and 363, 17–27 Sept. 1685.
20 SP 63/340, ff. 76–82; *CSPD 1686–7*, Nos. 195 and 576; *HMC, Ormonde MSS.*, n.s., vii. 425, Blessington to Ormonde.
21 NLI MSS. 4166, 1686.
22 *HMC, Hastings MSS.*, ii. 397, 19 June 1685, Thomas Stanhope to Sir Arthur Rawdon.
23 *Clarendon Correspondence*, i. 474–80, 4 July 1686, Clarendon to Rochester.
24 *CSPD 1686–7*, No. 779; *Clarendon Correspondence*, i. 474–80.
25 Rycaut, p. 129.
26 *HMC, Ormonde MSS.*, n.s., vii. 428–9, 12 July 1686, Dublin.
27 BL Add. MSS. 15,894, f. 213, 30 Sept. 1686.
28 Parker, *Military Transactions*, pp. 5–6; NLI MSS. 4166, 1687.
29 *HMC, Ormonde MSS.*, n.s., vii. 483–6; *HMC, Downshire MSS.*, i. 237.
30 NLI MSS. 4166, 1688; WO 9/1, Abstracts of Army Pay in Ireland, 1679–1688; *HMC, 2nd Report*, pp. 211 and 214–15.
31 *Clarendon Correspondence*, i. 474–80; *HMC, Ormonde MSS.*, n.s., viii. 345–6.
32 *Clarendon Correspondence*, i. 468–9.
33 *HMC, Ormonde MSS.*, n.s., viii. 346.
34 Rycaut, p. 152, 5 July 1686, Sir Paul Rycaut to John Cooke.
35 *The State Letters of Henry, Earl of Clarendon*, ed. Richard Powney (Oxford, 1765), ii. 140–1, 26 Dec. 1686, Clarendon to Rochester.
36 *HMC, Ormonde MSS.*, n.s., vii. 462–3.
37 *Clarendon Correspondence*, ii. 1–2, 22 Sept. 1686.
38 Simms, *Jacobite Ireland*, p. 24.
39 Rycaut, pp. 134–5, 153–8 and 161–2; *Clarendon Correspondence*, i.440–5.
40 King, *State of the Protestants*, p. 60; *Secret Consults*, pp. 56–7.

The great purge in Ireland

41 *CSPD 1686–7*, No. 802, 15 July 1686.
42 King, *State of the Protestants*, p. 62; *CCSP*, v. 657 and 679.
43 Miller, 'Tyrconnell', pp. 804–5; Simms, *Jacobite Ireland*, p. 34; Rycaut, pp. 127 and 148–9.
44 J. G. Simms, 'A Jacobite Colonel: Lord Sarsfield of Kilmallock', *Irish Sword*, ii.(1955), pp. 205–10.
45 *Clarendon Correspondence*, i. 339–42, 470–1, 512–13 and ii. 92–3; Francis Grose, *Military Antiquities respecting a History of the English Army* (London, 1812), i. 314.
46 Robert Steele, *A Bibliography of Royal Proclamations of the Tudor and Stuart Sovereigns* (Oxford, 1910), ii. Nos. 978 and 992.
47 *Clarendon Correspondence* i. 330–4.
48 Dalton, *Army Lists*, i. 209; *HMC, Ormonde MSS.*, o.s., i. 406–50; WO 26/4, p. 282; WO 26/5, p. 57.
49 *Wild Geese*, No. 2662; SP 63/351, f. 31.
50 *CSPD 1685*, No. 395; *HMC, Ormonde MSS.*, o.s., i. 425; Dalton, *Army Lists*, i. 209 and ii. 33.
51 D'Alton, i. 111–16; Childs, *Army of Charles II*, pp. 169 and 238; Dalton, *Army Lists*, i. 209.
52 Childs, *Army of Charles II*, p. 245; King, *State of the Protestants*, p. 368; *HMC, Ormonde MSS.*, o.s., i. 429.
53 *Wild Geese*, Nos. 2105 and 2806; *HMC, Ormonde MSS.*, o.s., i. 422.
54 D'Alton, i. 39; Dalton, *Army Lists*, i. 207 and ii. 221; *HMC, Ormonde MSS.*, o.s., i. 411; *Analecta Hibernica*, xv. 400–1, Dunsandle Papers.
55 *Clarendon Correspondence*, i. 470–1.
56 *CSPD 1687–9*, No. 1097.
57 J. C. O'Callaghan, *History of the Irish Brigades in the Service of France* (Shannon, 1969), pp. 152–3; SP 44/41, p. 10; *CSPD 1687–9*, No. 686.
58 *HMC, Hastings MSS.*, ii. 395–6; SP 63/340, f. 51; Steele, *Proclamations*, ii. No. 957; *HMC, Ormonde MSS.*, n.s., viii. 353–5 and 371; *Clarendon Correspondence*, i. 335–6, Rycaut, pp. 138–9.
59 King, *State of the Protestants*, p. 58.
60 *Clarendon Correspondence*, i. 259–63 and 436–7; Rycaut, pp. 148–9.
61 PRO SO 1/12, f. 44, 24 May 1686.
62 PRO SO 1/12, f. 52, 21 June 1686; *CSPD 1687–9*, No. 712.
63 King, *State of the Protestants*, p. 61.
64 *HMC, 7th Report*, Part 1, Appendix, p. 501, 17 Nov. 1686, Dr. William Denton to Sir Ralph Verney.
65 *The Negotiations of Count D'Avaux* (London, 1754–5), iv. 136; *HMC, Stuart MSS.*, vi. 21, Sheridan's, 'Historical Account'.
66 From the biographical material cited in chapter II, note 16; BL Add. MSS. 41,822, ff. 230–1.
67 SRO E 100/40/32, 'A List of those officers whom we are informed are to repair from Ireland to this Kingdom.'
68 *Calendar of the Orrery Papers*, ed. E. Maclysaght (Dublin, 1941), p. 325, 12 March 1687, Lord Burlington to Dowager Countess of Orrery.

69 BL Add. MSS. 41,822, ff. 230–1; BL Add. MSS. 9,962, p. 2; *HMC, Ormonde MSS.*, o.s., i. 402, 423 and 437.
70 BL Add. MSS. 28,938, ff. 314–15.
71 BL Add. MSS. 41,822, ff. 230–1; BL Add. MSS. 9,762, p. 1; *DNB*.
72 N. Japikse, *Correspondentie van Willem III en van Hans Willem Bentinck, eersten Graaf van Portland* (The Hague, 1935–7), ii. 772.
73 *CSPD 1687–9*, No. 1086; Dalton, *Army Lists*, ii. 230; *Papers Illustrating the History of the Scots Brigade in the Service of the United Netherlands, 1572–1782*, ed. James Ferguson (Edinburgh, 1899), i. 513.
74 Rycaut, pp. 152, 155 and 175.
75 *Orrery Papers*, p. 311, 10 Sept. 1685, Lord Inchiquin to Dowager Countess of Orrery.
76 *Council Books of the Corporation of Waterford, 1662–1700*, ed. Seamus Pender (Dublin, 1964), p. 268, 21 Oct. 1686.
77 Steele, *Proclamations*, ii. No. 971.
78 *Clarendon Correspondence*, ii. 2–6, 23 Sept. 1686, Clarendon to Rochester.
79 King, *State of the Protestants*, p. 61.
80 *Clarendon Correspondence*, ii. 114–15; *CSPD 1686–7*, No. 919; Parker *Military Transactions*, pp. 6–7; *HMC, Egmont MSS.*, ii. 162.
81 King, *State of the Protestants*, p. 62; *HMC, Ormonde MSS.*, n.s., ii. 378–84.
82 *HMC, Hastings MSS.*, ii. 398, 16 Nov. 1687, Drogheda, Isabella, Lady Graham to Sir Arthur Rawdon.
83 NLI MSS. 4166, 1687; *CSPD 1686–7*, Nos. 250 and 779; SP 63/351, f. 53; Bagwell, *Ireland under the Stuarts*, iii. 180; *Journal of the Hon. John Erskine of Carnock, 1683–1687*, ed. Walter Macleod (Edinburgh, 1893), pp. 201–2.
84 See chapter VI.

IV

Popularity and politics

One of the hallmarks of European government in the latter half of the seventeenth century was the development and political employment of the standing army. Between the conclusion of the Thirty Years' War and the end of the wars of Louis XIV most major and minor continental states created regular armed forces for the defence of the homeland, offence against an international opponent, to repress internal political and social opposition, and in slavish imitation of the fashionable French. Armies were frequently the only formed and disciplined institutions at the disposal of government and had to serve as labour forces on public works, execute police duties, and act as the right hand of administrative authority. Brandenburg–Prussia evolved an entire political system around the organisation and personnel of the army, and the French troops of Louis XIV helped to enforce religious and political conformity as well as undertaking numerous foreign campaigns. During this period standing armies became the storm troops of the absolute monarchs who were wrestling with the problems of centralising their authority in order to make their governments more effective. England, supposedly, lay beyond these developments. The whig interpretation of the seventeenth century, with its emphasis upon the steady rise of parliament at the expense of the royal prerogative, placed England in a different tradition to that of her European neighbours. Yet the modernisation of the central and local administration was one of the principal points at issue between Charles I and the Long Parliament, and after the Restoration the Commons persistently imagined that it could detect the beginnings of 'arbitrary government'. The miserable experience of military rule during the Interregnum undoubtedly made English politicians extraordinarily sensitive on this point, but their fears about the nature of Charles II's domestic policy were unfounded. Although the Lords and Commons dreamt that they could see a standing army being groomed for absolutism, Charles II had neither the money nor the personal energy for radical innovations. His army was small and remained firmly beyond the arena of politics. Principally, the 'guards and garrisons' were employed as an escort for the royal family and as a routine police force to uphold the law in town and country.[1] Civil servants of the Restoration period did indeed admire the French methods of administration, and as secretary-at-war William Blathwayt took huge pains to emulate the systems of the great Louvois. The regulations which governed l'Hôtel des Invalides provided the model for the operation of the Chelsea Hospital, and Blathwayt was also very interested in the French methods of mustering soldiers and of controlling seniority and precedence.[2] This was politically harmless and practically beneficial to the English army but, since the furious campaign against the Dutch in 1672, France had shown that she was demonstrably catholic, aggressive, and militarily powerful. It took little for Englishmen to make the connection between absolutism and catholicism and standing armies, an unfortunate combination, as James II was known to be somewhat abrupt and arbitrary in government and an avowed follower of Rome. All the ingredients for absolutism seemed to be present in England in 1685 and, following the refusal to disband the increased army after the Battle of Sedgemoor, this latent threat became a real danger in the minds of contemporaries. The extant military evidence strongly suggests that James both used and intended to use his enlarged army in an overtly political manner in order to increase the royal power in the provinces and in the City of London and generally to repress political opposition.

James was intent upon employing the regular army in the counties rather than the militia in order to lengthen the arm of the central government and to ensure that the provinces became more responsive to the king's authority. The changing composition of the officer corps provided him with great opportunities for the pursuit of this policy. Gone was the majority of gentlemen officers and courtiers who had infested the army under Charles II, to be replaced by professional career soldiers from Tangier, the colonies, France, the Spanish Netherlands, and the United Provinces. This was nowhere more apparent than in the three regiments of foot which were formed in March 1688 out of the officers and men who had returned from the

Anglo–Dutch Brigade; they were professional down to the most junior ensign. Such an officer corps depended for its livelihood, progress, and very existence upon obedience to the royal command and did not display a well developed sensitivity to the prejudices and vested interests of the English gentry and aristocracy. Charles's army had been nearly a mirror of its parent society: the army of James II increasingly detached itself from that bedrock. The enlarged percentage of catholics, both officers and men, gave a further assurance that the army would be loyal to the king rather than to the existing political, religious, and social structure of England. Whereas in Ireland James had been able to create a catholic army from the majority of the population to dominate the protestant minority, in England his religion was in the minority and he had to rely upon an army which was protestant but sufficiently professional and anaesthetised to do his personal bidding. In this policy he was highly successful. From the evidence of biographical information on 500 officers who served continuously with the English army between 1685 and 1688 only 127 took commissions under William III. One hundred and forty-seven fought in the Jacobite armies in Ireland and Scotland, and the remainder resigned their appointments and retired from military life in England. These figures show a huge proportion of the officers unwilling to transfer their allegiance to the new sovereign. In 1688 only a tiny number of English officers revolted against James, and their action was stimulated by adventurism and fears that the king was about to cleanse the English officer corps politically, not by objections to the royal policies. This reliance upon the army helps to explain James's love of the military and his intense interest in the smallest detail of drill and martial administration. His desire to advance the military education of his officers and to involve himself wholeheartedly in the army was born of a practical and political necessity as much as by nostalgia for his own youth. James did not occupy the throne for long enough to be able to develop his absolutist tendencies fully, and the historian can glimpse only the vague opening manoeuvres, but the military evidence is real and definite.

As its officer corps was deliberately created to detach the military from society, so the army's actions and behaviour in England enhanced this development. An important issue was the quartering of troops. Legally, the position on the billeting of soldiers was abundantly clear. Under the terms of the Disbanding Act of 1679 no private householders could be 'compelled against their wills to receive soldiers into their houses ... without [their] consent' and any subject was entitled 'to refuse to soujourn or quarter any soldier or soldiers notwithstanding any command, order, or billeting whatever'.[3] Occasionally it was possible to make this act apply to individual house owners but not to the keepers of public houses. Given the almost total absence of barracks for the soldiery, owners of inns and taverns were in no position to refuse to quarter troops, although some publicans of Fleet Street did lodge an objection in January 1686 'but to little purpose'.[4] Billeting upon private citizens was more contentious. Through his desire to extend the power of the army all over England, and by increasing its numbers substantially, James created enormous difficulties in accommodating his men. Hull, a vital fortress and port, had a garrison which was never less than 500 soldiers throughout the reign but, according to Blathwayt's 'Particular Account', there were only 195 beds in public houses in the town, leaving three-fifths of the soldiers to find lodgings in private houses. Portsmouth possessed a garrison of over 700 men yet had public accommodation for just 164. Small towns with no experience from the previous reign of housing troops found the pressure upon their public and private beds very considerable.[5] Apart from the illegal lodgings with private householders, the other abuse of the billeting system was the frequent recourse to 'free quarter' – the refusal to pay for food, drink, or accommodation. Colonel Percy Kirke was specifically ordered to restrain his men from taking free quarter in the months following the Battle of Sedgemoor, when the temptation to treat the West Country as a conquered territory must have been irresistible. James issued a proclamation on 25 August 1685 insisting that the army did not quarter upon private houses without the consent of their owners, that all bills were promptly paid, no game disturbed, and no threats of violence offered to civilians.[6] After a group of soldiers had left their quarters they were obliged to obtain a certificate from the chief magistrate of that town or village stating that they had behaved themselves decently and had discharged all their debts before their departure. If one of these vital pieces of paper was witheld by a civic authority, then a senior officer was sometimes sent to investigate the matter.[7] Officially, householders who billeted troops were paid the princely sum of 8*d* per week per man, a sum which the soldiers could easily afford, as the average daily pay of the lowliest soldier came to the same amount. Once all the bills had been met, then the town chamberlain issued the relevant receipts to the officers, an occasion which could be very civil.[8]

Paid for wine when Captain Barnes and other officers of the Earl of Huntingdon's [regiment] come to me at the Red Lion to receive ticks for part of his regiment's quartering in town, 3s.

However, all the abuses of quarters were still prevalent in September 1688, when James made another proclamation in an effort to regulate affairs. Again, it was repeated that no officer or soldier could quarter in a private house without the permission of the owner and all misdemeanours committed by the troops were to be reported direct to the king.[9] As the army dramatically increased in size in September and October 1688 so the problems of quarters increased.

The soldiery had lived with very little discipline in the times of peace and now the war was opening became more insolent so that the ill-observing this order [see note 9] was one of those things which tended as much as anything to the ruin of that army they being reduced to a great want of all necessaries by the people who feared their payment and hated both them and the cause they were embarked in.[10]

At certain times the pressure on all available lodgings was acute. As the army concentrated upon Hounslow Heath in every summer of the reign the villages and towns along the major routes into London were crowded with soldiers. James Yonge rode up to town during May 1686 and found most of the road between Dorchester and London full of marching troops and all the inns and taverns oversubscribed.[11] However, it was during the increase and deployment of the army in the autumn of 1688 that the shortage of accommodation was most keenly felt: the major garrisons of Hull, Plymouth, Portsmouth, and the Medway towns were packed with soldiers. At Sheerness Sir Charles Littleton was ordered to use the town chapel in order to house Sir Edward Hales's regiment of foot 'if it be necessary', for they had to be 'quartered within the garrison, as well as maybe, without distinction or reserve of quarters and there must be no scruple to lodge any of them'.[12] Not until after the Revolution did the situation improve. The Mutiny Act of 1689 declared that it was illegal to quarter any soldier upon a private citizen and empowered local magistrates to fix their own county and borough rates for providing billets in public houses.[13]

Throughout the reign there were recorded instances of soldiers seizing free quarter. Some officers of Henry Cornwall's regiment of foot exacted money from their landlords during September 1687 and when Reresby investigated the subsequent complaints he was informed by the officers that 'they had done it in other garrisons'.

Immediately after James's proclamation to the contrary on 25 August 1685, a captain and twenty grenadiers were reported to be on free quarter at Sir Walter Young's house in Colliton. In a rather bizarre incident the twelve soldiers who had the misfortune to spend their lives garrisoning Holy Island requested that beds be put into the castle for their use so that they would no longer be obliged to quarter upon the inhabitants, whose 'poverty' was causing the soldiers 'hardship'.[14] The areas which suffered most severely from having to billet soldiers were those situated on the main roads to and from London. Leicester was affected badly in this respect from 'soldiers passing and repassing and quartering within the borough', whilst Chelsea no sooner lost soldiers who had overstayed their welcome by three weeks than another detachment marched in. Colnbrook and Uxbridge had tolerated the presence of troops of cavalry since the Restoration but by 25 October 1688 even the patience of these long-suffering villages had worn out and the innkeepers removed their signs in an effort to keep the soldiers at bay. Several of the inhabitants and publicans of Barnet petitioned the Privy Council on 20 January 1687, complaining about the activities of Captain Thomas Hussey and his men. Unfortunately, the Privy Councillors decided that the complaint was frivolous and found the petition to be 'vexatious and causeless'. With its reputation for being a 'factious town' and its supposed support for Monmouth in 1685, Bristol was singled out for special treatment. Colonel Charles Trelawney's regiment of infantry, which had been well educated in the gentle finishing school of Tangier, was billeted on the city from the autumn of 1685 until May 1686, when it finally departed for the camp on Hounslow Heath, during which time it terrorised the town with its 'insolence, rapacity, and debauchery'.[15] This was one of the earliest incidents of the army being employed to punish a politically suspect community. In February 1686 James made it plain that he wished to extend his royal authority into the hitherto forbidden territory of the City of London. His method of partially achieving this end was highly offensive. Technically, the monarch had to ask the permission of the mayor and corporation if he wished to march troops through the streets of the Square Mile. Charles II had never attempted even this, but had maintained troops beyond the Temple Bar in the Savoy; south of the river in Southwark; north of the City in Holborn; in the Tower of London, which could be reached by water; and in the City of Westminster. With his customary forthrightness James abandoned such circumspection. In the area around Broad Street there were several dissenters' meeting houses 'which have lately been made use of by persons disaffected to our government', and these were requisitioned and converted into army barracks. At the same time troops were moved up from the Savoy and Charing Cross and billeted within the City limits in Fleet Street. This high-handed manoeuvre struck at the hallowed independence of the City and at the nonconformists with one blow and the overall impression was unmistably gallic.[16] Chester was usually unable to quarter all of its garrison in public houses and was forced to make use of private dwellings but the governor, Peter Shakerley, sent his 'people' around the military billets in the city once every two months to inspect them and make certain that the soldiers were paying their landlords. Sir John Reresby in York made sure that his soldiers' quarters were duly visited once a month but, in April 1688, he was ordered by the king to abolish this 'caution' without being offered any explanation. Many towns must have been similar to Leeds in that one of the first notable effects of the accession of James II was the 'quartering soldiers in gentlemen's houses and private families. I had two for my share and afterwards an officer of a good family in the neighbourhood, Sir Henry Goodrick's kinsman, but himself no saint.'[17]

In regular garrison towns like Berwick-on-Tweed the army was part of the way of life, but it could still represent a considerable burden to municipal finances. When a regiment left the garrison, an event which could occur three or four times in any one year, it was the custom for the corporation to give a dinner to the out-going officers which cost £14 10*s* 10*d* on 16 March 1687. Even a large garrison such as Berwick was not equipped with barracks, and on the imminent arrival of a new formation the General Guild of the town assembled and discussed with the mayor the arrangements for accommodating the expected soldiers.[18] For towns and cities which were unused to acting as hosts to troops the frequency of military visitations during James's reign represented unwelcome additions to civic expenditure. Soldiers left behind mountains of debts in Nottingham, and the city council felt obliged to reimburse individual burghers for sums of money which they had advanced to soldiers but had not been repaid: the city chamberlain gave £2 4*s* to Gregory Melton, who had loaned some horses to soldiers but had seen neither beasts nor men again. On 8 December 1688 Nottingham entertained a party of soldiers to guard the Princess Anne of Denmark, who was resident in the city, causing it to be 'much in debt' to the extent that the council had to go cap-in-hand to the citizens asking for voluntary contributions.[19] Sometimes the burden of quarters fell very heavily upon individual householders and the town council felt obliged to relieve them: Leicester city chamberlain paid the quartermaster of the Duke of Berwick's regiment of foot the sum of £1 'to ease the town'.[20] The mayor of Northampton was most earnest in treating the officers of all the regiments who marched through the town, no doubt as an attempt to buy the good behaviour of both officers and their men.[21]

James placed the need to quarter his army above his concern for civilians. In April 1688 he decided to increase the size of the Portsmouth garrison in order to man the new fortifications which had been built in 1686 and 1687. As a preliminary, he ordered Blathwayt to have the available accommodation in the town surveyed to ascertain the number of beds in public houses and the 'ability of the housekeepers to quarter soldiers'. Upon the results of this undertaking soldiers were ordered to sleep two to a bed and all the troops who could not be fitted into inns and taverns were instructed to lodge in private houses. This, together with the presence of a considerable body of inadequately disciplined catholic Irish soldiers, caused great friction between the town and the army and it was not until after the accession of William and Mary that the billeting of troops in that garrison was put upon a regular footing.[22] Hull was another garrison town adversely affected by enforced quarters. So grave were the difficulties in 1685 that landlords were prepared to lodge soldiers free of charge, provided that they paid for their food and drink, to lessen the risk of the military seizing free quarters. Two years later additional soldiers were drafted into the town for political reasons, all of whom were ordered by the king to quarter upon private householders. Early in 1688 Henry Cornwall's regiment of foot was directed to Hull and, although James ordered a survey to be taken of all the public houses in the town, the vast majority of these new troops had to be lodged in private accommodation at the rate of 8d per week per man. No sooner had these new soldiers arrived in the town than they refused to pay for their billets until, by 30 June, the town council reckoned that Cornwall's men owed a total of £127 18s 6d in unpaid bills. Unfortunately, the mayor's filing system was slack and he lost many of the relevant papers, leaving the town unable to press its claim.[23] North of the border, the tiny Scottish army was also remarkable lax in paying for its quarters. Proclamations in 1685 and 1688 insisted that soldiers met their debts once every eight days, 'yet many of their quarters remain unpaid for the soldiers threaten the tenants when they offer to exact payment'.[24] Without barracks and a well developed military administration the problem of how to accommodate large numbers of soldiers was insoluble, but the difficulties during James's reign were especially acute. Not only was the army suddenly expanded in 1685 and 1688 but quartering was used for political purposes in a number of instances, a factor which greatly increased public hatred of the army and assisted in divorcing the military from everyday society. To civilians the army appeared to be thoroughly arrogant and aggressive and whilst attempting to uphold the law paid scant regard itself to the legislation regulating billets.

Closely connected with quarters was the overall question of military discipline and legal control of the soldiery. In a charmingly off hand letter Colonel Percy Kirke, of Tangier reknown, asked Blathwayt what course he was to follow with those of his soldiers who should 'plunder and murder'. The secretary-at-war's reply established the legal practice which was to be current for the majority of the reign: any soldier who committed an offence against a civilian was to be tried before the 'common and statute law'.[25] This directive was reiterated in 1687 when Captain Charles Macarty in Guernsey informed Blathwayt that he had court-martialled Private George Holmes for stealing two silver cups from Alexander Hall a civilian inhabitant of the island. According to Blathwayt, the king thought these proceedings 'very irregular', as courts-martial could only be employed where one soldier 'in pay' wronged another 'in pay'; if a soldier abused a civilian the case had to be tried before civil magistrates.[26] These pronouncements run contrary to the statements of George Clarke, the judge advocate-general of the army, who clearly said that James altered the legal status of the military by referring all its judicial business, relating to both civil and military cases, to a weekly standing court-martial which sat at the Horse Guards in Whitehall. Clarke also recorded that, in his opinion, the creation of this court effectively removed the military from the competence of the civil power and made it an independent force reliant solely upon the orders of the king.[27] Just as the army largely ignored the legislation relating to quarters and made itself into an extra-legal estate, so these remarks of George Clarke suggest that it was progressively transformed into a force regulated solely by the exercise of the royal prerogative. Such an interpretation is more in keeping with James's political employment of the army and, given Clarke's intimate knowledge of the army's legal organisation, his evidence ought to be definitive. The available information indicates that Blathwayt naively tried to enforce both the strict letter and spirit of the regulations but that Clarke knew more of the actual practice.

On 10 July 1685 a general court-martial was appointed to sit in order to 'examine the several matters . . . touching any soldiers having deserted his colours or our service and all other crimes and misdemeanours whatsoever relating to our said service'. This was a very wide brief indeed and was imprecise about whether the jurisdiction of the court extended to crimes against civilians as well as to specifically military offences.[28] Probably, this partial declaration of martial law was intended to assist with the government of the army during Monmouth's Rebellion and was revoked after the cessation of hostilities. Martial law had been declared in Berwick-on-Tweed on 10 February 1685 to assist in the peaceful and unopposed accession of James II. A curfew was laid upon the town and no one was allowed into the streets 'under pain of death which begot a great surprising consternation in most of the town and many apprehended a massacre'.[29] During the second camp on Hounslow Heath in 1686 a council-of-war decided to establish a court-martial to enforce martial law within the bounds of the encampment on the grounds that James had discovered that civil magistrates tended to encourage deserters rather than punish them severely. Another court-martial was appointed to the camp in the summer of 1688, whilst earlier in the same year, on 11 March, a standing court-martial was commissioned to sit at the Horse Guards every Friday morning to hear all cases concerning military personnel and to entertain all civilian complaints against the army.[30] This was the weekly court-martial referred to by George Clarke. Until the establishment of this machinery, crimes by military men against civilians were generally tried by civil magistrates, with periodic courts-martial handling the army's internal discipline. After 11 March 1688 there appears to have been a definite trend towards making the army legally independent of the common and statute law, a force reliant on the king and not on parliament and society. The proceedings against desertion offer a practical illustration of this development.

The new regiments which had been raised to face Monmouth were thought to be temporary formations recruited solely for the duration of the conflict. When they were continued on foot beyond the Battle of Sedgemoor it came as an unpleasant surprise to many of the volunteers, and as a result James was faced with a high rate of desertion for the remainder of his reign. It is difficult to gauge the precise numbers who ran from their colours, but in some formations it was considerable. During May 1686 new regulations governing pay were introduced for the Scottish army in an attempt to reduce desertion and to improve the administration of the pay system. Despite these comprehensive standing orders, the first battalion of the Scottish Foot Guards, consisting of a paper establishment of 560 privates, succeeded in losing thirty-eight soldiers through desertion in the two-month muster period which ended on 23 April 1687. If this figure had been repeated throughout one full year, then the regiment would have lost from desertion 7 per cent of its strength in addition to the 2 per cent who died each year and the 1 per cent who managed to secure a discharge. The Scottish Foot Guards were a regular regiment which had been in existence since 1662, yet it suffered a minimum annual loss of personnel in the region of 10 per cent of its paper strength. Probably the wastage of the actual effective strength was higher, as the regiment would not have contained its full complement of 1,120 soldiers for most of the year, the ranks being artificially completed on muster day. In the newly raised regiments of 1685 the level of desertion was probably greater than that of this Scottish regiment.[31]

During the campaign against the Duke of Monmouth a variety of methods were employed to bring deserters to justice. One soldier, Charles Twist, was tried before the Western Assizes, whilst another private from the Holland regiment was hanged immediately after Sedgemoor, having been convicted before a drumhead court-martial.[32] Cases of desertion came before the Quarter Sessions in Wiltshire and Middlesex in 1686 and 1687. Private William Ward of Charles Trelawney's foot was sentenced to death by the Exeter Assizes on 25 February 1687 for running from his colours, and two soldiers were similarly convicted at the Old Bailey on 16 June 1688.[33] Without declaring a state of martial law in England, which was technically illegal except during a war or internal rebellion, James thought it vital to have desertion accounted a felony before the common law, as it continued the fiction that the military was subordinate to the civil and gave the army a bogus air of legality. More important, recourse to the common law provided him with a tried and proven weapon to employ against his deserters and removed the necessity of having to retain martial law during peacetime. Unfortunately, not all the common law judges thought that desertion in time of peace was a felony. In 1686 Sir John Holt, the Recorder of London, considered that desertion could only be regarded as a felony if the king was at war, an opinion based upon two statutes which gave the impression that a deserter could be tried as a felon if he served the king overseas and was thus, presumably, on active service.[34] Upon Holt's decision, Jeffreys sought the views of nine other judges, all of whom sycophantically confirmed that desertion in England during peace was a felony. Holt was reluctant to depart from his own interpretation but as the tide of deserters grew larger and he was the principal judge of London, the centre of the largest concentration of troops in England, he was not allowed to remain in office and Jeffreys appointed a more pliant recorder.[35] For a while matters continued as before – Reresby was instructed to take his deserters before the common law to have them proceeded against as felons on 4 January 1687 – but in the August of the following year came a vital change in policy. Sir Thomas Haggerston, the lieutenant-governor of Berwick, was informed that he could try deserters before either a regimental or a general court-martial; there was no need to bother with the civil law courts.[36] No doubt the increasing numbers in the army late in the autumn of 1688 made the old arrangements highly inconvenient and time-consuming but this step was taken without the necessary and legal preliminary of a declaration of martial law. When considered in conjunction with the creation of the standing court-martial on 11 March 1688, this evidence provides real substance for the views of George Clarke. The army in England was becoming independent of the law and increasingly divorced from society. More and more it became the king's force.

This separation of the army from the law was reflected in the attitude of the soldiers towards civilians and civil institutions. Men attempting to escape from the processes of the law had only to be mustered into the army to avoid its clutches, and even in the midst of a series of appearances in court enlistment was a sufficient cause to have the case abandoned. Soldiers showed no respect for the workings of the law and regarded themselves as above its jurisdiction. Jacob White, a private soldier who had been imprisoned for debt, was rescued from the custody of the deputy goaler of Warwick 'by several soldiers to the number of about fourteen which quarter in Warwick'. Following the murder of a townsman of Loughborough by a trooper from the Earl of Arran's regiment of horse, he was spirited away to Leicester by some of his colleagues and was there taken into military custody by Major John Parker. Presumably, Parker had not wanted his man to be tried before the common law and had accordingly taken affairs into his own hands. He was reprimanded by Blathwayt and reminded of the correct procedures. A 'scuffle' between the constable's watch of Aldgate and some Scottish soldiers of Dumbarton's foot led to the latter carrying the constable to the main guard. The lord mayor and the sheriffs of the City of London demanded the immediate release of the unfortunate constable but the soldiers' captain merely gave them 'insolent language', forcing the City authorities to appeal to the king in person. James duly suspended Captain Robert Hodges, adding blandly that he never intended the military to overawe the civil.[37] Possibly James meant what he said but his actions belied his words. The military generally despised the common law and saw themselves removed from its authority, an attitude which he did nothing to dispel. Until the establishment of the standing court-martial in 1688, James had to rely upon the common law to maintain the discipline of his army, but martial offenders were taken before the common law courts out of necessity rather than respect. After the army obtained its own judicial organ little more was heard of the common and statute law.

Onerous in their demands for quarters and increasingly divorced from the law of the land, the army in England was abominably behaved and thoroughly ill-natured. Two men were killed and a third badly wounded when three soldiers from the Earl of Huntingdon's regiment fought in the streets of York with three men from Sir Theophilus Oglethorpe's foot. Often differences over religion led to military quarrels as in Oxford in 1688 when a catholic soldier killed his protestant corporal. After an Irish private had murdered a sleeping protestant soldier in his tent it took the personal intervention of the king to calm the enraged English soldiers.[38] The military were arrogant, haughty, and well armed.

A soldier pistolled a watchman in Southampton Buildings saying, some time before he had been affronted by a watchman there of which he was resolved to be revenged and therefore went to them and killed one, whether he that affronted him or another it mattered not.[39]

Troopers killed civilians in Grantham, York, London, Henley-on-Thames, and many more places. Every town or village visited by soldiers was liable to murder and robbery.[40] The Scottish army was no better; soldiers were drunk on duty, killed civilians, murdered their own officers, and took every available opportunity to ruin property and abuse civilians. Under the threat of an invasion from the United Provinces, James attempted to improve the discipline of his forces on 8 September 1688, realising that some rapport between the army and society was necessary if England was to be immersed in an internal war. Yet, after sending out the orders to observe proper discipline and not to quarter soldiers upon private householders, Blathwayt issued a series of instructions to the mayors of Rochester, Great Yarmouth, Canterbury, Gravesend, Wilton, and Sittingbourne which insisted that they take additional troops into their towns whether or not there was sufficient room in public houses. William of Orange was well aware of the advantages to be gained by an army which maintained good discipline and did not disturb civilians and took considerable pains to ensure that his invasion force was impeccably behaved.[41]

Without committing any political act or being used for any political purpose, the army was unpopular with most ranks of English society.

Our rebellion is now over, Monmouth and all his party being routed. Instead thereof we have now got a standing army, a thing the nation hath long been jealous of, but I hope the king will no otherwise use it than to secure our peace. The war now from the field, I suppose, will pass into the roads which we must expect will awhile be infested with the remainder of those rogues.[42]

In the summer of every year of James's reign this hated army assembled upon Hounslow Heath in a huge camp which was initially 'ill resented all over and everyone says that a standing army will be England's ruin'. The purpose of an annual military concentration so near to London was immediately questioned: was it intended to overawe the City?[43] This was almost certainly one of the objectives of the exercise but it was also a genuine attempt by James to drill and train his soldiers into an effective and professional army in the European style. The king visited the camp at least twice a week and took a very personal interest in the progress of his forces, supervising much of the large-scale training himself.[44] During the camp of 1687 an imitation fort was built on the Heath 'about the bigness of Sheerness' which was later 'attacked in form by the whole army', an operation which took 'some days' to complete. This manoeuvre was supposed to represent the famous siege of Buda from the previous year, and these elaborate exercises were not solely confined to the annual musters at Hounslow – the Battle of Sedgemoor was re-enacted in Hyde Park on 16 March 1686.[45] Hounslow Heath was situated midway between Windsor and Whitehall and was thus highly convenient for James to make visits to the camp but it was also a strategically significant site. Charles II had used the heath for the concentation of his army in 1678, as it stood at the intersection of three major roads: the Great West Road, the Great North Road, and the Portsmouth Road. Any force gathered at Hounslow could be easily dispatched to counter a threat in any part of England, particularly on the south and east coasts. The great advantage of the institution of the annual camp was that it enabled an army which spent most of its time in garrisons scattered across England and Wales to drill and train in large formations up to regimental and brigade level. Initially, the Hounslow Camp was probably designed to remind the City of London of the monarch's potential power, an aim which James had already declared by quartering soldiers within the hallowed Square Mile in the early months of 1686. Unfortunately, the camps could only serve as periodic demonstrations of military might; as they were in existence for just six weeks every summer they were not able to maintain a consistent pressure upon the independent spirits of the City. They actually achieved the opposite effect to that intended by the king. Instead of reducing Londoners to hushed admiration for the strength of the monarchy, the camps became great popular spectacles and assumed all the characteristics of a funfair. Charles Petty, the son of Sir William Petty, included Hounslow Heath in his itinerary of the 'sights of London' and witnessed 'the noble appearance of his Majesty's forces', whilst Sir John Reresby took his wife and daughter, Frances, to view the camp, a sight which could not have proved too edifying for the young lady, as the tents were full of 'lewd women . . . to debauch the soldiers'.

The camp here at Hounslow is very glorious. His Majesty is there almost every day. There is great concourse to it and great feasting at it; often exercising and much powder burnt.[46]

The first assembly on Hounslow Heath took place in the summer of 1685, when the 'new' army which had defeated Monmouth stayed for a few weeks under canvas to be reviewed by the king and to undertake some basic training. In the following year the Hounslow Camp was due to open on 20 May but the tents were not actually pitched until eight days later because of heavy rain. At the height of that summer's rendezvous 10,144 infantry and cavalry were present on the heath, encamped in a line of tents about a mile and a half in length. Wet weather caused the camp to break up earlier than had been intended, and by 11 August all the regiments and the train of artillery had departed to their winter quarters. A similar number of troops came on to the heath in the May and June of 1687 and stayed in residence until 10 August. The camp of 1688 did not pitch its tents until 27 June, having been delayed by a spell of unseasonably damp weather, and departed sooner than was customary to enable the troops to be in their billets before the writs were issued for the election of a new parliament: contemporaries presumed that the troops would be required 'to keep order' during the ensuing parliamentary campaign.[47] Apart from learning how to exercise and operate in battle-sized formations, the Hounslow Camps confronted the English army with the realities of life in the field. The summer of 1688 was 'excessively hot' and subject to frequent violent thunder storms, a metereological combination which led to chronic ill-health amongst many of the common soldiers. The inadequacy of the commissariat under the incapable command of John Shales guaranteed that their condition was further reduced by a shortage of basic provisions.[48]

The spectacle and gallantry of the Hounslow Camp was an exception in the history of civil–military relations under James II. More typical was the dilemma of James Nimmo, who was worried about having to travel to London, as it involved leaving his wife at Edinburgh, 'alone in a garrison town', or the decision of Sir William Frankland that 'Peggy should have come out last Wednesday but, there being none but men and most of them soldiers in the coach, we thought it better to defer to another day'.[49] Mrs. Jane Pinney considered it safe for her husband to journey from Dublin to Axminster because all the soldiers were assembled on Hounslow Heath: 'you may travel as safe here as there till the soldiers do come back from the camp'.[50] This enormous hostility and fear of the army and its personnel sometimes expressed itself in violence. Several inhabitants of Great Yarmouth were 'very abusive to the soldiers there', and relations between the army and the civilians on Guernsey were exceptionally strained. Following the military protection of a wreck some of the islanders uttered 'seditious words' and threatened to cut the throats of the soldiers. Nottingham common council was obliged to pay compensation to Private James Carruthers, who had been beaten up by some townsmen, and a number of people from Sherborne in Dorset fell upon and wounded a party of soldiers under the command of Captain James Courtney on 6 November 1688.[51] After a London mob had assaulted the catholic monastery in Clerkenwell on 11 November 1688 the army intervened and killed some of the demonstrators. At the subsequent inquest into these deaths the jury proclaimed that they were public-spirited persons who had been done to death by the army whilst opposing the actions of traitors.[52] Whereas Charles II's army had rarely penetrated beyond London, the southern counties of England, and the major garrisons, James spread his forces over most of England, bringing a large proportion of the population into contact with the military. 'The country people complain much of the new army,' wrote Christopher Jeaffreson to Colonel Thomas Hill in St. Kitts, 'the roads are full of robbers.' John Evelyn recorded the 'great complaints' which had occurred since the 'forces were dispersed into several quarters throughout the kingdom'.[53] Between January 1686 and May 1687 there were incidents involving soldiers in Bideford, York, Honiton, Guernsey, Oxford, Cornwall, Exeter, Bristol, Brentwood, Wigan, Berwick, Gravesend, Salisbury, Pendennis, Windsor, and Great Yarmouth, and these represent only those events which evoked official objections; many more probably passed by unrecorded.[54] To Anthony Wood's horror, the proctors of Oxford were unable to 'walk ... because of the troopers for fear of being affronted by them. Whore houses increase, surgeons have work, and great salivation used. O tempora! O mores!'[55] To darken this dismal picture, Irish troops sailed to England in August and September 1688 to bolster the English army for the threatened Dutch invasion. Many of them were posted to Portsmouth, with the immediate corollary that many civilians refused to enter the town to work in the dockyards or on the fortifications. Apparently, the Irish soldiers lived in Portsmouth without discipline, beating the mayor and finally causing a vast riot which was sparked off when some Irish soldiers fired into an Anglican church during divine service. This brought about a battle between the protestant soldiers of the Duke of Berwick's regiment and the catholic Irish of Dennis MacGillicuddy's foot in which over fifty soldiers lost their lives.[56] Edmund Verney watched some of the Irish troops march through East Claydon in Buckinghamshire.

This day [29 October 1688] passed by here five hundred Irish foot soldiers in their march to London and just at the town's end they quarrelled amongst themselves about going over a stile in Newfield. One of them was knocked down and his skull much broken and he now lies insensible at Thomas Miller's. 'Tis thought he will die very shortly if he is not dead already.[57]

The catholic Irish soldiers were described as 'the rudest fellows that ever were seen', but the Scottish soldiers gained an equally unsavoury reputation. As Dumbarton's regiment of foot marched south they stayed for a while in the small town of Loughborough. They paid for nothing and extorted money from civilians; they lodged in private as well as in public houses; wounded a number of townspeople; were rude to the mayor and corporation; robbed some local gentlemen; and left the town worse off by over £100.[58]

Burdensome, indisciplined, and anti-social though it was, the army did perform some useful social duties. At Hull, Portsmouth, and Gosport many of the soldiers in garrison were employed as day labourers on building the new fortifications. In lesser garrisons where there was no official employment and even less entertainment, the troops were permitted to work at their own trades.[59] For the formations quartered in and around London, Westminster, and the home counties, numerous reviews, ceremonial parades, and the need to escort members of the royal family between Whitehall and Windsor occupied the majority of their time.[60] Ceremonial duties were also an important part of military life in the larger garrison towns. Thomas Cartwright, the new bishop of Chester, was conducted into the city on his first entrance to his new see on 30 November 1686 by 'a great train of the gentry on horseback and ten coaches with the guards drawn up from the gates to the palace.' When the Earl of Clarendon left Chester for London during his return from Ireland, the Marquis of Worcester's foot stood in a single line from the deanery to the East Gate with the officers saluting.[61] A regular duty for parties of cavalry was to convoy bullion from the Navy Pay Office in Broad Street to the dockyards in Portsmouth.[62] Patrolling the highways, reducing riots in London and Edinburgh, arresting notorious robbers or highwaymen, and delivering the post — these were social tasks which drew little public complaint, but James II also used his army in a number of ways which suggested that it was developing into a political force.[63] Two soldiers stood guard as the Ecclesiastical Commission interviewed Henry Compton, the Bishop of London, for the second time on 16 August 1686 and when that same Commission visited Magdalen College, Oxford, on 20 October 1687 its members were escorted into the university city by the Earl of Peterborough's regiment of horse. As the reaction to affairs at Magdalen became more unruly, these troopers were reinforced to enable them to maintain order within the town.[64] There were numerous indications that James employed his army to extend his authority into London and the provinces with a studied disregard for local privileges and the law. Between 1685 and 1688 the army began to act in the interests of James's personal policies by reducing political opposition to his objectives.

Henry Newcome, a dissenting minister, 'was at James Smethurst's [when] the soldiers and officers came in upon us but we were but four and so nothing was made of it'. James authorised a Huguenot church in Dover in 1685 on the condition that the French refugees said only the Anglican liturgy, 'wherein if they fail', the lietenant of Dover Castle was ordered, 'we do authorise and require you or the mayor ... to shut up the church doors and suffer them to meet no more'.[65] Not only was the army called upon to suppress noncomformists but it had to protect the numerous roman catholic chapels and religious institutions from attack and insult. Soldiers were required to quell serious anti-catholic riots in Bristol in May 1686, and on 24 December the Earl of Dumbarton detailed some of the catholics in his regiment to guard the popish chapel in Edinburgh. The decision of Obadiah Walker, the master of University College, Oxford, to hear a daily mass in the company of four of his college fellows and eleven commoners, was sufficient to demand the attentions of Lord Ailesbury's troop of horse to keep the peace in the city and reinforcements had to be dispatched to maintain order in the future.[66] During the public holiday on Shrove Tuesday in 1688, some bored apprentices put a stone through a window in the catholic chapel in York. Immediately the acting governor, Lieutenant-Colonel James Purcell, a catholic who had picked up a multitude of bad habits during his service with the French army in the 1670s, took two files of musketeers to deal with the affray. In a massive over-reaction which he could only have learnt in France, Purcell arrested fifteen boys and apprentices and took them to the main guard, where they were tied neck and heels and forced to ride the wooden horse.[67] As the bulk of James's army marched towards Salisbury to face William's invasion force, the two infantry regiments which remained in London were hard put to prevent serious anti-catholic rioting and attacks upon foreign nationals and their property.[68]

Dr. Miller is of the opinion that 'the army could not be used for wholesale repression or to impose catholicism as it was predominantly protestant and its loyalty to the king was far from unconditional'. Professor Kenyon says that James's army was too small to coerce the nation and because of a lack of sufficient revenue James was unable to increase his armed forces further after 1687.[69] These views imply a basic misunderstanding of the nature of the officer corps of the English army and of the potential of the Restoration military establishment. During his three and a half years on the throne James steadily purged his officer corps of political malcontents and went some considerable way towards converting it from a body of gentlemen and courtiers into a professional institution whose members were dependent on the king for their livelihood and prospects.

He caresses the officers much and explains himself openly enough, that he will keep none but those on whom he may entirely depend.

This process was far from complete by the time of James's flight but considerable progress had been achieved. Taking into account the addition of the Tangier garrison to the English establishment in the early months of 1684, the English army increased in size by 400 per cent between January 1684 and 31 December 1685. Three-quarters of the officers of the royal army were appointed between these two dates, mostly professional soldiers or young men setting out on a military career. The survivors of Charles II's 'guards and garrisons' were further depleted between 1685 and 1688, leaving James with an army which was very different in both personnel and complexion. An officer corps that was substantially professional did not have the same tender regard for the laws and liberties of England as the gentry and aristocracy who had played at soldiers after the Restoration, whilst the catholic officers had everything to gain by their overthrow. This army had little respect for the law and after the establishment of the regular court-martial it moved further away from legal contacts with society and became a separate organisation governing itself with reference to no authority but that of the monarch.[70] In the face of the universal opprobrium thrown against it, the army was a compact and tightly-knit force, and it represented the only organised and disciplined institution which James could use to extend his personal control into the provinces. As he steadily alienated the traditional loyalty of the country gentry and aristocracy James was forced back on to his army as the main pillar of his regime, the only organisation upon which he thought he could rely. Naturally, there were frictions within the officer corps. Protestant officers were sometimes less than enchanted by the presence of catholics, although many had experience of working closely together in France, Tangier, and the Dutch service and the idea of a 'military brotherhood' seemed to promote unity, and the career officers were constantly aware of Tyrconnell's progress in Ireland and looked over their shoulders for the signs of the beginnings of any purge in England. This nervousness was brought into sharper focus when James 'disobliged' some of the officers by removing their commissions without compensation during 1686 and 1687. However, in the acid test of 1688 the majority of the army and its officers remained loyal and it was only a tiny fraction who comprised the active conspiracy which demoralised the king and prevented William's invasion from turning into a protracted civil war. Even then, the military conspiracy only came into being as a part of the overall machinery of the Dutch invasion. In the bizarre conditions of 1688, James discovered that he had inadvertently created sufficient ill-will among a few of his officers to ruin his own cause, but this only became apparent after the conspirators in the army were in possession of the knowledge and the promise of William's impending armed assault. If James's reign had been blessed with peace or even allowed the privilege of a normal, foreign war in 1688, then, in all probability, there would have been no overt opposition to the monarch from within his own armed forces. That a large number of officers offered their swords to William after the campaign of 1688 had been decided gives no true indication of either the size of the conspiracy or the essential allegiance of most of the English army. When the 'war' was over men had to decide whether to serve under the new king or follow the old, but during the campaign itself the army's basic devotion to James was not in doubt.

The curious and unique circumstances of 1688 give the historian no reason for believing that James did not and could not have used his army to pursue his own personal policies. The army of James II was very different to that of his brother and was well advanced along the road to being an absolutist force by the time of William's intervention. Moreover, there is no substantial evidence that the army officers objected to being exploited in this way; the military rebellion of 1688 was not about the use of the army or the rights of the monarchy but about property. Nor was it too small to coerce the country. During the 1680s Louis XIV possessed a standing army of between 80,000 and 100,000 men to control a population of some twenty millions; James II had an army of 20,000 to dominate a population that was no larger than five and a half million people.[71] France thus enjoyed a ratio of one soldier to 225 civilians whilst England had one soldier to every 275, not a remarkable variation. The English population was far less widely spread than that of France, with the bulk living south of the river Trent and the great majority of these residing in London, the south-east, and the West Country. Military coercion in England would have proved difficult and the army might, ultimately, have proved to be too small, but a policy which aimed in that direction cannot, on these grounds, be dismissed as a bizarre dream. Because of the abbreviation of his tenure of office, it is only possible to catch glimpses of the policies which James might later have developed if he had been awarded a full span of years. These fleeting insights offer something very positive in the military field: the officer corps was reformed, the army was trained, the whole military organisation was made increasingly dependent on the king and it was often employed in the pursuit of political ends.

In July 1671 James had told Colbert de Croissy that Charles II would have been well advised not to summon parliament until after the actual opening of the third Dutch War on the grounds that, following a successful campaign, 'they would be in a position to obtain by strength what they cannot have by gentleness'.[72] Although this somewhat ambiguous reference is the sole evidence of James vocally advocating the use of military force against parliament, it is indicative that such thoughts were not totally absent from his mind. Whenever it was practicable, James stood for the extension of royal control and the centralisation of government. All the colonies in New England were stripped of their separate charters and were organised into one governorship in 1685 under the king's old associate, Sir Edmund Andros, who ruled the Dominion of New England by decree. The representative assemblies of the old colonies were abolished and the colonial militias became an arm of Andros's authority, a policy which reflected James's belief that government had to be fully subordinate to the royal will. Sir Edmund's position was reinforced when two regular companies of foot were raised in England in the autumn of 1686 and sent to New York, the 'capital' of the Dominion.[73] Biased contemporaries assumed that the logical corollary of James II's theories of government was an absolutism in the French style, with the suppression of individual liberties and parliamentary institutions. Lord Delamere accused Charles II of founding many of the bases for a popish absolutism and thought that James greatly benefited from his brother's groundwork but improved upon it by adding 'a great army, who lived in a manner upon free quarter, committing all manner of insolencies, and no redress could be had upon any complaint'.[74] The exaggeration in these remarks was only slight, whilst the opinion of Edmund Bohun was founded upon a wealth of evidence:

To prevent the worst they resolved to keep up a numerous army, to suppress betimes any party that might stir in the nation, and to fix them the more to their interest they not only exempted the soldiers from the civil jurisdiction but suffered them to outrage and injure whom they pleased almost without restraint.[75]

A certain David Jones claimed that he had once been a secretary and translator to Louvois, and his account of James's reign, published in 1717, was supposedly based upon the official French sources that had passed through the author's hands. Jones alleged that James had planned to discard the militia and rely entirely upon the standing army by quartering the soldiers all over England in order to assist the lords lieutenant in effecting a religious toleration. Furthermore, according to Jones, the king formulated plans to convert Whitehall into an armed citadel by constructing barracks, stables, and fortifications, and by building a new bridge across the Thames to give direct access to the south bank from the palace of Whitehall without having to depend upon London Bridge. Evidence of this description is extremely difficult to quantify. Jones might indeed have assisted Louvois at some time, and his book did not appear until the second decade of the eighteenth century, when the majority of the principal politicians of James's reign were dead, and long before the works of Dalrymple and Macpherson began the slow process of basing the history of the reign upon fact rather than prejudice and misconception. If there is any accuracy in Jones's statements the references must be to designs which the king harboured for the future; the records of the Ordnance Office provide no corroboration and make no mention of any projects for martial edifices in the environs of Whitehall. However, there was a precedent for using Whitehall as a military base. Following the sudden dissolution of the Oxford parliament in 1681, Charles II ordered the 660 soldiers who had protected him at Oxford to march to London to reinforce the 1,890 men who were already stationed in Westminster and around the City. On that occasion, with his heavy and extraordinary concentration of troops in the capital, the additional soldiers were billeted in Whitehall and Westminster, where 'the Mews is filled with horse and foot'. Similarly, Charles II showed a distinct preference for residence at Windsor Castle not solely on the grounds that it was a pleasant rural retreat but because it was the only royal palace which could be, and was, effectively garrisoned. These precedents in no way provide substance for the observations of David Jones but merely indicate that the employment of the palace of Whitehall as a military as well as a governmental base was at least quite possible. In all probability, Jones's accusations arose from a simple misunderstanding. In 1687 the Royal Mews at Charing Cross occupied the site of the modern Trafalgar Square, and although they accommodated three hundred horses, thirty coaches, and over thirty staff, James considered the buildings to be 'ancient and incommodious' and decided to erect 'a noble structure for his coach-houses and stables and an apartment for a court of horse and foot guards'. The scheme, which was entrusted to Sir Christopher Wren, was to situate the new mews on the west side of

St. James's Park and link them to Piccadilly by the construction of a new street. If the existing mews at Charing Cross were sold, Wren calculated that the total cost to the crown would be a mere £734 but, despite this, no work was undertaken before James lost his throne. By exaggerating this modest and non-military plan into something threatening Jones possibly arrived at his own conclusions, which cannot be verified and must be set aside.[76]

The principal foreign observer of affairs in England, Paul Barrillon, the French ambassador, was in little doubt concerning the objectives of James's domestic policy and reported to his master on 25 June 1685 'that the king of England is very glad to have the pretence of raising troops and he believes that the Duke of Monmouth's enterprise will serve only to make him still more master of his country'.[77] English contemporaries fully realised the potential which an increased army had presented to their monarch. In writing to Thomas Hill, the lieutenant-governor of St. Kitts in the West Indies, Christopher Jeaffreson ventured to suggest that 'St. Christopher's may be a good retirement and a better abode than this in a short time [as the king has] six regiments of new-raised foot and, I think, no less horse to keep us quiet.'[78] The definition of the exact aims of James's government – religious toleration, extension of royal control – mattered little when the methods which he adopted to achieve either or both were the same: the employment of the military to enforce the wishes of the central government, often at the expense of the law.

In the first place, the army was naturally used to present an example of enthusiastic loyalty to the royal family. The military were called upon to celebrate publicly the pregnancy of Mary of Modena, and upon the birth of the Prince of Wales all the governors, lieutenant-governors, and commanders-in-chief of the king's garrisons were ordered 'to cause suitable public demonstrations of joy and rejoicings within their respective garrisons'.[79] Many career-minded officers, anxious to please, began their celebrations before the appointed day, as in Cambridge, where 'Great St. Mary's bells rang and a bonfire was on the great hill ... and the soldiers there met and gave several volleys of shot.' In the other university city, soldiers fired their muskets in the air and busied themselves with the bottle, whilst in Carlisle

they drank wine till, with that and the transport of the news they were exceedingly distracted, throwing their hats into the fire at one health, their coats at the next, their waistcoats at a third, and so on to their shoes. And some of them threw in their shirts and then ran about naked like madmen.[80]

These were mere routine shows of loyalty by the army to their monarch but the response to the order for these celebrations was widespread and few, if any, of the army commanders refused to obey on grounds of political or religious conscience.

James expected co-operation and obedience from his army officers. All over England the governors of garrisons were important sources of information for the government and they were usually active correspondents of the secretaries of state or of the secretary-at-war. Sir John Reresby of York wrote regularly to Blathwayt, as did Peter Shakerley from Chester, especially concerning affairs in Ireland. Garrison towns were almost entirely subject to crown control in matters relating to parliamentary and local government elections and frequently returned their governors or other army officers as their members of parliament: Sir Christopher Musgrave sat for Carlisle from 1661 to 1689 and the regulators of Robert Brent and the Earl of Sunderland recommended army officers to sit for the garrison towns of Queenborough, Scarborough, Carlisle, and Berwick in 1688. Once chosen for a borough or a county, an officer was expected to attend the sittings of the House and to vote in favour of the court, and those officers who were elcted to the parliament of 1685 each received a letter instructing them to give their 'attendance at the House of Commons as soon as possible'.[81] In the absence of any discernible swell of opinion in favour of the repeal of the Test Acts and Penal Laws, the government of James II was obliged to fall back on the support of catholics, dissenters, and placemen, the latter category including a considerable number of army officers.[82] In Cornwall, the Earl of Bath entered the names of army officers into many of the borough charters in 1685 to ensure that loyal and devoted members were returned to parliament for those constituencies. During their Cornish tour in 1687 and 1688 the regulators suggested eight army officers to serve as members for some of that county's many boroughs. Following the king's decision on 24 August 1688 to summon a new parliament, Sunderland wrote a series of letters between 13 and 15 September to several lords lieutenant strongly recommending certain gentlemen as suitable candidates for county seats and directed other gentry to offer themselves as potential parliamentarians in various boroughs. Fifty-six serving army officers were suggested as court candidates by the regulators, and in September 1688 thirty-eight were instructed by Sunderland to offer themselves for election. Seven were to stand in the garrison towns of Carlisle, Scarborough, Queenborough, and Berwick, whilst the remaining officers were nominated to counties or boroughs which did not enjoy definite connections with the army. Probably, if William's invasion had not halted the campaign to select a new parliament, many more army officers would have been officially put forward as members of the House of Commons, perhaps in Hull, Portsmouth, Plymouth, or Chester. Even without these potential additions, thirty-eight was a sizeable number of officers to direct into parliament, especially as a further twenty-one had been recommended by the regulators as likely court supporters; if a parliament had met in 1689 it might well have contained sixty or seventy officers. In comparison, at the army's maximum size under Charles II in 1678, only forty-one officers had sat in the lower house.[83]

During the regulating of the borough charters the army had again provided some loyal placemen devoted to the interest of the court. The revised charters of the Cornish boroughs were 'more than half filled' with the names of serving army officers but these gentlemen have, unfortunately, avoided identification. Neither the original reports of the regulators nor the transcripts of those documents which were taken by Sir George Duckett identify army officers. It seems probable, despite Duckett's statement to the contrary about the charters in Cornwall, that very few army officers were drafted into the corporations, as they were unsuitable for such employment, being constantly on the march from one station to another. Only nineteen of the remodelled corporations appear to have included serving officers in 1688 and, with the notable exception of Berwick-on-Tweed, none of these boroughs could boast of the services of more than four military men.[84] In Berwick, however, the army ruled the town. After 16 December 1686 all field officers serving with the Berwick garrison were elected to the common council of the town and all subalterns were made burgesses. When a new regiment entered the garrison to relieve another, all the captains and field officers automatically joined the common council to replace their departing colleagues and the incoming subalterns completed the roll of bugesses.[85] Field officers in the Portsmouth garrison were usually put on to the commission of peace and were succeeded on their departure by their reliefs.[86] The lieutenant-governor of Hull adopted a very superior tone when writing to the mayor, suggesting that the military were also the dominant power in that city:

Since I left you I am informed that you have thought fit to return Baker upon bail. I am sorry [that] the very first, nay the only act you have done since you received your charter proves to the king's disservice especially when you might have excepted against the bail in Baker's case. I desire you will favour me with a copy of [the] commitment this night.[87]

When the regulators came to tackle the deputy lieutenancies and the commissions of peace they found the army a ready source of recruits. Late in 1686 Sir John Bramston noted that James had appointed a committee of the council to inspect the commissions of peace in order to remove those who were not amenable to the court and to replace them with more reliable candidates; 'the new are, for the most part, papists ... the officers of the army too are everywhere'.[88] Thirty-eight English and Welsh counties had eighty-two officers appointed as new deputy lieutenants, ranging from Kent and Northumberland with seven apiece down to Staffordshire, Herefordshire, and Hertfordshire with only one each.[89] Some contemporaries were of the opinion that army officers were used in large numbers to refill the revised commissions of peace but the available evidence does not support such an exaggeration. Luttrell reported that the officers of the English army were to be made justices in the counties where they were quartered, and a newsletter of January 1687 noted that sixty officers were to be inserted into the Middlesex commission. In fact, it has only proved possible to identify one military justice in that county in 1688. Forty-seven English and Welsh counties had 154 army officers recommended as their magistrates; Kent had a total of seventeen, Worcestershire seven, and many had just one.[90] Sixty-six of the military justices appear to have been roman catholic, whilst forty-three of the new deputy lieutenants were followers of Rome. This is not especially significant. Many catholic officers served as both justices of the peace and as deputy lieutenants in the same county, and some, like Lord Montgomery, held multiple offices in ten or more counties in England and Wales. Although 109 deputy lieutenancies and places on the commissions of peace were occupied by catholic army officers only fifty-seven gentlemen were actually involved. The majority of these catholic officers came from the English peerage and gentry and were thus able to boast of some interest in the counties. Ralph Sheldon of Warwickshire was made a deputy lieutenant in two counties and a justice in another, whilst Captain John Gifford of Sir Edward Hales's foot officiated in Kent and Staffordshire. None of the professional catholic veterans was elevated into local government. As far as it has proved possible to identify army officers they do not appear to have been over-used in the remodelling of the corporations or the counties, largely because of their unsuitability for these posts. They were itinerant and technically unable to devote much time to provincial affairs. Officers were more useful as members of parliament and, as a whole, the army was a splendid and ready instrument for coercing voters and suppressing political opposition. There seems to be no evidence of military men refusing to serve as members of parliament, in remodelled corporations, or in the new commissions of peace and deputy lieutenancies, neither is it possible to discover any adverse reaction from army officers to their political function. On the contrary, there is some evidence to suggest that parts of the army were strongly in favour of royal policies which placed the military in a dominant position in the country and ensured the primacy and importance of military officers and military commissions. Thirteen of the officers of Henry Cornwall's regiment of infantry signed the 'Berwick Address' in April 1688 which stated that they would positively concur in the choosing of parliament-men who were in favour of the repeal of the Test Acts and Penal Laws.[91] James began to elevate the army from a despised and hated profession into a position of social and political importance, to the great advantage of the professional officers who formed a sizeable majority of the officer corps.

Bristol received a protracted visitation from Charles Trelawney's foot in 1685 and 1686 as a reward for its suspected sympathy towards Monmouth. Cheshire and Lancashire had also shown signs of disaffection. Troops of dragoons were quartered on Lancaster, Warrington, Liverpool, and Preston, whilst 'Ormskirk will not be forgotten and you may be assured that Wrexham will have its turn before the dragoons leave your part.' By contrast, 'the honest town of Wigan' was spared the attention of the dragoons.[92] Clearly, the enforced billeting of soldiers was a powerful political weapon. During the campaign before the general election of 1685, John Sellicock, a vintner and former mayor of St. Albans, declared that Lord Churchill would stand as burgess for the borough even though the inhabitants preferred Sir Samuel Grimston and Sir Thomas Pope Blunt. Sellicock threatened the innkeepers and publicans that if they did not declare for Churchill their licences would be revoked and his lordship's dragoons quartered upon them at the ruinous rate of 8d per week.[93] In October 1686 three troops of Colonel John Berkeley's dragoons were lodged in the city of Gloucester and were duly enrolled as municipal voters so as to assist in the election of a roman catholic mayor.[94] The corporation of Hull was solidly protestant and hence lukewarm about sending an address to James expressing thanks for the second declaration of indulgence. To add to this sin, Hull was liable to return members of parliament in a future election who would not be to the court's liking. The punishment for this recalcitrance was the immediate revocation of the town's charter and the drafting of 1,200 soldiers into its already stretched accommodation. There was at this time, January and February 1688, no military purpose in committing more soldiers to Hull apart from the reduction of its citizens to the king's will.[95] Another victim was the town of Warwick. Because of its refusal to comply with the king's wishes in 1687, Warwick was made to suffer 'from the misery of a standing army' represented by three troops of cavalry, the same size of force which was also quartered in neighbouring Coventry to protect catholics at their worship.[96] In the garrison town of Carlisle the governor, Francis Howard, put the 'Three Questions' to the members of the corporation, and later, in December 1687, Sir John Hanmer, the lieutenant-colonel of Lord Montgomery's foot, suggested to the mayor that 'he would make him and all the rest of the officers in the garrison, freemen, that they might be capable to serve the king in electing parliament men for the city'.[97] No doubt Hanmer was under orders when making this 'request'.

Huntingdon's mayor and corporation were removed from office by the king's orders on 28 April 1688 and, in their places, the officers of the Duke of Berwick's regiment of foot were duly elected. As an additional blow, soldiers from Sir John Fenwick's horse and Irish troopers from Richard Hamilton's regiment of cavalry were quartered in Huntingdon and made freemen of the borough to assist in the future selection of 'right' members of parliament.[98] In the same month Winchester was subjected to a combination of political deprivation and 'dragonades'. When the corporation refused to surrender the remainder of its charter in 1688, James arbitrarily ejected the magistrates and replaced them with commissioners. The catholic lieutenant-colonel of Robert Werden's horse, Bernard Howard, was sent to the city and

> sought to gain them by persuasions and afterward with threatenings even so far that for their further compulsion he has marched six or seven more companies above the regiment of horse which is quartered there to burden the poor inhabitants ... this is looked upon by some as the commencement of dragooning.[99]

Howard was also created Recorder of Winchester and a justice of the peace for Wiltshire. Many of these dragooning tactics were also current in Scotland, although, north of the border, the army was accustomed to administering a rougher variety of justice. The Scottish forces were regularly employed in arresting felons and apprehending political or religious suspects, and just before the Scottish army marched south into England in 1688 sixty dragoons and two hundred infantry were ordered to move against the MacDonnells to destroy 'man, woman, and child pertaining to the Laird of Cappagh and to burn his houses and corn'.[100] Scotsmen who were unwilling to pay their taxes were visited by regular soldiers who lived at free quarter until the debt was considered to have been paid, even if the debtor had died in the meantime.[101]

James loved his standing army and enjoyed the fellowship of soldiers.[102] He introduced some catholics into the officer corps, increased the army to 20,000 men in peacetime, purged politically unreliable officers, and attempted to professionalise its ranks to the extent that it became dependent upon himself and not upon the society from which it had grown. To utilise some of the methods of continental rulers, he needed a detached, professional, and effective military weapon, and in the three and a half years of his reign he made notable progress towards this military objective. Although James was fully prepared to evict catholics from central and local government during his panic-stricken reversal of policy in September and October 1688, he did not lay a hand upon those in the army. The military was the sole pillar of his regime.[103] In the abusive behaviour of the army in public, the demands and burdens of its billets, its disregard for and ultimate avoidance of the common law, the use of some of its officers in the political regulations, and in the French tactics used against some corporations, James's intentions seem to be apparent – an authoritarian monarchy supported by a loyal army. In the military field, his actions during his reign must be taken as only the beginnings of a policy: neither the machinery nor the precise intentions of government had been fully worked out by the time of William's invasion. Certainly it would have been exceedingly difficult to enforce a toleration through the army, but it was quite possible to create an absolute style of government with its support and then employ the reformed administration to introduce a toleration. Throughout his long apprenticeship to monarchy and during his heavy responsibility for government between 1682 and 1685 James had shown himself to be direct, insensitive, and unsophisticated, a bull in a political and religious china shop. The ideal of government by the sword fits well with James's political character and with the military policies and evidence of his reign. Unfortunately, in his pursuit of this goal he made one fatal mistake. Against the uncomfortable background of the purge of the protestant officers in Ireland, his tactless attempts at ridding the English army of all but the most devoted to his service caused sufficient ill-will and suspicion among a small number of officers to ruin his whole design.

So King James got confirmed and also got a standing army which, contrary to his expectation, was his overthrow.[104]

Notes

1. F. L. Carsten, *Princes and Parliaments in Germany* (Oxford, 1959); J. B. Wolf, *Louis XIV* (London, 1968), pp. 199–265; D. T. Witcombe, *Charles II and the Cavalier House of Commons, 1663–74* (Manchester, 1966), pp. 127–72; Childs, *Army of Charles II*, pp. 220–32.
2. *HMC, Downshire MSS.*, i. 263; J. H. Plumb, *The Growth of Political Stability in England, 1675–1725* (Harmondsworth, 1969), pp. 106–16; Childs, *Army of Charles II*, p. 103.
3. 31 Charles II, c. 1.
4. Luttrell, *Historical Relation*, i. 370.
5. BL Add. MSS. 15, 897, ff. 78–81; BL Add. MSS. 38,695, f. 27; WO 30/48.
6. *CSPD 1685*, No. 1338; Steele, *Proclamations*, i. No. 3815.
7. SP 44/69, p. 190; *CSPD 1686–7*, No. 827.
8. *HMC, Hastings MSS.*, ii. 181–2; *Leicester Records*, p. 588.
9. Steele, *Proclamations*, i. No. 3871, 2 Sept. 1688; Edmund Bohun, *The History of the Desertion* (London, 1689), p. 7.
10. *Ibid*, pp. 43–4, 9 Nov. 1688.
11. *The Journal of James Yonge, 1647–1721*, ed. F. N. L. Poynter (London, 1963), pp. 192–3.
12. WO 4/1, p. 94, 30 Aug. 1688, Blathwayt to Sir Charles Littleton.
13. Steele, *Proclamations*, i. No. 3946; *Nottinghamshire County Records: Notes and Extracts from the Nottinghamshire County Records of the 17th Century*, ed. Hampton Copnall (Nottingham, 1915), pp. 97–8; *Buckinghamshire Quarter Sessions*, i. 380–1.
14. *Reresby*, p. 468; *HMC, Portland MSS.*, iii. 387; *HMC, Dartmouth MSS.*, pp. 134–5.
15. *Leicester Records*, p. 590; *HMC, 7th Report*, Part 1, Appendix, p. 506, 10 Jan. 1688; WO 4/1, p. 107; PC 2/71, ff. 199 and 200, 20 Jan. and 4 Feb. 1687; John Latimer, *The Annals of Bristol in the Seventeenth Century* (Bristol, 1900), pp. 434–8 and 477–8.
16. SP 44/164, pp. 301–2, 19 Feb. 1686.
17. BL Add. MSS. 38,694, f. 111, 6 Dec. 1687, Peter Shakerley to Blathwayt; BL Add. MSS. 9,735, ff. 30–1, 18 April 1688, Reresby to Blathwayt; *The Diary of Ralph Thoresby, F.R.S.*, ed. Joseph Hunter (London, 1830), i. 181.

18 Berwick-on-Tweed Corporation MSS. Berwick Guild Book, 1681–97, 16 March and 7 Sept. 1687.
19 *Nottingham Borough Records*, v. 348 and 354–5.
20 *Leicester Records*, p. 588.
21 Northamptonshire Record Office, Mayor of Northampton's Accounts, Nos. 7 and 8, 1686–7 and 1687–8.
22 SP 44/164, pp. 344–5; WO 4/1, pp. 74–5; Portsmouth City Record Office, Portsmouth Corporation MSS. S3/B/47 and R/1/10; *Extracts from Records in the possession of the Municipal Corporation of the Borough of Portsmouth and from other Documents relating thereto*, ed. Robert East (Portsmouth, 1891), pp. 190–1; *CSPD 1689–90*, pp. 108–9.
23 City Record Office of Kingston-upon-Hull, Hull Corporation Letters and MSS. L. 1106; Davies, 'Letters on the Administration of James II's Army', p. 75; Hull MSS. L. 1111 and L. 1117; WO 4/1, p. 70; Hull MSS. L. 1113.
24 Steele, *Proclamations*, ii. Nos. 2602 and 2738; *Historical Notices of Scottish Affairs selected from the Manuscripts of Sir John Lauder of Fountainhall, Bart.*, ed. David Laing (Edinburgh, 1848), ii. 634; *RPCS 1686*, pp. 340–1.
25 WO 4/1, p. 12, 21 July 1685, Blathwayt to Percy Kirke; WO 4/1, p. 15, 29 Aug. 1685, Blathwayt to Charles Trelawney.
26 WO 4/1, pp. 46–7, 27 Jan. 1687.
27 *HMC, Leyborne-Popham MSS.*, pp. 262 and 265, 'Autobiography of Dr. George Clarke'.
28 WO 89/1, pp. 82–92, 10 July 1685.
29 *Narrative of Mr. James Nimmo*, ed. W. G. Scott-Moncrieff (Edinburgh, 1889), p. 75.
30 *CSPD 1686–7*, No. 619; BL Add. MSS. 9,760, f. 7, 16 July 1688; *Bramston*, p. 306; Luttrell, *Historical Relation*, i. 434, 11 March 1688.
31 Jones, *Revolution of 1688*, p. 61; Portsmouth MSS. S3/B/41, 25 June 1688; SRO GD 16/53/32, Airlie Muniments, 22 May 1686; SRO E 100/10/116, 23 April 1687.
32 *CSPD 1685*, No. 745; 'Iter Bellicosum: Adam Wheeler His Account of 1685', ed. H. E. Malden, in *Camden Miscellany*, xii. (Camden Society, 1910), pp. 164–5.
33 *HMC, Various Collections*, i. 158; *Middlesex County Records*, iv. 290, 310–12, 315 and 327–8; *CSPD 1686–7*, No. 1495; *Ellis Correspondence*, i. 351–2.
34 7 Henry VII, c. 1, and 3 Henry VIII, c. 5.
35 *Bramston*, pp. 245–6 and 276; *CSPD 1686–7*, No. 975.
36 WO 4/1, pp. 44–5; Davies, 'Letters on the Administration of James II's Army', p. 73; WO 4/1, p. 89, 16 Aug. 1688, Blathwayt to Sir Thomas Haggerston.
37 PC 2/72, p. 70, 23 Dec. 1687; *Warwick County Records*, viii: *Quarter Sessions Records, Trinity 1682 to Epiphany 1690*, ed. H. C. Johnson (Warwick, 1953), pp. 184 and 256; Davies 'Letters on the Administration of James II's Army', p. 72, 11 Dec. 1686; *HMC,*

Downshire MSS., i. 240.
38 *Reresby*, p. 443; Wood, *Life and Times*, iii. 264; *Portledge Papers*, p. 39; Luttrell, *Historical Relation*, i. 449; *HMC, Portland MSS.*, iii. 409–10.
39 *Verney Memoirs*, ii. 449, 2 Dec. 1686.
40 SP 44/69, p. 193; BL Add. MSS. 9,735, f. 28; *CSPD 1687–9*, No. 1005; *Portledge Papers*, pp. 29–30; Wood, *Life and Times*, iii. 263–4; *Reresby*, p. 479.
41 Lauder, *Historical Notices*, ii. 700 *et passim*; *Extracts from the Records of the Burgh of Edinburgh, 1681–1689*, ed. Marguerite Wood and Helen Armet (Edinburgh and London, 1954), p. 266; Clarke, *Life*, ii. 133; Davies, 'Letters on the Administration of James II's Army', p. 79; *HMC, Le Fleming MSS.*, pp. 225 and 227.
42 *Letters of Humphrey Prideaux to John Ellis*, ed. E. M. Thompson (Camden, Society, 1875), pp. 142–3, 9 July 1685.
43 *Pryme's Diary*, p. 8; Evelyn, *Diary*, iv. 514.
44 *Ailesbury's Memoirs*, i. 150; *Ellis Correspondence*, i. 120 and 122; *Reresby*, p. 427; *Hatton Correspondence*, ii. 69 and 88; *CSPD 1686–7*, No. 778.
45 *Hatton Correspondence*, ii. 69, 13 July 1687, Sir Charles Littleton to Lord Hatton; Luttrell, *Historical Relation*, i. 410; *HMC, Portland MSS.*, iii. 395.
46 Childs, *Army of Charles II*, p. 188; John Carswell, *The Descent on England* (London, 1969), p. 74; R. E. Boyer, *English Declarations of Indulgence, 1687 and 1688* (The Hague and Paris, 1968), p. 140; Turner, *James II*, pp. 498–9; Jones, *Revolution of 1688*, p. 164; *The Petty–Southwell Correspondence, 1676–1687*, ed. Marquis of Lansdowne (London, 1928), p. 139; *Reresby*, p. 426; *CSPD 1686–7*, No. 721; Jeaffreson, ii. 303–4, 4 Aug. 1686.
47 *Ailesbury's Memoirs*, i. 110, 121 and 150; Dalrymple, *Memoirs of Great Britain and Ireland*, ii. app. Part 1, p. 167; *HMC, Downshire MSS.*, i. 163; *CSPD 1686–7*, Nos. 601–2; BL Add. MSS. 34,516, ff. 46–9; BL Add. MSS. 15,897, ff. 86–7; *CSPD 1687–9*, No. 887; Luttrell, *Historical Relation*, i. 383; BL Add. MSS. 9,760, ff. 1–5; *Ellis Correspondence*, i. 125, 271, 331, 335, ii. 1, 82, 108 and 116.
48 *HMC, Downshire MSS.*, i. 177; Jeaffreson, ii. 289–90; Evelyn, *Diary*, iv. 513–14.
49 Nimmo, *Narrative*, p. 76; *HMC, Frankland–Astley–Russell MSS.*, pp. 67–8, 27 Sept. 1688, Sir William Frankland to George Skaife.
50 *Letters of John Pinney, 1679–1699*, ed. G. F. Nuttall (Oxford, 1939), pp. 39–40, 2 June 1686, Jane to John Pinney.
51 BL Add. MSS. 29,563, ff. 5–6, 1686; *CSPD 1687–9*, No. 1883; W. L. Sachse, 'The Mob and the Revolution of 1688', *Journal of British Studies*, iv. (1964), p. 34.
52 Luttrell, *Historical Relation*, i. 474; Sachse, 'Mob', p. 28.
53 Jeaffreson, ii. 244–5, 9 Dec. 1685; Evelyn, *Diary*, iv. 490; Luttrell, *Historical Relation*, i. 356–7; WO 4/1, p. 34; *Portsmouth Sessions Papers*, p. 121.

54 WO 4/1, pp. 26–52; *HMC, 7th Report*, Part 1, Appendix, p. 505.
55 Wood, *Life and Times*, iii. 207 and 241.
56 *HMC, Dartmouth MSS.*, i. 235; BL Add. MSS. 41, 805, f. 89; BL Add. MSS. 34,510, ff. 152 and 161; *HMC, Le Fleming MSS.*, pp. 213 and 218; *Portsmouth Extracts*, pp. 190–1.
57 *Verney Memoirs*, ii. 468.
58 *Pryme's Diary*, p. 14; *HMC, Hastings MSS.*, ii. 186–7.
59 Tomlinson, 'Ordnance Office and the King's Forts', p. 18; *Reresby*, p. 470; SP 44/164, pp. 344–5; WO 4/1, p. 48.
60 Childs, *Army of Charles II*, pp. 66–72; Evelyn, *Diary*, iv. 504 and 536; *HMC, 7th Report*, Part 1, Appendix, p. 482; *HMC, Downshire MSS.*, i. 131.
61 *The Diary of Dr. Thomas Cartwright, Bishop of Chester*, ed. Joseph Hunter (Camden Society, 1843), p. 15; *HMC, Dartmouth MSS.*, i. 131.
62 WO 5/2, pp. 37 and 60.
63 *HMC, Downshire MSS.*, i. 122; WO 4/1, p. 69; *HMC, Rutland MSS.*, ii. 92–3 and 106; Japikse, ii. 741–2; *RPCS 1686*, pp. 15–16 and 23; *CSPD 1685*, Nos. 266–7.
64 *Bramston*, p. 242; *Cartwright's Diary*, p. 86; G. W. Keeton, *Lord Chancellor Jeffreys and the Stuart Cause* (London, 1965), p. 427.
65 *The Autobiography of Henry Newcome, M.A.*, ed. Richard Parkinson (Chetham Society, 1852), ii. 261, 26 Feb. 1686; R. D. Gwynn, 'James II in the light of his treatment of the Huguenot refugees in England, 1685–1686', *EHR*, xcii. (1977), p. 830.
66 *Annals of Bristol*, pp. 438–41; John Miller, *Popery and Politics in England, 1660–1688* (Cambridge, 1973), p. 258; Lauder, *Historical Notices*, ii. 772; *Ellis Correspondence*, i. 55; BL Add. MSS. 15,897, ff. 78–81; Wood, *Life and Times*, iii. 194 and 196.
67 *Reresby*, pp. 487–8.
68 John Lowther, Lord Lonsdale, *Memoir of the Reign of James II* (York, 1808), p. 55; *Bramston*, p. 332; *Hatton Correspondence*, ii. 99–100.
69 Miller, 'Militia and the Army', p. 664; Kenyon, *Sunderland*, p. 169.
70 Childs, *Army of Charles II*, pp. 75–9; Dalrymple, *Memoirs of Great Britain and Ireland*, ii. app. Part 1, p. 170.
71 *New Cambridge Modern History*, vi. 741–2; Philippe Sagnac, *La Formation de la Société française moderne* (Paris, 1945), i. 66–70.
72 John Miller, *James II: A Study in Kingship* (Hove, 1977), pp. 62–3.
73 D. E. Leach, *Arms for Empire: a Military History of the British Colonies in North America, 1607–1763* (New York and London, 1973), pp. 74–7; Viola F. Barnes, *The Dominion of New England* (New Haven, 1923), p. 219 *et passim*.
74 Henry Booth, Lord Delamere, *Works* (London, 1694), p. 623.
75 Bohun, *History*, p. 1.
76 David Jones, *The Secret History of Whitehall from the Restoration of Charles II down to the abdication of the late King James* (London, 1717), i. 270–2; WO 48/24–6; WO 55/334–5; Childs, 'The army and the Oxford

parliament of 1681', pp. 581–4; *HMC, Kenyon MSS.*, p. 186; *The History of the King's Works*, ed. H. M.Colvin (London, 1976), v. 313–15; *HMC, Downshire MSS.*, i. 282, newsletter of Dec. 1687; *King's Works*, v. 207–10.

77 Dalrymple, *Memoirs of Great Britain and Ireland*, ii. app. Part 1, pp. 169–70.
78 Jeaffreson, ii. 223 and 262–3.
79 *CSPD 1687–9*, No. 1169; PC 2/72, p. 130; BL Add. MSS. 38,361, f. 156.
80 *The Diary of Samuel Newton, Alderman of Cambridge, 1662–1717*, ed. J. E. Foster (Cambridge, 1890), p. 94; Wood, *Life and Times*, iii. 271–2; *Memoirs of the Life of Mr. Ambrose Barnes*, ed. W. H. D. Longstaffe (Surtees Society, 1866), pp. 431–2.
81 Peter Fraser, *The Intelligence of the Secretaries of State and their Monopoly of Licensed News, 1660–1688* (Cambridge, 1956), pp. 31–2; WO 4/1, p. 19, 3 Nov. 1685.
82 Jones, *Revolution of 1688*, pp. 157–8; J. R. Jones, 'James II's Whig Collaborators', *HJ*, iii. (1960), pp. 71–2.
83 Duckett, *Penal Laws*, ii. 214–17; Western, *Monarchy and Revolution*, p. 224; *CSPD 1687–9*, pp. 273–7; BL Add. MSS. 34,516, ff. 50–4; Childs, *Army of Charles II*, p. 38; See Appendix A.
84 Duckett, *Penal Laws*, ii. 134; *CSPD 1687–9*, pp. 275 *et passim*; *HMC, Various Collections*, i. 328 and 249.
85 Berwick MSS. Berwick Guild Book, 1681–97, unpaginated.
86 Portsmouth MSS. S3/B/47.
87 Hull MSS. L. 1115, 1688, Lionel Copley to the Mayor of Hull.
88 *Bramston*, p. 251.
89 See Appendix B.
90 Luttrell, *Historical Relation*, i. 388; *CSPD 1686–7*, No. 1361; See Appendix C.
91 *CSPD 1687–9*, No. 1042, 27 April 1688; Kenyon, *Sunderland*, p. 174.
92 WO 4/1, p. 23, 28 Nov. 1685, Blathwayt to Peter Shakerley.
93 *HMC, Verulam MSS.*, pp. 99–101, 'The Case of the Borough of St. Albans'.
94 Dr. Williams' Library, London, Morrice MSS. P. p. 639; BL Add. MSS. 38,695, f.27; BL Add. MSS. 15,897, ff. 78–81.
95 Hull MSS. L.1111 and L.1112; Thomas Gent, *History of Hull* (reprinted, Hull, 1869), pp. 186–7; J. J. Sheahan, *History of the Town and Port of Kingston-upon-Hull* (Beverley, 1866), pp. 186–7. Sheahan's book relies almost entirely upon the earlier work of Gent.
96 *VCH, Warwickshire*, ii. 460; BL Add. MSS. 15,897, ff. 78–81; BL Add. MSS. 38,695, f. 27.
97 *HMC, Le Fleming MSS.*, pp. 207–8.
98 Cambridgeshire County Record Office, Huntingdon Borough MSS. Chamberlain's Accounts, Box 6, Bundle 6, 28 April 1688; *VCH Huntingdonshire*, ii. 33; BL Add. MSS. 34,510, f. 122; BL Add. MSS. 38,695, f. 27; PC 2/72, pp. 92, 126 and 154.

99 R. H. George, 'The Charters granted to the English Parliamentary Corporations in 1688', *EHR*, lv. (1940), pp. 48–9; WO 5/2, unpaginated, 3 April 1687; BL Add. MSS. 34,512, ff. 77–8. Bernard Howard was a catholic and the eighth son of the Earl of Arundel. He was quarrelsome, tactless, thoroughly undiplomatic, and typical of the gentlemanly ruffians whom James had attracted in his days as Duke of York. He was a second to the Earl of Shrewsbury in his fatal duel with the Duke of Buckingham in 1667; he ran the Earl of Pembroke twice through the chest in another duel in 1674; and in 1677 he killed Lord Sherard after a challenge. The corporation of Winchester had already enjoyed dealings with Howard, as, in 1685, he had forced the town to choose the Tory pamphleteer, Sir Roger Le Strange, as one of its members of parliament by threatening to bring the king and court to Winchester that summer if his wishes were rejected (*HMC, 7th Report*, App. pp. 486a, 491–2 and 494; J. P. Kenyon, *The Popish Plot* (London, 1972), pp. 33 and 266; Reresby's Letters, 29/5, 24 March 1685, Thomas Yarburgh to Reresby). J. R. Jones, in *Revolution of 1688*, p. 158, assumes that the dragonades in Winchester actually took place in Queenborough on the Isle of Sheppey but this seems to be a misreading of BL Add. MSS. 34, 512, f. 77.

100 SRO GD 30/51/2074, Shairp of Hounstoun Muniments, 1687; John Creichton, *Memoirs*, dramatised by Jonathan Swift (1731), p. 114.

101 SRO GD 16/51/64, Airlie Muniments, 1687; *RPCS 1686*, pp. 68 and 71–2; *RPCS 1686–9*, p. xxxvi.

102 Burnet, *History of His Own Time*, iii. 163; *Reresby*, pp. 419–20; *Ellis Correspondence*, i. 60; *HMC, Downshire MSS.*, i. 187–8; *Bramston*, p. 237; Miller, *James II*, p. 51; Turner, *James II*, p. 237.

103 Clarke, *Life*, ii. 181; Jones, *Revolution of 1688*, pp. 17 and 292.

104 *The Autobiography of William Stout of Lancaster, 1665–1752*, ed. J. D. Marshall (Manchester and New York, 1967), p. 82.

V

The Anglo-Dutch Brigade

In 1585 the Earl of Leicester led 5,000 British soldiers into the United Provinces to assist the protestant Dutch in their struggle against the might of Imperial Spain. Eight years later they were joined by a corps of 6,400 Scottish mercenaries, and together the two elements became known as the Anglo-Dutch Brigade. During the Thirty Years' War the Brigade was organised into three English and three Scottish regiments of infantry, and it was in these ranks that many of the principal military figures of the English civil wars learned their trade, amongst them Aubrey de Vere, Sir William Constable, and Sir John Meldrum. The Brigade was continued in the Dutch service after the Peace of Westphalia and was recognised as one of the veteran formations of the army of the States General and a great school of the art of war. However, in 1665 this continuity came to a temporary halt. On the outbreak of the second Anglo-Dutch war Charles II recalled the three English regiments and formed the Holland regiment of foot from the officers and men who returned to England. Many of the officers chose to disobey the royal instruction and remained with the Dutch army, a decision which was made easier by the fact that the three Scottish regiments were unaffected by these alterations. It was not until 1674 that the English portion of the Brigade was reformed. Following the wholesale disbandment of the newly raised forces for the third Anglo-Dutch war, a considerable number of professional officers found themselves without employment. Their offer to recreate three English regiments was eagerly accepted by the States General and, in conjunction with the three existing Scottish regiments, a new Anglo-Dutch Brigade came into existence. Between 1674 and 1685 the Brigade engaged a large number of English, Irish, and Scottish professional soldiers who were unable to find employment elsewhere. Some officers like William Middleton, Henry Lillingstone and his son Luke, and Arthur and Philip Babbington, settled permanently in Holland and regarded the Anglo-Dutch Brigade as their sole career, whilst others – Sir John Fenwick and John Beaumont – viewed the Brigade as yet one more foreign service station in which to gain valuable experience and money whilst awaiting a vacancy on the English establishment.[1]

In terms of seventeenth century military practice, the position of the Anglo-Dutch Brigade was unexceptional. The regular Dutch army contained contingents of soldiers from Denmark, the Spanish Netherlands, and some of the smaller German states who were hired by the States General on long-term contracts. The famed army of Louis XIV was composed of Germans, Spaniards, Scots, Irishmen, Swiss, Italians, and even one or two Frenchmen. Under this system, lesser European powers like Saxony, Hesse-Cassel, Württemberg, or Weimar were able to maintain very large standing armies relative to the size of their populations and economies by leasing their troops to the major countries, who were thus partially spared the expense and social inconvenience of raising all their military requirements from within their own frontiers. Also, on the outbreak of war, it was often cheaper and more expedient to rent trained regiments from abroad than to rely wholly upon whipping raw recruits into passable soldiers. Naturally, within these basic principles there were many variations in the agreements between the contractors and the hirers, but the rules governing the allegiance and employment of the Anglo-Dutch Brigade were more imprecise than most. Legally, the six regiments formed a part of the Dutch standing army and were accordingly paid and equipped by the States General but, if the monarch of England had sufficient occasion, he could summon the brigade into England to assist him in a military emergency. At the termination of such a crisis it was understood that the brigade would return to the Netherlands. Thus the regiments fought in the Confederate army between 1674 and 1678 and then remained in garrison in the United Provinces until 1685, when James was able to call upon their services to help in the reduction of Argyll and Monmouth, after which they sailed back across the North Sea. These sensible arrangements, which provided the Dutch with an élite corps and the king of England with a reserve of highly trained soldiers whose upkeep cost him nothing, were confirmed in a convention which was drawn up between William of Orange and the Earl of Ossory in 1678. Unfortunately, this was merely a private compact between the stadtholder and the commander of the Brigade and did not receive a ratification by the States General.[2] Ultimately, neither the king of England nor the Dutch government were to feel themselves bound by the terms of this unofficial convention. The inexact legal status of the Brigade was further weakened by the traditionally easy loyalties of seventeenth century army officers. Gentlemen were free to enter the Brigade or to give up their commissions in order to serve in the English or any other army as and when they chose; there was no suggestion of being tied to the Dutch service for eternity, although some officers did adopt such a course voluntarily. The sole technical restriction upon their freedom of movement was that as subjects of the king of England they were obliged to obey any orders that he might make. It mattered little that there was an arrangement between the Prince of Orange and the commander of the Brigade when the monarch of England always enjoyed the undoubted right of summoning his own subjects into his own service. There were, however, two serious complications. Some Huguenot and Dutch officers had acquired commissions in the Brigade and these gentlemen were pre-engaged to no authority other than the States General, and a number of the English and Scottish officers were political and religious exiles who had no desire to return under the government of James II.

Each regiment in the Anglo-Dutch Brigade consisted of 500 private soldiers, giving the formation an overall strength of 3,000 men who were commanded by 234 officers. In peacetime the Brigade represented approximately ten per cent of the Dutch armed forces, which numbered 34,666 in 1679, 30,855 in 1684 but increased substantially to 53,834 in October 1688 as the United Provinces readied themselves for a general European war and for the invasion of England. Both the officers and the men were experienced veterans; Blathwayt considered the Scottish regiments to be 'the best men and [the] best prepared for service that ever were seen, having their tents and all other necessaries of their own with them'.[3] Many of the 1,500 Scottish soldiers were recruited from men of that nationality who were already sheltering in the United Provinces from the wrath of Lauderdale and from the retribution which followed the Battle of Bothwell Bridge in 1679. The papers of the Earl of Middleton in the British Library give numerous indications that a considerable number of the Scottish troops were political and religious exiles.[4] Try as they might, neither Lauderdale nor James was able to drive enough convenanters into the United Provinces to fill all the ranks of the three

Scottish regiments, and Anglo-Dutch officers had to undertake frequent visits to Scotland to bring back suitable volunteers.[5] In contrast, the three English regiments appear to have been raised mainly in England itself. Major Robert Parsons was given permission to recruit 100 men 'anywhere in England' on 12 February 1686 for the Anglo-Dutch regiment of Lieutenant-Colonel John Hales. At the same time, Sir Henry Bellasise was allowed to take another hundred men out of the kingdom to fill the ranks of his own regiment. As late as 30 August 1688 there were substantiated reports of an officer from the Anglo-Dutch Brigade recruiting both soldiers and seamen 'in and around London and Westminster'.[6] There were probably many more recruiting parties sent to England during James's reign, as the rate of desertion in Holland was relatively high and service with the Brigade less than popular.

On 4 November 1688 one of the fluyts which was conveying William's army to England had the misfortune to lose her rudder and was consequently captured by the *Foresight*. On board were 200 men of Philip Babbington's English regiment under the command of Major Ventris Colombine and, 'as I am told, the common men rejoiced when they were taken but I do not find the officers so though the major pretends a great deal'.[7] Nine years before the invasion, eight English battalions marched to Brussels ready to embark for England at the end of their futile excursion into the Spanish Netherlands. As they entered the city Anglo-Dutch officers hovered about the quayside and the soldiers' quarters, trying to tempt men into the service, but 'not one single soldier would have their colours upon any terms they could propose'. The officers were also watching for any deserters who might have taken the opportunity to slip away.[8] Further evidence of the unpopularity of the Anglo-Dutch Brigade occurs after the invasion in 1688. Following the defection of Lord Cornbury, some of the troopers from the Duke of St. Albans' regiment who had been duped into deserting their king were placed in the custody of Thomas Talmash's Anglo-Dutch regiment.

The Scots soldiers that had the guard of the Duke of St. Albans' regiment treated them very civily and gave them drink and drank king James's health to them on their knees and declared their great dislike to them of the service they were engaged in . . . and of the great hardship and smallness of their pay and wished they were so happy [as] to be in the King's pay.[9]

These might have been no more than soldierly grumbles about pay and conditions, for there is some evidence that a number of both the English and Scottish soldiers settled happily in the United Provinces and became more Dutch than British. Sixty-two English, Irish, and Scottish soldiers married Dutch women between 1674 and 1679, as indeed did a number of officers, including Major-General Hugh Mackay and Captain John Gibson.[10] Probably, service with the six regiments was no better and no worse than with other European armies, although the business of the recall in March 1688 caused an excess of ill-feeling amongst those men who wished to leave the United Provinces but were forcibly prevented from so doing.

As the Brigade was technically an English formation on permanent loan to the Dutch, Charles II was especially concerned that the commander of the force ought to be his own nominee rather than a protégé of William, thereby giving a reasonable guarantee that the six regiments would return to England *en bloc* when summoned. It was also thought that a general who met with the approval of the king of England would ensure that the regiments maintained their distinctive national character and did not become submerged into the overall anonymity of the Dutch army. 'His Majesty is very sensible of the necessity of having an English general of his own nomination over his subjects in Holland and will do all in his power to procure it for the Duke of Albermarle.'[11] Unfortunately, as the regiments were paid and materially supported by the Dutch, there was little that Charles could do effectively to press the claims of Albermarle above those of William's friend, Henry Sidney, who was accordingly appointed to the command. When James came to the throne there developed a tacit understanding between himself and William that they would jointly agree on candidates for commissions to the ranks of captain, major, lieutenant-colonel, and full colonel but would leave the filling of subalterns' places solely to William. As a general rule, James recommended captains and senior officers to the Prince of Orange, who, provided that he could find no violent objection, duly signed their commissions. This was a bizarre arrangement, for James recognised that his son-in-law was a better judge of the suitability of many of the candidates, as he knew most of them personally, whereas 'what I know of some of them is only hearsay from their respective colonels who recommended most of them to me'. However, William did have the power to veto any prospective appointment if he so wished, and this he exercised in 1685. Under pressure from James, Sidney was withdrawn from his command in June 1685 because of his whiggish inclinations and, in his place, James suggested the Earl of Pembroke. Although he was most reluctant to dismiss a personal friend, William bowed to his father-in-law's wishes for the sake of political amity, but he refused to appoint Pembroke. William wanted a military and not a political general at the head of the Anglo-Dutch Brigade; Pembroke had handled some militia formations with competence during Monmouth's Rebellion but he was otherwise without any martial experience. Even James could see the force of this argument and instead put forward the name of William Taafe, the second Earl of Carlingford, an Irish catholic with some limited knowledge of continental warfare. Such a man was hardly appropriate to command a force consisting of Scottish covenanters and political exiles from England, and William himself did not wish to see a catholic assume an important command within his own army. On religious and political grounds William rejected Carlingford's candidature, a decision which was deeply resented by James and regarded by him as a peronal insult. After this unhappy episode William abandoned the attempt to find a suitable commander for the Brigade. There was no military necessity for such an officer, as the brigade structure in the Dutch army was only a temporary institution introduced during a campaign and there was no reason why the six regiments should not be administered and commanded through the normal governmental machinery. When William did require a senior officer within the Brigade he relied upon Major-General Hugh Mackay, who had served with the regiments since their reformation in 1674.[12] Mackay was forty-five years of age in 1685 and in that time he had amassed considerable martial expertise derived from fighting for France, England, Venice, and the United Provinces. He was to meet his end at Seneffe in 1692.[13] Thereafter, until the recall of the entire Brigade in 1688, James appears to have made no further efforts to influence unduly William's choice of either junior or senior officers.

This surrender to William is surprising, as the Brigade undoubtedly contained a number of officers and soldiers who were hostile to James on the grounds of religion and politics. During his five years of command, Henry Sidney had attracted many officers with whiggish attitudes into the corps and in the aftermath of the Rye House Plot more political dissidents had sought places in the Brigade. Once in Holland, even political innocents were subjected to the propaganda of the English and Scottish exiles. During 1685 James did his best to persuade William to remove some of the most rabid of these officers, whose presence in a section of his army James found thoroughly offensive. Among them was John Gibson.

Though I have heard he is a good officer yet he is such a shuff lying [*sic*] kind of man and was such a favourer of the late Duke of Monmouth that I cannot agree to his having any employment amongst my subjects. In God's name give him what command you please amongst any of your other troops and 'tis very important for me not to have such sort of men in any of the regiments of my subjects where there are yet too many of the common men that have been infected by some of their former officers.

Philip Babbington, who had sold all his lands in England in 1677 and had devoted himself to the Dutch service absolutely, was another officer who had been sympathetic towards Monmouth and whose removal was requested by James.[14] No notice was taken by William of these pleas: Gibson was still a captain in 1687 and Babbington continued as the lieutenant-colonel of Sir Henry Bellasise's foot. Many of the Anglo-Dutch officers were known to Monmouth through their previous campaigns together in the English corps in France between 1672 and 1678 and from the Scottish campaign of 1679. John Foulkes was a personal acquaintance of the protestant duke and as a captain in Bellasise's foot in the Brigade he attempted to induce some of his fellow officers and men to join Monmouth's expedition. He himself had the courage of his convictions and sailed with Monmouth to England as the colonel of his white regiment, being fortunate enough to escape back to Holland after the defeat at Sedgemoor. As a sop to James's tender feelings Foulkes was cashiered from the Brigade on his return but he had his reward in 1689, when he was made a colonel of foot, and he died three years later as commander-in-chief of the West Indies.[15] Closely associated with Foulkes was Ensign James Fox, who also managed to escape from Sedgemoor and was subsequently dismissed from the Brigade on his return. He was promoted to a majority of foot in 1689 only to be killed at Aughrim.[16] Having served in the English army in Tangier and during the mass levies of 1673 and 1678, Edward Mathews was admirably suited to liaise between Monmouth and the regular officers in England. In addition, he was the son-in-law of the late Sir Thomas Armstrong, a relationship which gave him political credibility with the exiles in Holland. Mathews went over to England before Monmouth's invasion and tried to persuade regular officers to alter their allegiance. In this aim he was singularly unsuccessful and was forced to flee to the United Provinces, where he took to the bottle and, for a time, became the leader of the 'ungodly' exiles in Amsterdam. After the Revolution his erstwhile efforts at subversion were recognised with the grant of the colonelcy of the Royal Dragoons.[17] When these Anglo-Dutch officers who had been implicated in Monmouth's unhappy venture returned to Holland, Bevil Skelton, the English envoy at The Hague, 'used his utmost endeavours' to persuade the more loyal officers from the six regiments to arrest their errant colleagues for desertion. He met with no co-operation, and the rebellious officers, although they were cashiered from the Brigade, received all their belongings from their old comrades and had their debts paid as well. Assistance for these displaced gentlemen was not limited to these measures but attempts were made to find them military employment in some of the German states. A Captain Burrage was cashiered from Alexander Cannon's Scottish regiment in 1685 yet was found a lieutenant-colonel's commission in the army of the Elector of Brandenburg. Captain James Thompson and Edward Mathews, who was parted from his beloved drink for the purpose, were given commissions under the Prince of Friesland in June 1686. Needless to say, most of these cashiered officers were able to free themselves from their new commitments in time to accompany William to England in 1688.[18]

To James in 1685 the Anglo-Dutch Brigade must have appeared to be riddled with political and religious dissent, a thoroughly unreliable body of officers and men who were as likely to fight for Monmouth as against him. So suspect was their allegiance that James took the precaution of not ordering either the Scottish or the English regiments to march towards the theatre of war in the West Country but retained them in camp on the open spaces at Hounslow and Blackheath. Before they had embarked for England, Bevil Skelton had tendered them the Oaths of Allegiance and Supremacy but the regiments had demonstrated no enthusiasm for swearing the oaths or for leaving the United Provinces. The English regiments were more reluctant to sail than their Scottish comrades; possibly many of the officers and men feared arrest for their numerous past crimes and misdemeanours.[19] Until they set foot in England in June 1685, the Anglo-Dutch Brigade was an unknown quantity. James had been reasonably well informed by Skelton about the state of the regiments but it was not until he was able to see them for himself that he realised the magnitude of their religious and political extremism. Nine soldiers from the Scottish regiments, 'having drunk the health of the Duke of Monmouth and having engaged in some unseemly talk', were court-martialled on 20 July 1685. Two of their number were condemned to be shot and one was sentenced to be flogged beneath the gallows. It was with a deep sigh of relief that James ordered the Brigade back to the United Provinces early in August. He had seen enough to realise that the majority were ill-disposed towards his religion and his style of government.[20] Throughout the next two years there was ample reinforcement of his suspicions. Robert Parsons murdered a gentleman in Bishops Stortford in 1680, but he fled to the United Provinces to escape apprehension and had become an ensign in the Anglo-Dutch Brigade by 1685, when he was described by his lieutenant-colonel, Alexander Cannon, as one of 'the most horrible, rebellious villains that ever lived . . . which he hopes that his Majesty will require should be cashiered'. On the contrary, Parsons was promoted to a captaincy within three years.[21] Sir Patrick Hume fled to Holland after the *débâcle* of the Rye House Plot but had sufficient fortitude to accompany Argyll to Scotland in 1685. His son, Patrick, was arrested in London and held as a hostage for his father but on his release in the following year he crossed the North Sea and entered the Prince of Orange's foot guards as a volunteer,

among persons of very good quality till we learn the Dutch way of exercising and when we are perfect in that I have very good ground to expect to be an ensign in his guards or some far better place in some other regiment but pray do not talk of this except to Grissell and very good friends for fear something may stop it.

Hume's expectations were over-sanguine, for his first commission was not in the prestigious Blue Guards but as a lowly ensign in the Anglo-Dutch Brigade.[22] During 1686 and 1687 James made some attempts to counter the increasing number of political and religious opponents in the Brigade by recommending more catholics for commissions. Usually, on foreign service stations, catholics and protestants were accustomed to working side by side as a matter of course, but after 1685 a definite clique formed within the six regiments of catholic officers who were known to favour the domestic policies of James II. If any political employment was to be found for the Brigade in the future, then William did not want it to contain a proportion of officers upon whom he could not entirely rely. James placed great importance upon military affairs, and the state of the Anglo-Dutch Brigade was a major item in the relations between the king and his nephew. As a result, in order to preserve tolerable and reasonably harmonious links with England, William permitted some catholics into the Brigade during 1686, but after the following April he refused to admit any more and insisted upon protestant officers. This still left the Prince with the problem of how to remove the catholic officers who already held commissions, but this was solved by his father-in-law's decision to recall the Brigade to England in March 1688, which allowed William to cleanse the regiments of the undesirable catholics and to introduce some agents into James's own army.[23]

Not all the officers and men of the Brigade were followers of radical politics and the covenant. George Etherege recalled how, in 1685, he had found the officers 'so well inclined that I could not have imagined in so little time to see that notable ardour extinguished which they had for his Majesty's service. I do not doubt but much pains and address had been employed to debauch them.'[24] Perhaps the greatest demonstration of loyalty to James by Anglo-Dutch officers was during the infamous Peyton Affair. Sir Robert Peyton of East Barnet was a City magnate and a 'firebrand' and 'the hottest of all the City Whigs' during the first twelve months of the Exclusion Crisis.[25] As a result of his political leanings he was forced to seek refuge in the United Provinces, where he took the prudent precaution of having himself made a Dutch citizen and a burgher of Amsterdam. On 12 October 1686 Bevil Skelton was about to embark on his yacht at Rotterdam to return to England when Captain Solomon Slater, an officer of the Anglo-Dutch Brigade and a client of Skelton, recognised Sir Robert in the crowd about the quay and attempted to seize him and force him on board Skelton's vessel with the transparent intention of taking him back to England and justice. Peyton shouted out that he was being kidnapped and a throng began to gather in the street, whereupon Slater, assisted by some more officers from the Brigade, rushed Peyton into a house, beat him with a cane, and stole his papers. At this point the magistrates of Rotterdam arrived, rescued the bedraggled Peyton, and arrested the officers who had been involved in this 'scuffle'. There was little doubt that the whole affair had been carefully stage-managed by Skelton and Slater, and in this they were much at fault, as Sir Robert was known to be a Dutch citizen and Skelton had ordered officers in the pay of the United Provinces to execute a political action for the king of England. Slater himself later admitted that Skelton had been the instigator of the scheme and that 'the king has very well approved of what he did'. How many officers were involved is unrecorded. Slater led the abductors with the assistance of Lieutenant-Colonel William Middleton, the brother of the English secretary of state, but no other names have come down to us. Some of the officers appear to have avoided the consequences of their actions but Slater resigned his commission and fled to Paris, whilst four more offenders were tried and cashiered.[26] If it achieved little else, the Peyton Affair served to illustrate that the officers of the Anglo-Dutch Brigade were not all enemies of the king. Indeed, this caustic mixture of catholics, whigs, and loyalists must have led to an officer corps which was torn by friction and internally divided. On those grounds alone the recall of the Brigade must have been a blessing to William.

Although James was less than favourably impressed with the political and religious views of some of the officers and men he was most struck by their military bearing when they came over to England in 1685. On 3 July he reviewed the three Scottish regiments on Blackheath and 'was pleased again and again with various expressions to testify that he had never seen better or finer soldiers'. Two days later he and the queen watched them exercise in Hyde Park, an experience which moved James to write to William that 'there cannot be, I am sure, better men than they are and do truly look like old regiments and one cannot be better pleased with them than I am and must again thank you for them'. Other observers were equally enthusiastic. John Evelyn thought them 'excellently clad and perfectly disciplined and were encamped on Blackheath most formally with their tents'. However, once away from the parade ground the Brigade displayed most of the undersirable characteristics of seventeenth century soldiery. Initially the Scottish regiments under the command of Hugh Mackay were destined to assist the tiny army in Scotland in reducing Argyll's insurrection and they actually landed in that country before being redirected into England. During their short soujourn in Scotland the three regiments undertook 'a dry march' during the course of which 'many of the common soldiers deserted and ran away with their officers' clothes, money, and arms'. Once back in the United Provinces the smart appearance of the soldiers disappeared as they became the victims of the embryonic military administrations of the later seventeenth century; Captain Joseph Studd's company, which was quartered in Zealand, was reduced to 'great want' because of the difficulties of squeezing money out of the Estates of that province.[27]

Upon the issue of the first declaration of indulgence in Scotland, on 12 February 1687, some of the Scottish exiles in the Netherlands drew up a memorial which eloquently expressed the widely held fear that James would establish catholicism by law and enforce uniformity with the support of popish standing armies in England, Scotland, and Ireland. Although the memorial only claimed to see the beginnings of these possible developments it prophesied the future of the Anglo-Dutch Brigade with remarkable precision.

It is a step of advantage, if it can be done or when it can, to have the six regiments put out of the king's power, by either setting British officers, trusty to the Prince, over them and so the soldiers might be made or got to be all such, or else to break and disband so as honest British and Dutch officers might levy and take on again the whole soldiers in companies to be divided among the Dutch regiments.[28]

By 1687 the Anglo-Dutch Brigade was known to be a dangerous foreign legion which was attracting political and religious partisans and was acting as a prop to the numerous English and Scottish exiles lurking in the United Provinces. One of the most promising of James's officers, Lieutenant-Colonel Thomas Talmash of the Royal Fusiliers, had resigned his commission in 1686 in protest at the admission of catholics into the English army and had taken his sword and his whiggish principles into the Anglo-Dutch Brigade. After covering himself with glory at the siege of Buda and at the battle of Mohacs, the whig John Cutts, who had previously fought with Monmouth, found his way into the Anglo-Dutch Brigade in April 1688. He would, so he informed Lord Middleton, have returned to the English army 'were not the present measures of state visibly opposite to the principles and interest of that religion which is dearer to me than all things in this world, or than life itself'. The fact that he would undoubtedly have been arrested had he set foot in England was conveniently omitted from his letter. William had refused to permit any more catholics into the Brigade and had adopted the contrary policy of admitting renegades like Talmash and Cutts, Huguenots, and as many of the disbanded officers from Ireland as the Brigade could accommodate. If James was unable to control the patronage and personnel of his overseas reserve, then it was a useless instrument and no longer fulfilled any political or military function for the king. In 1686 he tried to create another foreign force by supporting James Porter's scheme for the Governor of the Spanish Netherlands to entertain 4,000 English, Scottish, and Irish soldiers on terms very similar to those which governed the Anglo-Dutch Brigade. If these negotiations had reached a favourable conclusion then James might not have shown such profound disquiet over the deterioration of the Anglo-Dutch Brigade, as an Anglo-Spanish force would have provided him with a substitute. The failure of Porter's design spelt the end of the Anglo-Dutch Brigade. James was fully aware that an order for the Brigade to return permanently to England would be disobeyed by many of the officers and men, but the point of the recall of 1688 was not to transfer it as a solid formation from Holland to England. The whole exercise was designed to break up the Brigade once and for all, to deprive William of one of his élite corps. If a number of experienced officers and soldiers did come across to England, then that was a pleasant bonus, but it was more important to destroy the nest and refuge of military men who were ill-disposed towards James and his government. Precedents for such an action were encouraging. After his brother had recalled the three English regiments upon the outbreak of the second Anglo-Dutch war in 1665, the Dutch had been forced to disband the remnants of the regiments which remained in the United Provinces, thereby ruining the Brigade as a distinct formation. There was nothing James could do to prevent English exiles taking commissions in the Dutch army, but he could remove the one institution which concentrated them into a politically dangerous force.

It was Tyrconnell who probably first suggested the total recall of the Brigade during his meeting with James at Chester on 7 September 1687 but the idea could hardly have come as a surprise to the king. The initial difficulty was one of finance. James was able to pay for his English army of 20,000 men with the assistance of £30,000 per annum from the Irish treasury but the assumption of a further 3,000 would have been a very heavy burden. Some expedient had to be discovered. Louis XIV was sympathetic to the military and political objectives of Tyrconnell and James, for any weakening of the Dutch armed forces was bound to work to his benefit. Through the good offices of Paul Barrillon, James approached his French cousin to see whether he could be persuaded to accommodate the regiments on French soil, where the troops could live in a healthy catholic climate away from the evil influences of the United Provinces and enjoy the advantages of being trained and drilled in the company of the premier army of Europe. This proposal was for the Anglo-Dutch Brigade to be translated into an Anglo-French Brigade, but Louis was not in the habit of hiring foreign soldiers on any terms other than his own. He was not prepared to take 3,000 men into his army on the understanding that they might be withdrawn at any time upon the orders of the king of England. The unfortunate experiences in 1674 and 1678, when English forces had been recalled from the French army on the orders of Charles II, had led Louis to regard English troops as more of a hindrance than a help. However, the Sun King was prepared to pay for the maintenance of these soldiers in England, and he let his decision be known on 8 December 1687. Barrillon made over the first two months' pay to Godolphin on 26 July 1688.[29]

Although James explained that he fully expected 'a great number of the officers and soldiers will remain in Holland', he was hopeful that the catholics would return as well as 'those who are not entirely gained by the Prince of Orange'. James emphasised this realistic approach by asking Louis to provide pay for just 2,000 soldiers and not for the full strength of the Brigade. Colonel John Wachop was entrusted with making the practical arrangements for the return of the six regiments, and on 14 March 1688 James issued a proclamation summoning home all officers, soldiers, and sailors in the service of the United Provinces. Neither William nor the States General were willing to let the Brigade disband without a struggle; accordingly they ordered all officers and men to their garrisons and there did their best to persuade them to remain with the Dutch army. These exhortations were directed mainly at the soldiers. William did not want to lose 3,000 trained men, as they were difficult and expensive to replace, but the officers were another matter. No obstacles were placed in the path of catholics who wished to sail to England, as there were a considerable number of protestant Irish officers and Huguenots already in the United Provinces ready to step into the vacancies. It would be wrong to suggest that William encouraged catholics to depart, but he did nothing to prevent them, as James had provided him with the opportunity of purging the Anglo-Dutch Brigade and making the officer corps entirely loyal to himself. Non-catholic officers he was anxious to retain. The protestant officers and soldiers were subjected to long harangues about how they were certain of employment and promotion in the Dutch army whereas the English army might suddenly be forced to contract under pressure from parliament; those who decided to leave would be 'quitting a certainty for an uncertainty'. Because the agreement about the procedure for recalling the Brigade which had been made between William and Ossory had not been ratified by the States General, the Dutch did not feel themselves obliged to obey James's request to send the Brigades into England. Moreover, the recall went against the spirit of the 1678 concordat, which only referred to the Brigade being summoned into England for a finite period to deal with a definite emergency; the agreement said nothing about the permanent recall of the six regiments. In the end such details mattered little. Officers were at liberty to resign or sell their commissions and return to England if they so wished, and those who took the opportunity enjoyed the wry blessing of the stadtholder.[30]

Gradually the officers reached their decisions and either remained in the United Provinces or sailed over to England. For the Mackays, the Lillingstones, the Erskines, and the Babbingtons their lives were in Holland and there they stayed, but the catholics and some others stood by their essential loyalty to their monarch and sacrificed certainty for uncertainty. James made very adequate provisions for the returning officers. They were paid at English rates from James's treasury from the moment they resigned their Dutch commissions, and this remuneration continued until they received an appointment in the British Isles. Three new regiments of foot were created to employ the loyal officers, commanded by John Hales, John Wachop, and Roger MacElligott. Each regiment contained 530 non-commissioned officers and private soldiers under the direction of forty-three officers. As far as was possible the officers were given equivalent ranks to those that they had enjoyed in the Anglo-Dutch Brigade. James did not press the Anglo-Dutch officers to come to England, as he did not want his own armed forces filled with politically and religiously suspect officers; he merely wished to recall those who were loyal to himself and his cause. William's intentions formed a perfect dovetail with those of James. He was delighted to watch the catholics and loyalists depart, safe in the knowledge that he could use the opportunity to remodel the Brigade into a corps which was entirely reliant upon himself and his own patronage. To be able to spearhead any possible future intervention in England with 3,000 protestant and English troops would consistute a very astute political manoeuvre. Most contemporary and modern authorities suggest that the number of officers who obeyed James's order was between forty and sixty but this appears to be a serious under-estimate. Working from biographies of 213 of the 234 officers in the Brigade during the early months of 1688, it seems that 104 withdrew from Holland and all of these were given places in the three new infantry regiments. This movement resulted in over one hundred vacancies in the Anglo-Dutch Brigade, enabling William to commission a number of the disbanded protestant Irish officers, to recommission some of the officers who had been forced out of the Brigade through James's insistance in 1685, and to provide for some Huguenot refugees – Jean Martin de Plantte and Henri de Caumont, Le Marquis de Rade. As the number of officers who obeyed the recall roughly equalled the number of new commissions made available by the foundation of the three regiments of foot, it seems probable that the response to the royal summons matched James's expectations.[31]

Very few private soldiers returned. D'Albeville, the English envoy in the United Provinces, was instructed to assist soldiers with money to enable them to clear their debts and travel to England, and Sir Richard Bulstrode, the English resident in Brussels, was asked on 24 February to help all officers and soldiers from the Anglo-Dutch

Brigade who passed through Spanish Flanders *en route* to England. Without money or influence, and confined to their quarters by the Dutch authorities, only a trickle of Anglo-Dutch soldiers succeeded in reaching England, a fact which probably accounts for the unhappiness of the Scottish soldiers in Talmash's regiment in 1688 and for the glee of the soldiers 'liberated' from the rudderless fluyt. In June a soldier who escaped from his garrison at Breda was recaptured and hanged as an example to other would-be deserters. Anglo-Dutch officers went to extraordinary lengths to prevent their soldiers from leaving the United Provinces. John Moody, a roman catholic private from one of the three Scottish regiments, slipped away from his garrison at Bergen-op-Zoom and managed to reach Antwerp, where he gained shelter in the English monastery. An English Jesuit from that institution, Father Visconti, wrote to Bulstrode that 'several parties' were looking for Moody and his captain, the Marquis de Rade, had sworn to take him and then hang him. Eventually the clamour died down and Visconti sent Moody by water to Brussels, where Bulstrode was able to help him take passage for England. Between mid-April and October 1688 forty-four soldiers from the Anglo-Dutch Brigade, most of them catholic, slipped through the Spanish Netherlands and succeeded in reaching the British Isles. Some of these soldiers, whom Bulstrode met, talked of being 'threatened' by their officers and there is every indication that quite sizeable bodies of troops, often up to thirty in number, attempted to escape but were mostly captured before they could leave the United Provinces. If only a handful of loyal soldiers could effect their desertion through the supposedly neutral Spanish Netherlands, even fewer were able to escape through the United Provinces themselves.[32]

As only a tiny number of Anglo-Dutch soldiers deserted their service, the three new regiments which had been created to provide for the loyal officers had to be manned from within the British Isles and not, as the intention had been, with returning soldiers from Holland. MacElligott's was recruited by reducing all the foot companies in Ireland by ten men, a procedure which produced approximately one thousand soldiers, enough to fill MacElligott's and leave 450 to help complete the ranks of John Hales and John Wachop. Louis XIV had been persuaded to pay for 2,000 soldiers most of whom, he had been led to believe, would be coming home from the United Provinces and would thus be a new burden on the English establishment. In reality, the French king unwittingly assumed the responsibility for paying 1,000 soldiers who were already in the Irish army and 400 who were not raised at all. Louis's decision to allow payment of these bogus troops to lapse after he had met the first two months' instalments was perfectly understandable.[33]

The Anglo-Dutch Brigade was of vital importance in the Glorious Revolution. Not only did the issue of the Brigade cause considerable ill-feeling between William and his father-in-law but the actual regiments themselves formed one of the cornerstones of the operation of the conspiracy in the army and in the mechanics of the invasion. The numerous personal and official contacts between the officers of the armies in England, Scotland, Ireland, and the United Provinces allowed the conspiracy within the English officer corps to function smoothly and without causing undue suspicion. More than any other institution, the Anglo-Dutch Brigade was the instrument by which William was able to prepare the way for his descent on England in November 1688.

Notes

1. Childs, *Army of Charles II*, pp. 240–2; C. G. Cruickshank, *Elizabeth's Army* (Oxford, 1966), p. 236; C. H. Firth and G. Davies, *The Regimental History of Cromwell's Army* (Oxford, 1940), ii. 689–92; Childs, *Army of Charles II*, pp. 35–6 and 171–3; Ferguson, *Scots Brigade*, i. 511 and 513; G. H. Jones, *Charles Middleton: The Life and Times of a Restoration Politician* (London and Chicago, 1967), p. 73; Dalton, *Scots Army*, pp. 163 and 164n.; Dalton, *Army Lists*, ii. 228 and 236.
2. Carswell, *Descent on England*, pp. 121–4; Jones, *Revolution of 1688*, p. 181; PRO SP 84/220, State Papers, Dutch Republic, f. 35, 12 March 1688.
3. WO 4/1, p. 9; *Het Staatsche Leger, 1568–1795* (The Hague, 1911–59), vi. 161–5 and 214; *The Dispatches of Thomas Plott (1681–1682) and Thomas Chudleigh (1682–1685), English Envoys at The Hague*, ed. F. A. Middlebush (The Hague, 1926), p. 34.
4. Earle, *Monmouth's Rebels*, p. 109; BL Add. MSS. 41, 823, f. 114.
5. Lauder, *Historical Notices*, ii. 847; *RPCS 1686–9*, p. viii.
6. SP 44/69, pp. 184–5, 12 Feb. 1686 and 13 Jan.1686; BL Add. MSS. 41,805, ff. 42–3.
7. *HMC, Darmouth MSS.*, i. 263.
8. PRO SP 77/52, State Papers, Flanders, f. 108, 25 Feb. 1679, Sir Richard Bulstrode, English resident in Brussels, to Sir Joseph Williamson.
9. Rawlinson MSS. D. 148, f. 7.
10. J. Maclean, 'Huwelijken van Militairen, Behorende tot het Derde Regiment van de Schotse Brigade in Nederland, onteend aan de Gereformeerde Trouwboeken van 1674 tot 1708', *De Brabanste Leeuw*, xx. (1972), pp. 90–6. For an interesting account of life in the Dutch Brigade

in the eighteenth century see, *Journal of John Gabriel Stedman*, ed. Stanbury Thompson (London, 1962), pp. 21–112.
11   *Plott & chudleigh*, pp. 70–1, 7 March 1682, Lord Conway to Sir Leoline Jenkins.
12   John Bernardi, *A Short History of the Life of Major John Bernardi* (London, 1729), p. 49; *CSPD 1685*, Nos. 358, 1503 and 1684; *Clarendon Correspondence*, i. 152–3; Japikse, ii. 708–9 and 736; *An Historical Account of the British Regiments employed since the Reign of Queen Elizabeth and King James I in the Formation and Defence of the Dutch Republic, particularly of the Scotch Brigade* (London, 1794), pp. 58–9; Dalrymple, *Memoirs of Great Britain and Ireland*, ii. App. Part 1, pp. 121, 136–7 and 141.
13   John Mackay, *The Life of Lieut.-General Hugh Mackay, Commander-in-Chief of the Forces in Scotland, 1689 and 1690* (Edinburgh, 1836), pp. 1–13; *Historical Account*, pp. 68–9.
14   Jones, *Revolution of 1688*, p. 181; Japikse, ii. 720, 13 Oct. 1685, James II to William of Orange; HPT.
15   BL Add. MSS. 41,819, ff. 1–12; Earle, *Monmouth's Rebels*, pp. 31 and 148; Dalton, *Army Lists*, ii. 244.
16   Earle, *Monmouth's Rebels*, pp. 31 and 72; Trench, *Western Rising*, pp. 93 and 98.
17   Earle, *Monmouth's Rebels*, pp. 32, 78, 148 and 154; Trench, *Western Rising*, pp. 92–3; Dalton, *Army Lists*, i. 81 and 220, ii. 250; *CSPD 1685*, No. 689.
18   *Historical Account*, pp. 55–6; BL Add. MSS. 41, 827, ff. 230–1; BL Add. MSS. 41,812, ff. 5–6 and 14–15; SP 84/220, ff. 10 and 18–19.
19   Clarke, *Life*, ii. 26–7; *Ailesbury's Memoirs*, i. 114–15; *D'Avaux*, iii. 233, 237 and 248; Dalrymple, *Memoirs of Great Britain and Ireland*, ii. App. Part 1, pp. 125–6, 129–30 and 131; *HMC, Buccleuch (Drumlanrig) MSS.*, ii. 74–5 and 78; Ferguson, *Scots Brigade*, i. 536–8 and 540.
20   WO 89/1, pp. 82–92, 10 July 1685; Jeaffreson, ii. 212.
21   BL Add. MSS. 41,812, ff. 5–6, 31 March 1685, Bevil Skelton to Lord Middleton; Dalton, *Army Lists*, i. 146, ii. 230. The other 'most horrible, rebellious villain' was a Lieutenant Carew.
22   *HMC, 14th Report*, App. Part 2, p. 115; *HMC, Laing MSS.*, i. 460.
23   Japikse, ii. 724–5; *D'Avaux*, iv. 117–18; Burnet, *History of His Own Time*, iii. 220–1.
24   *Etherege's Letters*, p. 184, 4 March 1688, Ratisbon, George Etherege to d'Albeville.
25   K. H. D. Haley, *The First Earl of Shaftesbury* (Oxford,1968), p. 405; J. R. Jones, *The First Whigs* (Oxford, 1970), pp. 110 and 168.
26   G. H. Jones, *Middleton*, pp. 183–5; James Walker, 'The English Exiles in Holland during the Reigns of Charles II and James II', *TRHS*, 4th series, xxx. (1948), p. 118; Erskine, *Journal*, p. 218; BL Add. MSS. 41,822, ff. 194–7; *Etherege's Letters*, pp. 273–4, 28 Dec. 1686, Paris, Slater to Etherege; *Ellis Correspondence*, i. 176–7; BL Add. MSS. 41,814, ff. 46–7, 8 Oct. 1686, 'Captain Slater's Evidence'; *The Correspondence of John Locke*, ed. E. S. de Beer (Oxford, 1976 ff.), No. 974, J. G. Graevius to John

Locke; SP 84/220, ff. 14 and 16.
27 Walton, *History of the British Standing Army*, p. 488; Evelyn, *Diary*, iv. 458; Ferguson, *Scots Brigade*, i. 538; Dalrymple, *Memoirs of Great Britain and Ireland*, ii. App. Part 1, p. 132; Lauder, *Historical Notices*, ii. 657; *HMC, Buccleuch (Drumlanrig) MSS.*, ii. 78; BL Add. MSS. 41,819, ff. 250–1.
28 Japikse, (1928), p. 20.
29 HPT; BL Add. MSS. 41,805, ff. 23–4, 12 April 1688, Het Loo, John Cutts to Lord Middleton; Dalrymple, *Memoirs of Great Britain and Ireland*, App. Part 1, pp. 260–7; *D'Avaux*, iv. 136; Mackintosh, *History of the Revolution*, p. 469; G. H. Jones, *Middleton*, p. 187; Clarke, *Life*, ii. 133; Carswell, *Descent on England*, pp. 112–13; S. B. Baxter, *William III* (London, 1966), p. 221.
30 Luttrell, *Historical Relation*, i. 429 and 432–3; BL Add. MSS. 41,815, ff. 157–8; Steele, *Proclamations*, i. No. 3861; Lauder, *Historical Notices*, ii. 860; Bernardi, *Life*, pp. 50–1.
31 BL Add. MSS. 28,087, ff. 107–18; G. H. Jones, *Middleton*, p. 189; WO 4/1, pp. 79–80; *Historical Account*, pp. 63–4; Ferguson, *Scots Brigade*, i. 477–8; *Bramston*, p. 305; J. L. Garland, 'The Regiment of MacElligott, 1688–1689', *Irish Sword*, i. (1949), p. 121; BL Add. MSS. 41,822, ff. 215–18 and 229.
32 *HMC, Portland MSS.*, iii. 405–9; SP 77/55, f. 337, 19 March 1688, Sir Richard Bulstrode to Sunderland; SP 77/55, ff. 397, 409–10, 421–2, 425, 464, 472 and 494; BL Add. MSS. 41,822, f. 229.
33 Simms, *Jacobite Ireland*, pp. 45–8; *Letters of Lady Rachel Russell*, (London, 1809), p. 152; Garland, 'Regiment of MacElligott', pp. 121–3; *HMC, Ormonde MSS.*, n.s. viii. 352; *Analecta Hibernica*, i. 39 and 41; *CSPD 1687–9*, No. 986.

VI

The conspiracy in the army

Conspiracies and all manner of clandestine affairs often defy accurate reconstruction as most of the vital business is conducted verbally, with as little as possible committed to potentially incriminating paper. In England and Scotland in 1688 there was a conspiracy which worked on behalf of the Prince of Orange to reduce the efficacy of the army and navy of James II. Whether this scheme actually fulfilled the expectations of both William and the conspirators remains a matter for debate and will probably continue so because of the paucity of direct evidence which forbids a detailed study of the precise aims of the conspiracy. The majority of the surviving evidence is heavily circumstantial but it contains sufficient steel to allow some useful observations to be made about how the undertaking operated, who was involved and why, and the means by which the participants communicated with one another.

Professor S. B. Baxter is of the opinion that the conspiracy was principally confined to the English army and that it failed to achieve its objectives. He points out that the task of Grafton, Churchill, Kirke, Trelawney, and the other senior officers who were parties to the design was to bring over the bulk of the army to William soon after his landing, and this they did not succeed in achieving. Furthermore, says Dr. Baxter, the army conspiracy was very shallow, concerning only a few officers of the rank of colonel and above; it did not extend to the rank and file who remained largely loyal to James. Viewed in this light, the conspiracy appears unimpressive and it is difficult to see how it could have made a significant contribution to the decision of the campaign in 1688, but Dr. Baxter misses the essential point. In the summer of 1688 there was no suggestion of a rebellion in England.

Certainly the English protestants were disgusted with James's domestic policies and were thoroughly disillusioned to the extent that they were unlikely to do much to assist their king if he was attacked. However, Englishmen had no love for the Dutch and just as there was no positive movement against James in the summer and autumn of 1688 so there was no important swell of opinion in favour of William's intervention. The famous 'Invitation' stated that William could expect to be joined by some of the most 'considerable' of the gentry and aristocracy 'whose interests would be able to draw great numbers' but this was less than strictly accurate. In 1688 the vast majority of the political classes in England remained studiedly neutral, only declaring themselves when the direction of the wind was definite and strong. Until then the Glorious Revolution of 1688 was a military campaign fought between the armies of William of Orange and James II, with neither side enjoying significant support from the bulk of the population. For the success of his gamble William relied entirely upon his own armed forces and upon the fact that there was a conspiracy within his uncle's army which was designed to rip the heart out of those troops before they came into contact with William's international corps. James also relied upon his army. Throughout his reign he had concentrated his attention upon making his soldiers politically secure and sufficiently professional to be relatively detached from religious and political prejudices. Supposedly, the English army would be loyal to James rather than to the country and, without any visible support among civilians, he was forced to rely solely upon the assurance of his troops. Conspiracies among the aristocracy and the protestant gentry mattered little provided that the army did its work and fought off the Dutch challenge. Unfortunately for James, a small section of his English officer corps was seriously infected with a Dutch-inspired conspiracy. His own high-handed disregard for the sanctity of commissions and the dismal example of the purge in Ireland had made a small yet vital number of officers less well disposed towards the king than he suspected. Within the three and a half years of his reign James had made enormous progress in transforming an *ad hoc* mixture of professionals, courtiers, and politicians into a detached standing army that looked solely to the monarch for direction, but the bouts of purging that were necessary for the success of this operation resulted in a handful of officers either holding personal grudges against their king or fearing for their own careers. The desertion of Lord Cornbury and Thomas Langston on 10 November 1688, although a minor event in seventeenth century terms, when officers frequently changed sides, shook James's confidence in his troops. He had already decided to abandon his position at Salisbury and retire on London when the defection of Churchill, Grafton, and Prince George of Denmark removed the small reservoir of faith which he still retained in his army. The conspiracy might not have achieved all its intentions but it was instrumental in separating James from his throne and ensured that the assumption of William of Orange was effected without bloodshed or unnecessary violence. It was an indispensable and crucial part in the machinery of the Glorious Revolution.[1]

The conspiracy against the king in his own army was neither large nor widespread. When Henry Sidney arrived at The Hague early in July 1688 bearing the Invitation, William of Orange

could not believe what they suggested concerning the king's army being disposed to come over to him, nor did he reckon, as much as they did, on the people of the country's coming in to him. He said he could trust to neither of these. He could not undertake so great a design, the miscarriage of which would be the ruin both of England and Holland, without such a force as he had reason to believe would be superior to the king's own, though his whole army should stick to him.[2]

Burnet might have been correct in asserting that William had very little confidence in the claims of the 'Seven', yet he had no alternative but to trust them if he was to fulfil his ambition. It was physically impossible for him to convey a sufficiently large army to England in order to be able to face James with an equal number of troops. The balance was heavily weighted against him to the extent that on Salisbury Plain James assembled almost twice as many soldiers as William had brought ashore at Torbay. Of neccessity, the core of the conspiracy had to be military in order to present William with a weapon which could replace his lack of numbers by making sure that James's army did not fight. The Dutchman had to appear as a deliverer, not as a conqueror.[3] The estimation of the Jacobite biography of James II that 'many officers of the army ... took the king's great pay and served another master' overstates the physical size of the conspiracy.[4] It was not large, it affected mostly the more senior officers, and it suffered greatly from having to combat the traditional loyalty of the gentry and aristocracy to their monarch as well as the professional detachment which James had tried to inculcate into his officers. Captain Charles Hatton's views on his duty towards his sovereign were typical of those held by many of the army officers.

I trust the nation in general will behave themselves with loyalty to their prince and regard to their country that the Dutch will succeed no better than the Spaniards did in 1558. As to my own particular, I shall endeavour to act according to those principles of loyalty in which I am obliged both by my religion and allegiance and submit myself to whatever state Providence designs.[5]

This letter illustrates a further vital aspect of 1688. William had to overcome the sizeable disadvantage of being a Dutchman, a nationality which inspired the utmost loathing amongst the English, from a country with which England had been at war on three occasions since 1651. To invade England peacefully in 1688 was a remarkable achievement.

Because of the shortage of evidence it is impossible to state when the conspiracy began or indeed to chart its progress and development in any useful manner. It probably had its origins in the unofficial gatherings at the Earl of Shrewsbury's house in the summer of 1687 and in the bundle of letters which Dyckveldt carried back to the Prince of Orange in June of that year.[6] From then until the writing of the Invitation on 30 June 1688 the conspiracy was probably little more than an intelligence-gathering organisation and a debating club. Only when the military intervention of William was a certainty did the conspirators earnestly begin the practical task of arranging for the future defection of sections of the army and navy.

The conspiracy was greatly assisted by the absence of security within the royal administration. In February 1688 Samuel de Paz, a translator in the secretary of state's office, was discovered to be a Dutch spy. Whether de Paz was an agent for the States General or for William was not ascertained, but he had been engaged in passing English state and military information into the United Provinces since July 1685.[7] This episode brought about a further deterioration in Anglo-Dutch relations, which were already under severe strain over the recall of the six regiments and because of William's persistent refusal to agree to the repeal of the Test Acts and Penal Laws. James was out of sympathy with all things Dutch to the extent that he was reluctant to allow Lord Dumblane, Danby's eldest son, permission to go into Holland for 'curiosity'.[8] Even with the slackness of both internal and external security that was a feature of most seventeenth century governments, there were well founded fears that the embryonic conspiracy might be uncovered before William was ready to launch his forces across the North Sea. Henry Sidney wrote to William on 30 June 1688 that if the martial intentions of the Dutch were made public as much as a fortnight before the armada actually left the shores of the United Provinces, then 'all your particular friends will be clapped up which will terrify others, or at least make them not know what to do, and will, in all probability, ruin the whole design'.[9] The existence of a conspiracy was undoubtedly well known in James's court, as were the names of the principal offenders. The Earls of Feversham and Ailesbury went on their knees before the king,

> humbly begging him to clap up seven or eight of the heads of them and with the most humble submission I ventured to name the Prince of Denmark, the Dukes of Ormonde and Grafton, Lord Churchill, Mr. Kirke, Mr. Trelawney, &c., but as it was found, and fatally, that the king could not resolve and, if he had, in all probability his army would have stood by him.[10]

James's reluctance to take the necessary measures has never been satisfactorily explained. Perhaps he refused to believe that officers like Churchill, Kirke, and Trelawney who had enjoyed his patronage during their military careers could be so base as to rebel against him. Maybe he was prepared to gamble upon the rumours proving to be inaccurate so that he was spared the painful necessity of having to disrupt the internal cohesion of his army on the eve of a major campaign. It is quite possible that, knowing of the poor relations between Feversham and the more competent professional officers, he regarded the rumours as deliberate malice. Not until the weeks immediately preceding the invasion were token gestures made to arrest some of the leading conspirators.

> Orders were sent . . . to secure Lord Lumley, then in the North Riding, but he that was commanded in that service, Colonel John Darcy, pretended he could not find him though it appeared afterwards that he was not far off and might have seized him if he pleased.

It was hardly surprising that Darcy was unable to locate Lumley, as he was most certainly involved on the fringes of the conspiracy which centred on the Earl of Danby, and Darcy was unlikely to render James any service, as he had been dismissed in 1685 from his twin commissions as guidon of the second troop of the Life Guard and lieutenant-colonel of Lord Shrewsbury's horse for voting against the court in the parliament.[11]

Although James would not recognise the existence of disloyalty in his armed forces, the conspiracy was a poorly kept secret. As early as 1687 the king was fully aware that the Earls of Halifax, Danby, Devonshire, and Nottingham were ill-disposed towards his government, and in July 1688 the Modenese resident in London was able to report the foundation of the Association of Protestant Officers among the military encamped on Hounslow Heath.[12] The knowledge of the presence of a growing number of political dissidents and their surreptitious activities was not confined to the court. Solid rumours of the invasion plans of the Prince of Orange were first heard in England around Michaelmas in 1688. On 10 August John Evelyn dined with Sir William Godolphin and in the company was Thomas Tenison, the future Archbishop of Canterbury, who 'told me there would suddenly be some great things discovered which happened to be the P. of O.'s intended coming'.[13] One month later Evelyn noted a general sense of apprehension 'and with reason, that his Majesty's forces would neither at land nor sea oppose them with that vigour requisite to repel invaders'.[14] Despite this general cognisance of the existence of a conspiracy and its broad aims, the plotters did attempt to cloak their detailed designs with secrecy even though an anonymous paper recorded that the mystery of William's planned invasion was kept by the impossibly large circle of nearly two hundred people.[15] Lieutenant-Colonel John Beaumont and John Churchill were both involved in the compact, yet, at the court martial which tried Beaumont and four of his regimental captains for refusing to receive Irishmen into their companies at Portsmouth, Churchill was in favour of exercising the utmost severity against the offending officers. His motives are not clear. The demand might have been an effort to conceal the existence of the army conspiracy or Churchill may have been genuinely unaware of Beaumont's interest in the army plot, although this is difficult to countenance.[16] Apart from the more elevated officers like Churchill, Trelawney, and Kirke it was less easy to identify a number of both the junior and the more senior of the conspirators. During the breathing space provided by the timely storm which dispersed William's first venture on to the North Sea, James ordered the Earl of Arran's regiment of horse, Richard Hamilton's Irish dragoons, and the Queen's regiment of horse, under Sir John Lanier, to march to Ipswich to cover Languard Fort in the event of a Dutch landing on the East Anglian coast. Lanier was given overall command of this brigade and yet he was one of the foremost of the conspirators.[17] The Earl of Huntingdon reached his command at Plymouth on 9 November 1688 and, reporting all in good order, added that his own regiment was unanimous in its desire to serve the king. On the very eve of the surrender of Plymouth to William by its governor, the Earl of Bath, Captain Charles Hatton wrote from the garrison that, to our unspeakable joy and happiness our governor, the Earl of Bath, is here, which, having told you, I need not say that I think myself more happy to be under his command than under that of any other person on earth ... Should the Dutch think fit to attack us here we think ourselves very secure under his conduct.[18]

The fact that there was a conspiracy within the army was well enough understood at Whitehall but there was no real appreciation of the extent to which the canker had infiltrated beneath the upper crust. Within the officer corps itself and among the higher echelons of society a detailed knowledge of the workings of the army conspiracy was clearly less than widespread; a letter from London on 17 November stated that 'on Thursday evening we were not a little surprised that part of some regiments had deserted to the enemy'. One possible explanation of why an officer like Charles Hatton, who was the son of a peer and himself politically well connected, should have been so ill-informed and naive about the loyalty of his commanding officer is that he had spent the majority of James's reign in the geographically remote garrisons of Guernsey and Plymouth. The army conspiracy was effectively founded during the summer camp on Hounslow Heath in 1688 and flourished in those formations which were in constant attendance on the court or were regularly stationed in or close to London: the regiments of horse and foot guards. Officers from provincial garrisons were very probably unaware of the political activities of their colleagues from the more prestigious corps. It was these élite units which formed the bulk of the regiments on Hounslow Heath in the summer of 1688, and over half the English army did not attend that rendezvous but continued in their garrisons. When the army concentrated upon Salisbury Plain in November 1688 many of the officers from Scotland, Ireland, and the outlying posts in England would have been in the same position as Hatton in that they were ignorant of the conspiracy and genuinely taken aback when the first desertions occurred. It is no wonder that the Earl of Huntingdon should have been unconscious of the suspect allegiance of some of the officers from his own regiment of foot, as, being an aristocratic colonel with but a limited aptitude for martial affairs, he spent as little time as possible with his soldiers and his arrival at Plymouth on 9 November was the first time that he had visited his own command for many months.[19]

The companion conspiracy in the fleet was neither as deep nor as successful. By the very nature of its environment, the fleet was a more disunited organisation than the army and it was difficult for a conspiracy to blossom once the ships were at sea. Even at the anchorage off the Buoy of the Nore, the physical separation of the vessels made regular contact between officers difficult unless they took extended, unofficial, and highly conspicuous shore leave. Lord Dartmouth mentioned 'caballing' amongst his captains and commanders in a letter of 17 October, and five days later he reported that Lord Berkeley had visited the fleet and spread his insidious influence.[20] It was not the conspiracy among naval officers that prevented the king's ships from intervening effectively in the campaign of 1688 but a combination of adverse weather and Dartmouth's curious tactics. When George Churchill did desert in the *Newcastle* the maritime aspect of the campaign had already ended. However, ill-defined though it was, the plot in the navy did possess close ties with the undertaking in the army. George Byng, the co-ordinator of the naval conspiracy, held a preliminary meeting in London with the Duke of Ormonde, Percy Kirke, and Captain Mathew Aylmer of the Royal Navy, before he went down to the Nore and won over Captain John Ashby and Wolfran Cornwall, the son of Colonel Henry Cornwall.[21] During Dartmouth's frustrated pursuit of the Dutch along the English Channel the naval conspiracy showed no sign of coming into operation. So ineffectual did the naval officers who were involved appear to be that they sent Byng on a hazardous overland journey to convey a verbal message to William to reassure him that 'those in the fleet who were well inclined to him thought it time to show themselves and even some that were timorous and silent hitherto'.[22] This had more of the ring of a frantic appeal for the recognition of services not quite rendered and an apology for inaction than a statement of intent.

One of the most important elements in the functioning of the conspiracy in the army was the close link between the Anglo-Dutch Brigade and the standing army in England and Scotland. As we have seen, the officers who obeyed James's order to return to England in March 1688 were formed into three new regiments of foot but a few were posted into established formations. Evidence that some of these officers acted as Dutch spies and were deliberately planted by William among the homecoming officers is only circumstantial but it is not unconvincing. Aeneas Mackay was the second son of John, Lord Reay and a nephew of Major-General Hugh Mackay of the Anglo-Dutch Brigade. Aeneas Mackay served as a captain in his uncle's regiment but sailed to England in answer to James's proclamation and was duly commissioned as a captain in one of the three new regiments of foot, that which was commanded by Colonel John Wachop, on 13 March 1688. A number of pieces of information indicate that Mackay was very probably an agent of William. On 1 May 1688 Major George Winraham, the governor of Edinburgh Castle, was instructed to arrest Mackay and to send to London any papers which might be discovered on his person.[23] A fortnight later, 'Captain Mackay, lately come from Holland, is imprisoned in the Castle of Edinburgh on suspicion of a secret correspondence with the Prince of Orange, or some of his servants about him.'[24] Even in captivity it proved impossible to prevent Mackay from remaining in touch with his fellow conspirators.

Doctor Blackader, new come from Holland, (who had been twice pardoned before, first for Bothwell Bridge and then for Argyle's invasion), was apprehended by the chancellor's order when he was visiting Captain Mackay in the Castle of Edinburgh and is put in close prison and at first in the irons on the suspicion of keeping an seditious intelligence and correspondence with some in Holland. And Patridge's Almanack, called Mene Tekell, and letters and verses are found on him reflecting on the birth of the Prince of Wales.[25]

The Earl of Balcarres said that Mackay came over to Scotland,

that he might be the better able to serve the Prince of Orange in his own country which was confirmed by a letter of his own found in his pocket which he had intended for his uncle. In it he expressed great affection to the Prince of Orange and desired his uncle to let him know that, although he had quitted his service, yet he hoped, from the condition he was in, to be more useful to him and that he only wanted his directions to show his good intentions.[26]

Mackay managed to secure his own release by swearing that his letter 'meant nothing but a compliment' but he remained under suspicion and was rearrested by the secret committee in Scotland in September and held in custody until after the Revolution.[27] Undoubtedly, Mackay was intended to be an active agent although his two spells in gaol must have limited his usefulness to the Orangist cause. He was in contact with Dr. William Blackader, a known gatherer of intelligence for William, and with Blackader's associate, William Cleland, who was to be rewarded for his espionage with the lieutenant-colonelcy of the Cameronians in 1689.[28]

Samuel Bonfoy was also an officer of the Anglo-Dutch Brigade who returned to England in 1688 and was subsequently commissioned as an ensign in the Earl of Huntingdon's foot.[29] During the period of the invasion and the Revolution, Huntingdon's regiment of infantry, a formation which contained a considerable number of roman catholics, was stationed in the vital fortress and seaport of Plymouth under the government of the Earl of Bath. Prior to the appearance of the Dutch fleet off Torbay, Bath had given the Prince of Orange 'but vague assurances'.[30] Between 14 and 16 November, Ensign Bonfoy and Captain John Tidcomb, the senior captain in Huntingdon's foot, disappeared from the garrison, only to turn up in William's camp around Exeter shortly afterwards.[31] In all probability, Bonfoy and Tidcomb carried either a verbal or a written message from Bath to William, in advance of his formal letter of 18 November, announcing his resolution to desert James and declare both himself and Plymouth for the Orange interest.[32] Communications between Plymouth and the royal field army had been cut by 20 November and, four days later, Huntingdon and all his catholic officers were arrested by Bath, Sir John Jacob, and Lieutenant-Colonel Ferdinando Hastings, a cousin of the unfortunate earl.[33] There is no absolute evidence that Samuel Bonfoy was actively involved in liaising between the conspirators in the Plymouth garrison and the Prince of Orange's camp but there is adequate cause for suspicion.

Anglo-Dutch officers made frequent official trips across the North Sea to recruit their companies and attend to their personal affairs, voyages which were often used to convey letters between centres of opposition in England and The Hague.[34] Emmanuel Scrope Howe, a younger brother of Sir Scrope Howe, was a captain in the Earl of Pembroke's regiment of the Anglo-Dutch Brigade and on several occasions during 1688 he carried letters to William from the Marquis of Winchester, the Earl of Danby, and the Earl of Devonshire. There were a number of close links between the English, Scottish, and Irish standing armies and the Anglo-Dutch regiments. Henry Sidney, one of the leading conspirators in England, had been the commander of the Brigade between 1681 and 1685, and many of the officers were professional soldiers who had served in branches of the English army under Charles II or had been displaced from their commissions in Ireland.[35] Hugh Mackay was a lifelong friend of John Churchill, 'with whom he kept up a friendly correspondence to the day of his death', an acquaintance which had originated when they were both young subalterns in France in the 1670s. The personal and professional contacts between the two forces were extensive and enduring, and the numerous channels which were opened by James's recall of the Brigade in conjunction with the passage of officers to and from Holland were much employed by the conspirators on both sides of the North Sea. Sir Henry Bellasise, colonel of one of the English regiments in the Anglo-Dutch Brigade, came over to England in April 1688.

Apparently he had somehow displeased William of Orange in the previous year and had been forbidden the Dutch court although he had been permitted to retain the nominal command of his own regiment. Sir Henry was not discouraged by the Prince's frown but operated on his behalf with the conspirators in the northern counties of England. 'Sir Henry Bellasise (who had commanded a regiment in Holland under the Prince and lurked long here in Yorkshire for his service)' was a principal in Danby's seizure of York.[36]

The best, indeed the only, contemporary account of the conspiracy in England is that presented by Gilbert Burnet, who was in a central position to observe its workings.[37] Henry Sidney, the son of the Earl of Leicester and himself the future Earl of Romney, was the person 'into whose hands the conduct of the whole design was chiefly deposited, by the Prince's own order'. The close personal friendship and respect between William and Sidney was 'well known over England so that all who desired to recommend themselves to the Prince did it through his hands ... all centred in him.' Because of Sidney's laziness much of the routine correspondence connected with the undertaking was handled by a kinsman of Burnet, James Johnston. Without providing a precise chronology, Burnet says that Sidney originally tried to involve Halifax and Nottingham before turning his attention to the more receptive person of Danby. Devonshire was the next to be approached and he entered into the plan with 'a great resolution'; his recruitment was followed by the successful overtures to three army officers: Charles Trelawney, Percy Kirke, and Lord Churchill. Significantly, all three of these gentlemen had fought together in France during the Franco-Dutch war from 1672 to 1678, had seen service in Tangier, and were very well known in military circles in England and in the United Provinces. Trelawney was able to bring in his brother, Sir Jonathan, the Bishop of Bristol, whilst Churchill seems to have been responsible for converting the faction centred upon the household of the Prince and Princess of Denmark through the influence of his wife, Sarah. Arthur Herbert and George Churchill assisted in spreading discord in the navy, and during the summer and autumn of 1688 a number of Anglican-Tories joined in the conspiracy: the Duke of Grafton, the young Duke of Ormonde, the Earl of Bath, the Marquis of Worcester, Sir John Lowther, and the Bishop of St. Asaph.[38]

Apart from Sidney, who seems to have controlled the means of communication between the Prince of Orange and the conspirators in England, the central figure in the military conspiracy was John Churchill, with his considerable contacts in the army, the navy, the court, and with the solidly protestant Princess Anne. By 4 August 1688 Churchill was definitely committed to the Orangist cause[39] and he began to organise the Anglican-Tory plotters at the court and in the army together with the small group of active whigs and republicans. The Anglican-Tory group was based upon the household of the Princess Anne at the Cockpit and principally consisted of the second Duke of Ormonde, who was smarting at the treatment of his father by Tyrconnell in Ireland; the Duke of Grafton, a natural son of Charles II and colonel of the First Foot Guards; Colonel John Berkeley, the commander of a regiment of dragoons; Lord Drumlanrig, son of the Duke of Queensbury; and Lord Cornbury, the eldest son of the Earl of Clarendon and Colonel of the Royal regiment of dragoons. Henry Compton, the suspended Bishop of London, was also closely connected with the Cockpit circle, having been the religious tutor to both Princess Anne and her sister, Mary. During September 1688 Compton travelled through the north of England trying to broaden the base of the conspiracy. He succeeded in winning over his nephew, the Earl of Northampton, his relative the Earl of Dorset, the Montagues of Horton, Lord Grey de Ruthin, and the Earl of Manchester. The Earl of Stamford was also willing to countenance the plot, as were Charles Bertie and his brother the Earl of Abingdon, both of whom were brothers-in-law of Danby, and Lord Willoughby, the son of the Earl of Lindsey and Danby's nephew. Other loyal Tory conspirators were John Darcy, the grandson of the Earl of Holderness, Sir Henry Goodricke of Ribston Hall in Yorkshire, Lord Fairfax of Cameron, and Christopher Tankard, all four being acquaintances of the Earl of Danby. Although the majority of the plotters were Anglican-Tories there was a small collection of whigs who assembled about Thomas Wharton, the Earl of Devonshire, Lord Delamere, the Earl of Stamford, and the 'Treason Club' which met at the Rose Tavern in Covent Garden, but even this group was related by family and marriage to the central Cockpit circle. Charles Godfrey, a whig and an ex-army officer, was a brother-in-law of Churchill, having married his sister, Arabella, whilst Thomas Wharton was a relative of the Berties. Thomas Wharton's father, Philip, the fourth Baron Wharton, allowed his house at Wooburn to be freely visited by his Bertie relatives, who were in close touch with Danby and his Yorkshire faction, whilst Thomas Wharton himself was a principal figure in the conspiracy, collecting a large store of arms at Winchendon and using his time in London to cultivate friendships with retired and serving army officers. He was greatly helped in this latter task by his brother Henry, who was a captain in the Earl of Lichfield's foot.[40] Apart from the risings of Danby in York, Devonshire in Nottingham, and Delamere in Cheshire, most of the non-military conspirators do not appear to have materially assisted the Dutch invasion. Even these three rebellions which were conducted by civilians were largely irrelevant to the main struggle between the two armies in the south-west of England, and William was somewhat displeased when Danby distracted attention from himself and created a rival centre of opposition to James. The conspiracy that mattered was the attempt to undermine the English army's will to fight.

Murmurings about the army's loyalty to James were current as early as 1686. In that year an anonymous writer warned the king that 'the protestants of your English army would, in case of a rebellion, be too inclined to fight for the king, parliament, and [the] protestant religion [and] against the king as papist, his popish cabals, and popery'. A year later the same correspondent announced that 'most of your protestant officers love your money but not your service. They serve you contre coeur and hate those that serve you zealously.'[41] These remarks hopelessly overstated the position, for the army raised no objection to being employed as a political force in 1687 and 1688 and James's open eye for political suspects made the officers increasingly devoted to himself. There were, however, limits to the objective loyalty of some of the officers. James seems to have made the elementary mistake of assuming that professionalism automatically eradicated political and religious sympathies. In the Prussia of Frederick the Great, where the standing army became the servant of the state, the emphasis upon career officers did result in a force which supported the monarchy and reserved its own political judgements but James could not achieve such an ideal within three and a half years. Even the aggressive Louvois was unable to anaesthetise the French army officers; the plan for the destruction of the Palatinate in 1688 was achieved only partially, because of the scruples of the senior officers. The allegiance of the soldiery was more straightforward and predictable. Much has been made of the way in which the rank and file of the army who were in London and at the camp on Hounslow Heath received the news of the acquittal of the Seven Bishops with such glee and obvious contentment. Was this a sign of the army's deep-seated hostility to the king's religious policy? Undoubtedly it was, but that did not necessarily mean that the soldiers would be disloyal to their monarch when England was invaded by a horde of Dutchmen and German mercenaries. On the contrary, the naive loyalty which the soldiers demonstrated towards the Anglican prelates was transferred into a similarly simple devotion to their king when his lands were violated. Many officers might have deserted to William in November and December 1688 but few soldiers willingly followed them and those who did were often ignorant of where they were being led and why.[42] Popery and Irishmen brought no pleasure to English soldiers, but they did not permit these problems to stand in the way of their sense of duty to their divinely appointed monarch. Their officers were rather more sophisticated.

Serious suggestions that all was not well within the officers corps first appeared in February 1688. Like all other holders of public positions, army officers were tendered the infamous Three Questions. Those who were on leave gave their replies in their own counties but officers on duty with their regiments were canvassed by the governor of their garrison or by their colonel. The young Duke of Berwick, James's illegitimate son, put the Three Questions to the officers of the two foot regiments which were within his government of Portsmouth but the results were most displeasing. Nearly all the gentlemen refused to sign until the first two questions had been totally erased, even though the officers who made 'difficulties' had been previously threatened with the loss of their commission.[43] Further trouble occurred in Portsmouth in September. The soldiers who had been withdrawn from Ireland to fill up the ranks of the three new regiments of foot which had been formed to accommodate the officers who had returned from the Anglo-Dutch Brigade proved to be too many, leaving between forty and fifty supernumeraries. Rather than send these men back to Ireland, James ordered Berwick to take them into his own regiment of foot, which was in garrison at Portsmouth. Reasonably enough, Berwick decided that these catholic Irishmen ought to be evenly distributed between the twelve companies. Unfortunately, his officers did not agree. Lieutenant-Colonel John Beaumont and Captains Thomas Paston, Simon Pack, Thomas Orme, William Cooke, and John Port refused to receive the Irishmen into their companies. Beaumont spoke to Berwick on their behalf.

Sir, I am desired by these gentlemen (with whose sense I do concur), to inform your grace that we do not think it consistent with our honours to have foreigners imposed upon us . . . We humbly petition [that] we may have leave to fill up our companies with such men of our nation as we judge most suitable to the king's service and to support our honours.[44]

The six 'Portsmouth Captains' were individually very different yet they were able to act in concert over the issue of recruiting catholic

Irishmen into the English army. John Beaumont was a professional soldier. Born in 1636, he was the brother of the third Viscount Beaumont and lived in Burton in Leicestershire. He almost certainly served in European armies until 1674, when he entered the English establishment as a captain in the Holland regiment of foot. This attachment in England did not last for long and in 1684 it was noted that 'he now liveth abroad' in Holland, where he held a captaincy in the Anglo-Dutch Brigade. On the expansion of the army to meet Monmouth's rebels, Beaumont returned to England to become the lieutenant-colonel of Lord Ferrers's foot, the formation which Berwick assumed in 1687. After the Revolution he was rewarded with a colonelcy of infantry and he served in Ireland, Flanders, and Scotland until his retirement from active service in 1695. He died six years later in 1701.[45] Also with aristocratic connections was Thomas Paston, the brother of the Earl of Yarmouth. Until 1685 he appears to have had no military experience, but in that year he entered Lord Ferrers' foot as a captain. In 1690 he reappears as the lieutenant-colonel of the Earl of Danby's volunteer dragoons and in the following year he was appointed to the same rank in the second regiment of marines. He was drowned in 1691 before he could enjoy the fruits of his new commission.[46] Simon Pack was the son of Sir Christopher Pack of Prestwould and his first taste of the military life came in 1678 when he was commissioned as a captain in Sir Henry Goodricke's foot. On the disbandment of this corps the next year Pack was without employment until 1685, when he entered Lord Ferrers's foot as a captain. Among fashionable society he had a reputation for being unlucky in love and possessing an 'unruly passion', and it was probably the latter characteristic that drew him into a duel with Captain Alan Bellingham in 1686 from which he appears to have escaped without injury. After the Revolution, Pack was promoted to the lieutenant-colonelcy of Berwick's old regiment, a rank which he seems to have retained throughout the War of the Grand Alliance.[47] Thomas Orme came from a Staffordshire family which suffered severely during the period of the Commonwealth, and after the Restoration he was forced to try his fortune at the court. During the great scramble for appointments after 1660 Orme could only secure a position as a Yeoman of the Guard to Charles II, although he did receive a promotion into the Gentlemen Pensioners in 1685. Also in that year, he was able to take advantage of the expansion of the army to become a captain in Lord Ferrers's regiment of infantry. His fortune somewhat repaired, Orme retired permanently from army life in 1688.[48] The fifth captain, William Cooke, was thoroughly committed to the army. A son of William Cooke of Highnam in Gloucestershire, he followed his father into the profession of arms. In 1678 he was first commissioned as a cornet in the Queen's regiment of horse and in 1681 he received a permanent commission in the Duke of York's infantry. On 24 May 1686 he was promoted to a captaincy in Lord Ferrers's corps. His stand at Portsmouth did not go unrecognised, and after the Revolution Cooke was appointed lieutenant-colonel of Lord Lovelace's regiment of foot. This signalled the end of his career, as Lovelace's formation turned out to be ill-officered and badly organised and Cooke himself was cashiered in 1689 for spreading illwill between the English and Huguenot regiments in the Williamite army in Ireland.[49] Of the final Portsmouth captain, John Port, hardly any information has come to light. He was commissioned as a captain in Lord Ferrers's regiment on 12 March 1686 but that is the sum total of our knowledge.[50]

As his behaviour towards the fellows of Magdalen College had shown, James reacted violently to any direct challenge to his authority. Beaumont and his five colleagues were arrested by Berwick and sent up to London under guard to face a court-martial in Windsor Castle. The verdict of the court was entirely predictable, and the six officers were cashiered and rendered unfit to serve the king on any future occasion.[51] Before it is possible to assess the political importance of the Portsmouth episode it is as well to clarify the actual issues involved. In the first place, the fact that Berwick's regiment was able to absorb between forty and fifty Irish recruits indicates that the formation must have been well below strength, because the officers were operating some system to cheat the muster-master and the treasury. This, in James's eyes, would have exaggerated their initial offence. Secondly, no contemporary evidence suggests that the introduction of these Irish soldiers into Berwick's regiment was the beginning of a policy of filling the English army with Irish catholics. There were surplus troops available from MacElligott's Irish regiment and as that formation was stationed in Portsmouth it made practical sense to use the men to recruit another under-strength regiment which was in the same garrison. That such a decision was inept and politically gauche cannot be doubted, but it does not appear to have been the thin end of a catholic military wedge. The objection by the six officers was to a single, specific event. Their stand won considerable support from among their fellow officers in Berwick's regiment, and three lieutenants and four ensigns resigned their commissions in sympathy with the deprivation of their senior officers. During these upheavals over a hundred private soldiers took the opportunity to desert.[52] Although the demonstration by the Portsmouth Captains probably had some effect upon James's attitude towards his officers, the fact that he moved rapidly to arrest, try, and evict the offenders might well have convinced him that he had gone some way towards making an example of them to other would-be men of principle and that he might have stamped out the trouble. James was probably correct in these assumptions. No other open incidents occurred, and similarly he did not repeat the mistake of trying to foist Irish soldiers on to English regiments. The Portsmouth episode was an isolated occasion caused by one tactless royal decision, and although it clearly showed that professionalism in officers did not yet mean total obedience to the royal will it does not seem to have been connected with the conspiracy in the army. John Beaumont was an active conspirator but his posture in Portsmouth must have been viewed with horror by his fellow plotters. There was every danger that his court-martial might have revealed the existence of the army conspiracy and ruined the whole design, and this probably accounts for Churchill's extreme hostility towards Beaumont at his trial. By acting hastily Beaumont could easily have jeopardised all William's careful planning.

The Portsmouth episode does raise the importance of the question of religion in the army. Given the enormous solidity of the average officer's loyalty to the king, James's policy of professionalising the officer corps, and the fact that William's intervention would have to be a barely disguised military invasion, religion was the one weak spot which could be readily attacked by Dutch-inspired propaganda. During the late spring and summer of 1686 Samuel Johnson, an Anglican clergyman, who was already in prison for having written *Julian the Apostate*, managed to smuggle the manuscript of a *Humble and Hearty Address to All the English Protestants in this Present Army* to a London printer. The resulting pamphlet was widely distributed in the streets of the capital and among its principal target, the army. The *Address* accused the protestant officers of allying themselves with 'bloody papists' and announced that it was the intention of the king to destroy the protestant religion. Rather than support such a government, Johnson exhorted the army to rebellion.[53] There is no reason to suppose that Johnson's libel caused much concern in the army at that time, but in 1688 William of Orange's *Letter to the English Army* pursued similar lines of argument, stressing that the officers had obligations to God and their religion as well as to their country.[54]

The principal institution in the army conspiracy against James II was the Treason Club, which met at the Rose Tavern on Russell Street in Covent Garden. The club was a loose collection of young whiggish army officers and would-be politicians bound together by common aims and interests. Unofficial president of the group was Richard Savage, Viscount Colchester, a whig and a member of the Oxford Parliament of 1681. Colchester was both an aristocrat and a professional soldier, having served in France in the 1670s and having occupied the lieutenant-colonelcy of the fourth troop of the Life Guard since 1686. After the Revolution, as the fourth Earl Rivers, he was to rise to the rank of lieutenant-general and become a soldier of very considerable distinction. However, in 1688 he was a young and adventurous man in his mid-thirties.[55] Thomas Wharton had connections in both the army and the whig interest, as did Charles Godfrey, who had been a captain in the Royal English regiment in France between 1672 and 1674 and had then transferred into the First Foot Guards in England. His captaincy was removed from him in 1681 because of his excessive partiality for Monmouth and the cause of exclusion.[56] Godfrey was a bosom companion of Wharton and acted as second in most of his duels. Jack Howe was the brother of Emmanuel Scrope Howe, a captain in the Anglo-Dutch Brigade, whilst William Jephson was another professional soldier whose career had been prematurely ended by his adherence to Monmouth. Jephson had served with the British force in France between 1672 and 1678 and had then returned to England as a lieutenant in the Duke of Monmouth's foot in 1678 and 1679. Following the failure of the Rye Plot, life became so uncomfortable for Jephson that he was forced to seek temporary refuge at The Hague, but he appears to have spent some time in England during James's reign and probably acted as a liaison between the plotters in England and the circle about the Prince of Orange. His reward in 1689 was the officer of secretary to the treasury, but he could only enjoy it for two years until his death in 1691.[57] Another vital member of the Treason Club was Thomas Langston, a professional officer who again had once been a protégé of the late Duke of Monmouth. Langston had served as a captain in Monmouth's regiment of horse in France in 1675 and when this formation returned to England in 1678 he continued in the same rank. After a three-year term of duty in Tangier Langston transferred into the Royal Dragoons, and by 1686 he had been promoted to the lieutenant-colonelcy of Princess Anne's regiment of cavalry. Contacts between Monmouth and Langston appear to have been very strong, as in 1685 he was one of the officers whom Monmouth attempted to persuade to assist in subverting the English army[58] The final member of the club was Thomas Talmash, the ex-lieutenant-colonel of the Royal Fusiliers and a colonel in the Anglo-Dutch Brigade. With the exception of Wharton, who had a brother in the army and was a leading whig, all the members of the Treason Club were either professional soldiers or ex-professionals most of whom had been followers of Monmouth. It was a tightly bound organisation both in background and aims, and the links with the United Provinces through Howe, Talmash, and Jephson were considerable and probably very frequent. Although there is no evidence it seems likely that the plans for the defection of parts of the English army were arranged through the club's auspices.

The second recognisable group in the army conspiracy were the so-called 'Tangerines', an informal gathering of army and navy officers who had enjoyed the dubious privilege of serving in Tangier. Colonels Charles Trelawney and Percy Kirke were the major figures among the 'Tangerines', but Thomas Langston was both a veteran of Tangier and a member of the Treason Club, thus forming a useful bridge between the two. George Byng, Mathew Aylmer, and Arthur Herbert represented the naval 'Tangerines' and then in April 1688 they were joined by John Cutts, who had entered the Anglo-Dutch Brigade as a captain after previous service with the Imperial armies in Hungary. Being an old associate of Monmouth, Cutts had considerable influence with many of the members of the Treason Club and his position in Holland created another tentacle of conspiracy across the North Sea. One feature emerges very clearly from these biographical surveys. With the exception of the Duke of Grafton, a natural son of Charles II, the officers who were actively involved in the military conspiracy were professional soldiers who relied upon their sword for their livelihood. Percy Kirke had fought in France from 1673 to 1676 and then with the Anglo-Dutch Brigade until 1679. In the following year he proceeded to Tangier as the lieutenant-colonel of the Earl of Plymouth's foot and in 1682 he became the governor of Tangier until its evacuation two years later. Throughout the reign of James II, Kirke commanded his own regiment of foot as well as receiving promotions which found him in the uniform of a major-general in 1688.[59] Charles Trelawney also began his military career in France between 1674 and 1677 before moving to Tangier as Kirke's deputy and then back into England as colonel of his own regiment of infantry.[60] Sir John Lanier lost an eye whilst fighting for the French in 1673 but that did not prevent him from pursuing a successful military career in England and Flanders until he received the colonelcy of a regiment of horse in 1687 and the rank of lieutenant-general in 1688. Perhaps the most notable of these careerists was John, Lord Churchill. Like his fellow plotters Churchill had served in France and Tangier in the 1670s and early 1680s, and he relied heavily upon the patronage of James II for his advancement, position, and his basic income. The common denominator of these professional soldiers was that none of them enjoyed sufficient financial security to enable him to forfeit his military commission. Even a seemingly aristocratic officer like Lord Cornbury came from a family which was not over-endowed with surplus wealth. The successful purge of the Irish army and the ominous direction which James's military policy seemed to be taking during the summer of 1688 did much to convince a section of these career officers that their future might be in jeopardy unless they took positive action to safeguard their interests. To an extent, the defection of a few English officers to William fitted into the accepted military *mores* of the age. European army officers tended to be professional soldiers in the first instance, with patriotism taking second place, and many were prepared to serve any state which offered them lucrative employment, prospects of promotion, and reasonable security of tenure. Although it was unofficial, this military internationalism was an accepted code of behaviour on the continent. Most of the conspirators who were serving officers had fought under a number of different flags before 1685 and were well acquainted with foreign practices; as a result they were less squeamish about changing sides and did not suffer from scruples of allegiance to the same extent as a Captain Charles Hatton. The manner in which these officers transferred their loyalty in 1688 was a trifle bizarre, being in mid-campaign rather than during the close season, but the principle was recognisable.[61] English officers who adopted this flexible stance were in a decided minority; the majority, including many who had fought in France, Flanders, and other foreign stations, regarded the armies of England, Scotland, and Ireland as their 'home' establishments and were less than anxious to exchange a career in their native countries for an itinerant life abroad. Loyalty to the English monarchy was exceptionally strong.

Exactly when the Treason Club and the 'Tangerines' first turned their attention to conspiracy is impossible to say. It is highly unlikely that either was operational before the middle of June 1688, as their sole *raison d'être* was to assist William's invasion by organising the collapse of the morale of the English army and the Dutchman did not reach a firm decision about armed intervention until about that time. The 'Tangerines' had been a force within the officer corps since the abandonment of the Mediterranean outpost in 1684, an association of hardened veterans united by drink and a hatred of Lord Dartmouth and Samuel Pepys, the twin villains who had supervised the evacuation of Tangier. Similarly, the Treason Club had its origins in an unofficial society which was in being long before 1688. It grew almost organically from among the fashionable young gentlemen who mixed with the Restoration wits, dramatists, and rakes in their lairs at the Rose Tavern and Will's Coffee House. George Etherege was a good friend of Charles Godfrey, Thomas Wharton, and William Richards, a young lieutenant in the First Foot Guards, and he was also well acquainted with William Jephson and Thomas Maulle, who was a groom of the bedchamber to Prince George of Denmark and very definitely involved in the conspirational circle connected with the Cockpit and the Churchills.[62] Sir Charles Sedley, Lord Dorset, William Wycherley, and Thomas Shadwell were, or had been, closely associated with the modish group at the seedy Rose Tavern. The future members of the Treason Club were thus already very well known to one another, and the general air of devilment and excitement which characterised that part of London may well have contributed to their eagerness to foment the conspiracy.

Until the army concentrated for the summer camp on Hounslow Heath it was difficult for any of the conspiratorial groups to come into effective operation, but once James officially opened proceedings on 28 June conditions for 'caballing' within easy reach of London could hardly have been better. To begin with, James himself spread distrust among his officers. By attempting to assess the number of officers and men in the Earl of Lichfield's foot who were in favour of the repeal of the Test Acts and Penal Laws, the king provided a catalyst for the formation of another underground organisation within the army, the Association of protestant Officers. Thomas Langston, already a member of both the Treason Club and the 'Tangerines', was the moving spirit behind this group and, using James's canvas of Lichfield's regiment as his sole evidence, he started to spread wild stories about James planning to evict all protestant officers from the English army; 'king James, so soon as his army was modelled to his purpose, would set up a mass in every church in England and Scotland; and he that was not a thorough papist would be hanged, quartered, or burnt'. There is no evidence whatsoever that James did intend to replace all the protestant officers with catholics and, even if this had been his wish, there were insufficient romanists available in England. However, Langston fastened on to the twin bogeys of religion and the very real fear among army officers that some sort of purge was not far in the future. These tales seem to have been widely accepted within the camp and succeeded in bringing 'over many to their party', and Langston was not afraid to employ vigorous persuasion; 'he frighted and wheedled several officers and soldiers to undertake with him in his design of deserting his Majesty'. Langston introduced some more officers to the Treason Club, among them Hatton Compton, a brother of the Earl of Northampton and a nephew of the suspended Bishop of London, and John Hope, the captain-lieutenant of the Coldstream Guards and 'a very bad man'.[63] Later, the Rose Taverners 'resolved that the regiment under the aforesaid Lieutenant-Colonel Langston's command should desert entire, as they did on Sunday the 9 November 1688, the which was better effected because the Lord Churchill, one of the lieutenant-generals, had ordered those regiments to go on the advanced post nearest the enemy'.[64] This last statement probably presumes too much too soon. Whilst it is almost certain that the Treason Club gave William assurances that they would be responsible for ruining James's army it would have been impossible for them to have drawn up any definite plans until after William had actually landed in England. Most of the conspirators, including Danby, were under the impression that the Dutch would land on the coast of Yorkshire to the north of the estuary of the Humber; the appearance of the invaders at Torbay must have upset some carefully laid schemes. Eleven days elapsed between the landing of the Prince of Orange and the defection of Langston and Lord Cornbury, a delay caused not by reluctance or reticence on the part of the conspirators but by the fact that all their designs had to be remade to meet the entirely unexpected theatre of operations. Apart from vague guarantees, the detailed plans for defection were probably not made until after 5 November.

However, despite the last-minute alterations, a great deal of planning and liaison was carried out between July and November 1688, most of it under the overall supervision of William's assistants and ministers. No conspirator was sufficiently indiscreet as to leave a memoir of how the organisations in England maintained contact with the Prince of Orange. Very probably, the army conspirators and the northern plotters who gathered around Danby, Devonshire, and

Delamere used the same channels of communication between England and Holland, although the frequent passage of some of the Anglo-Dutch Brigade provided the military group with an additional method of passing information. Lord Dumblane, Danby's eldest son, was the captain of a frigate and was thus able to cross and recross the North Sea at will, conveying letters and individuals. D'Avaux possessed precise information of a small vessel 'very well rigged and an excellent sailor' which ran between England and Maensluys, a small village at the mouth of the Meuse, from mid-July until the eve of William's invasion. It was this ship that carried Arthur Herbert to Holland complete with the Invitation. Many of these voyages sailed to and from Scotland rather than from England, as the ports north of the border were less well observed by government correspondents, and according to D'Avaux much of the money that was collected in England was transported to William from minor Scottish harbours. Even so, some information and secret journeys must have passed through major English ports. John Westbourne, a dissenting minister of Harwich, was suspected of holding a correspondence with contacts in the United Provinces; he seems to have 'transcribed' papers from Holland then distributed them. Perhaps he had something to do with encoding information. Danby received news of developments in Holland from one 'J.E.' of Hull, who began his letter of 4 November in highly conspiratorial language:

I hope my last came safe to your hands but having no answer would not entrust the enclosed to the post.

He added that William's fleet of six hundred ships ought to have landed near Southampton and Lord Langdale had received an express letter ordering him to call out the militia.[65] The spy-boat service across the North Sea was organised on a regular basis, for Lord Lovelace was able to leave from Holland on Sunday and return the following Monday, landing in the region of Lowestoft from a 'small vessel'. Lovelace had been granted a pass to travel to Spa to take the waters but his health obviously underwent a dramatic improvement before he had time to leave the United Provinces. On his return to England he put 'one of his men' ashore one day before he himself disembarked; any vital letters were almost certainly entrusted to this servant.[66] In the summer of 1688 Edward Russell sailed to The Hague, as 'he was desired by many of the great power and interest in England to speak very freely to the Prince and to know positively of him what might be expected from him', a voyage which was suitably camouflaged by Russell visiting his sister, who lived in Holland. Although he spent most of James's reign in the Dutch Republic, the Earl of Manchester returned to England in time to assist in the preparations of the conspirators. Shrewsbury and Russell sailed secretly for Holland in the middle of September 1688 in a small hired vessel, carrying with them 'a full scheme of advices' and a draft of what was to become William's *Declaration* which had been sketched by Danby. The secret of this voyage was so well kept that Shrewsbury's movements remained uncertain until October.[67] Sir John Guise, a notorious whig and an uncle of Emmanuel Scrope Howe, withdrew into the Netherlands in 1688 'not only to secure himself but to contribute also, as far as in him lay, to the Prince of Orange's expedition into England'. Just as James was about to sit down to his dinner on 23 October, the Earl of Argyll rode to Greenwich and embarked on a Dutch vessel which was waiting for him.[68]

James knew of these clandestine journeys and midnight voyages, and he must have been aware that their frequency increased dramatically from the beginning of July 1688, but he took no action to prevent them or to apprehend the principals. There was no contemporary method by which he could have stopped these sailings from the east coast of England and Scotland, and there was no effective means to halt the internal post service of the conspirators. Plots and rumours of plots were endemic in Restoration England, and James appears to have placed little importance upon the happenings in 1688; provided his army and navy remained loyal, then the tiny number of active conspirators would count for nothing. The deceit of the plotters and the implied affront to his authority and dignity hurt the king deeply but he did not translate this annoyance into definite action. James's curiously ambivalent attitude to the conspiracy is well illustrated by the following relation of a bizarre journey undertaken by his nephew, the Duke of Grafton.

When the late Duke of Grafton returned from Holland where he made a short visit to the Prince of Orange he came straight to Whitehall where the king was and stood near him. There came an express to the king from the Marquis d'Albeville, his envoy in Holland, and the king, who commonly upon receiving letters used to go to his bedchamber or closet, did however at that time pretty hastily open the packet in the same room where he was when it was brought to him and where all the company that attended him at the time was standing in a circle. The king pulled out d'Albeville's own letter to read it first and he read but a little part of it when he looked to the Duke of Grafton and said in my hearing, 'Well, my lord, you have made a very quick voyage to Holland and have returned very speedily,' or words to that effect.

The duke answered thus, 'Your Majesty knows I was here with you on such a day,' naming it, 'and here I am now so how can that be?' The king said, 'It is certainly so for here in this letter now in my hands the Marquis d'Albeville tells me of your arrival in Holland, where you went when there, how long you stayed, and when you left it.' The king then mentioned the particulars: that the duke had landed in Holland at such an hour and in such a place and then went to the Prince of Orange and was with him for so long &c. I can only remember that these particulars were mentioned by the king but I cannot, at this distance of time, remember them exactly yet I have not forgotten the duke's answer which was, 'Your Majesty may see by this what good intelligence you have from the Marquis d'Albeville for it is impossible to do what he says in so short a time.' These words I am positive in for the rudeness of the expression and the denying what was so notoriously true in fact and which all about the court believed.[69]

Apart from the great and powerful, there were a number of minor figures whose names appear from time to time who were very likely employed as couriers. Letters were carried by 'Captain Man and Mr. Foster, who hath a mind to be employed, and will talk to you of things of importance. You know how he is to be managed therefore I need give you no further caution.' On 23 October 1688, William Penn wrote to Lord Dartmouth of

one Greenwood [who] is apprehended for dealing with such of the king's officers of his army to revolt. Also Wicksteed for such practices and words against the lord president [and] for having a correspondence with the Prince of Orange. He is fled with his messenger.[70]

Which of these channels of communication was principally employed by the army conspirators it is impossible to say.

The number of active military conspirators was very small, probably no more than twenty or thirty, but they formed a tightly-knit group bound together by ties of blood, marriage, political allegiance, and a common concern for their future careers. This exclusive club was responsible for organising and executing the trickle of defections which wrecked James's confidence in his armed forces and removed the one obstacle which stood between the Prince of Orange and the throne of England. If they could achieve no more than the desertion of a few key officers, then this was a reflection of the tremendous devotion to the monarchy which James had been able to engender through his policy of detaching the army from society. The basic fact of an invasion by Dutchmen led many officers and men to stand by their king but, through his policies in Ireland, by his abuse of the sanctity of commissions, and by his tactless and clumsy attempts to interfere with the political and religious affiliations of his officers

James created enough ill-feeling for the army conspiracy to come into being. It is noteworthy that those senior officers who were involved in the conspiracy – Churchill, Langston, Lanier, Trelawney, Kirke, Colchester – had all risen high in the army during James's reign or had enjoyed his patronage under Charles II. They do not appear to have been unduly motivated by personal grudges against their king although, politically, many of them were old associates of Monmouth and held whiggish opinions. This is in contrast to the position amongst the civilian conspirators, many of whom harboured a very real loathing of James because of the way he treated them during his reign. Charles Godfrey and William Jephson might have felt aggrieved that their military careers had been brought to a halt in 1681 and 1679 respectively because of their political persuasions, but these were but minor complaints compared to the animus felt by Delamere, Hampden, Devonshire, Ormonde, and Danby. Of course, William may have made tempting offers of future promotions and perquisites to the principal military plotters but, if this was the case, no evidence has survived. Although our insight into the motives of the army officers is poor and our knowledge of the conspiracy woefully inadequate, it seems that the military design to defect to William was a direct result of James's mishandling of his officer corps. His clumsy policies in England and Ireland led a number of professional officers to fear the worst, and Thomas Langston and his friends had to turn the screw but a few more turns to convince a reasonable and significant number of colleagues that their future lay with William and not with James. There was, as far as it is possible to tell, no plan to purge the English army of protestant officers and to replace them with catholics but James succeeded by his actions in making some of his officers believe the contrary.

This played directly into William's hands. Because of the threats from France and the difficulties of transporting large numbers of troops, stores, and horses by sea, William knew that he would be outnumbered by the army of his father-in-law. To the Dutch a conspiracy in James's officer corps was a vital facet of their invasion plans, a necessary secret weapon which would ensure that the campaign would be bloodless, short, and victorious. How much positive assistance and encouragement were given to the army conspirators by William is an open question, as no evidence of Dutch instructions or directions had come to light. The rather vague nature of the conspiracy and the fact that William's landing took place at the opposite end of England from that which was expected probably meant that he had to be content with verbal guarantees and smooth words from the Treason Club and their associates. William must have placed a very high priority on bringing England into the war against France to have risked his own political future and the defence of the United Provinces upon the assurances of hard and dissipated men like Kirke and Trelawney and fashionable young rakes from the disreputable Rose Tavern.

Notes

1 Delamere, *Works*, pp. 59–63; J. P. Kenyon, *The Nobility in the Revolution of 1688* (Hull, 1963), pp. 13–14; Miller, *James II*, pp. 188–9; S. B.Baxter, *William III* (London, 1966), pp. 231 and 240; Lucile Pinkham, *William III and the Respectable Revolution* (Cambridge, Mass., 1954), p. 157; *HMC, Le Fleming MSS.*, p. 220.
2 Burnet, *History of His Own Time*, iii. 303.
3 W. S. Churchill, *Marlborough, His Life and Times* (London, 1933–8), i. 267–8; Simms, *Jacobite Ireland*, p. 47.
4 Clarke, *Life*, ii. 69–70.
5 *Hatton Correspondnece*, ii. 96, 16 Oct. 1688, Charles to Lord Hatton, ii. 109, 20 Nov. 1688, Same to Same.
6 Burnet, *History of His Own Time*, iii. 180–1; Dalrymple, *Memoirs of Great Britain and Ireland*, ii. App. Part 1, pp. 190–200; *HMC, 8th Report*, App. iii., Part 1, p. 560b; Jones, *Revolution of 1688*, p. 221; Turner, *James II*, p. 354; Baxter, *William III*, p. 230.
7 G. H. Jones, *Middleton*, pp. 121–2.
8 Japikse, iii. 9; Dalrymple, *Memoirs of Great Britain and Ireland*, ii. App. Part 1, pp. 217–18. For an account of security in contemporary English government see David Francis, *The First Peninsular War, 1702–1713* (London, 1975), p. 23.
9 Henry Sidney, *Diary of the Times of Charles the Second*, ed. R. W. Blencowe (London, 1843), ii. 269–71.
10 *Ailesbury's Memoirs*, i. 184–5; Lonsdale, *Memoir*, pp.59–60; G. H. Jones, *Middleton*, pp. 127–8.
11 Reresby, p. 524; Luttrell, *Historical Relation*, i. 472; BL Add. MSS. 41,805, f. 59; HPT; Dalton, *Army Lists*, ii. 2 and 8.
12 G. H. Jones, *Middleton*, pp. 127–8.
13 *The Diary and Autobiography of Edmund Bohum Esq.*, ed. S. Wilton Rix (Beccles, 1853), p. 81; Evelyn, *Diary*, iv. 592.
14 *Ibid.*, iv. 600, 6 Oct. 1688.
15 'Notes on the Follies of King James II and the causes of his defeat in 1690–2', in *The Tusmore Papers*, ed. L. G. Wickham Legg (Oxfordshire Record Society, 1939), p. 36.
16 Clarke, *Life*, ii. 169.
17 *Ibid.*, ii. 205–6.

18 *HMC, Hastings MSS.*, ii. 189–90; *Hatton Correspondence*, ii. 109.
19 *Ellis Correspondence*, ii. 304, 17 Nov. 1688; Churchill, *Marlborough*, i. 294; Dalton, *Army Lists*, ii. 37; WO 5/3, pp. 143–60.
20 E. B. Powley, *The English Navy in the Revolution of 1688* (Cambridge, 1928), pp. 67–9; *Ailesbury's Memoirs*, i. 185; *HMC, Dartmouth MSS.*, i. 260–1; Sir Almeric Fitzroy, *Henry, Duke of Grafton, 1663–1690* (London, 1921), pp. 58–9.
21 *The Memoirs relating to the Lord Torrington*, ed. John Knox Laughton (Camden Society, 1889), pp. 27–8.
22 *Ibid.*, p. 30.
23 *RPCS 1686–9*, p. xxii.
24 Lauder, *Historical Notices*, ii. 868.
25 *Ibid.*, ii. 878, 17 July 1688.
26 Colin Lindsay, Earl of Balcarres, *Memoirs touching the Revolution in Scotland, 1688 to 1690* (Edinburgh, 1841), p. 7.
27 Dalton, *Army Lists*, ii. 153 and 232; Carswell, *Descent on England*, p. 124n.
28 *The Life and Diary of Lieut. Col. J. Blackader*, ed. Andrew Crichton, (Edinburgh, 1824), pp. 19n., 30–1, 72 and 95n.; Dalton, *Army Lists*, iii. 82; Dalton, *Scots Army*, p. 144.
29 *HMC, Hastings MSS.*, ii. 191.
30 Mackintosh, *History of the Revolution*, p. 526.
31 *HMC, Hastings MSS.*, ii. 191, 16 Nov. 1688, Huntingdon to Lord Preston.
32 Sir John Dalrymple, *Memoirs of Great Britain and Ireland* (London, 1790), ii. 251.
33 *HMC, Hastings MSS.*, ii. 195–9; Clarke, *Life*, ii. 230; Japikse, iii. 69–70, 27 Nov 1688, Earl of Bath of William of Orange; *Hatton Correspondence*, ii. 108–9, 20 Nov. 1688, Charles to Lord Hatton.
34 Japikse, ii. 772.
35 Childs, *Army of Charles II*, pp. 29–36 and 172–3; Dalrymple, *Memoirs of Great Britain and Ireland*, ii. App. Part 1, pp. 213–18; *HMC, Kenyon MSS.*, p. 209; Carswell, *Descent on England*, p. 123; Mackintosh, *History of the Revolution*, p. 533.
36 Mackay, *Life*, p. 5; *Reresby*, p. 530; Dalton, *Army Lists*, ii. 228n.
37 Burnet, *History of His Own Time*, iii. 274–84.
38 K. Feiling, *A History of the Tory Party, 1640–1714* (Oxford, 1924), p. 227.
39 William Coxe, *Memoirs of the Duke of Marlborough*, ed. John Wade (London, 1905), i. 21; Mackintosh, *History of the Revolution*, p. 481; Dalrymple, *Memoirs of Great Britain and Ireland*, ii, App. Part 1, p. 239.
40 Hosford, *Nottingham, Nobles and the North*, pp. 34–43; Mackintosh, *History of the Revolution*, pp. 481–2; *Ailesbury's Memoirs*, i. 179–80; *HMC, Ormonde MSS.*, n.s. viii. pp. xix–xx; G. F. Trevallyn Jones, *Saw-Pit Wharton: The Political Career from 1640 to 1691 of Philip, fourth Lord Wharton* (Sydney, 1967), pp. 258–9.
41 Frazer, 'Anon. Letters', vi. 3 and 62.
42 *Ailesbury's Memoirs*, i. 170–1; *Reresby*, p. 500; T. B. Macaulay, *The History*

of England from the Accession of James II, ed. C. H. Firth (London, 1914), iii. 1066; Burnet, *History of His Own Time*, iii. 232, 233 and 237; Clarke, *Life*, ii. 163; John Gutch, *Collectanea Curiosa, or Miscellaneous Tracts relating to the History and Antiquities of England and Ireland etc.* (Oxford, 1781), i. 360–1; E. C. Legh, Baroness Newton, *Lyme Letters, 1660–1760* (London, 1925), p. 157; *HMC, Le Fleming MSS.*, p. 214.

43 BL Add. MSS. 34,510, f. 82, 13 Feb. 1688, Van Citters to the States-General.

44 Lonsdale, *Memoir*, p. 63; Campana de Cavelli, *Les Derniers Stuarts a Saint-Germain-en-Laye* (Paris, London and Edinburgh, 1871), ii. 265–6; *Bramston*, pp. 314–15; Bohun, *History of the Desertion*, pp. 7–8. The Duke of Berwick, the senior officer most concerned in this affair, has left no record of his actions or his motives. His memoirs contain not one word on the Portsmouth episode (James Fitzjames, Duke of Berwick, *Mémoires du Maréchal de Berwick* (Switzerland, 1778), i. 14–27).

45 HPT; Childs, *Army of Charles II*, p. 243; Cherry, *Convention Parliament*, pp. 17–18; *Bramston*, p. 314.

46 Dalton, *Army Lists*, ii. 138, iii. 135 and 213; *Ellis Correspondence*, ii. 184; *Bramston*, p. 315.

47 Dalton, *Army Lists*, i. 219, ii. 138, iii. 107; *Verney Memoirs*, ii. 448–9; *Etherege's Letters*, pp. 101n. and 275.

48 Dalton, *Army Lists*, ii. 29 and 138; HPT; Duckett, *Penal Laws*, ii. 203.

49 Dalton, *Army Lists*, i. 201 and 286, ii. 76 and 138, iii. 115.

50 Dalton, *Army Lists*, ii. 69 and 138.

51 Lonsdale, *Memoir*, pp. 59–60; *Reresby*, p. 509; Garland, 'Regiment of MacElligott', p. 123; Clarke, *Life*, ii. 168–9; Luttrell, *Historical Relation*, i. 460 and 462; *Ellis Correspondence*, ii. 167–8, 192 and 196. There is no record of this court-martial in the War Office Papers in the PRO (WO 89/1 and WO 92/1).

52 BL Add. MSS. 34,512, f. 98; BL Add. MSS. 34,510, ff. 145 and 157; Cavelli, ii. 265–6; *Analecta Hibernica*, i. 39 and 41.

53 Clarke, *Life*, ii. 70; *Bramston*, pp. 232 and 248–9; *Savile Correspondence*, ed. W. D. Cooper (Camden Society, 1858), pp. 290–1; Miller, *Popery and Politics*, p. 256; Wood, *Life and Times*, iii. 182; Luttrell, *Historical Relation*, i. 381–2.

54 *A Collection of Papers Relating to the Present Juncture of Affairs* (London, 1689), pp. 16–18.

55 Childs, *Army of Charles II*, p. 246; HPT.

56 HPT; *CSPD 1681*, 11 March 1681; Carswell, *Old Cause*, p. 45.

57 *DNB*; Childs, *Army of Charles II*, p. 246; Baxter, *William III*, p. 277; Dalton, *Army Lists*, i. 207; Carswell, *Old Cause*, pp. 55–6.

58 Childs, *Army of Charles II*, p. 249; Dalton, *Army Lists*, i. and ii. passim; Trench, *Western Rising*, p. 180.

59 Childs, *Army of Charles II*, p. 246; HPT.

60 Childs, *Army of Charles II*, p. 246; HPT; *DNB*.

61 Childs, *Army of Charles II*, pp. 30–43; Carswell, *Descent on England*, p. 124;

Francis, *First Peninsular War*, p. 23; *A Fragment of a Memoir of Field-Marshal James Keith, written by Himself*, ed. Thomas Constable (Edinburgh, 1843).

62 *Etherege's Letters*, pp. 121–2, 190 and 277n.; Bryant Lillywhite, *London Coffee Houses* (London, 1963), Nos. 1091 and 1548; V., de Sola Pinto, *Sir Charles Sedley, 1639–1701* (London, 1927), p. 107; *Ailesbury's Memoirs*, i. 179–80; H. J. Oliver, *Sir Robert Howard, 1626–1698* (Durham, North Carolina, 1963), pp. 252–5; Brice Harris, *Charles Sackville, sixth Earl of Dorset; Patron and Poet the Restoration* (Urbana, Illinois, 1940) pp. 114–18.

63 Edward Carpenter, *The Protestant Bishop, Being the Life of Henry Compton, 1632–1713, Bishop of London* (London 1956), p. 131; BL Add. MSS. 41,805, f. 65.

64 Rawlinson MSS. D.148, 'Letter about the Revolution in the Army in 1688', 16 Oct. 1713, London. This letter is anonymous but was probably penned by Ambrose Norton, who was major of the Duke of St. Albans' horse in 1688, a regiment which was effectively commanded by Thomas Langston. Although this account was written some twenty-five years after the event it is the only detailed description of the Association of Protestant Officers and the defection of Langston and Lord Cornbury. In the absence of any other substantial evidence, this version of the development of the conspiracy has been adopted. An incomplete and inaccurate version of this important document is printed in Macpherson, *Original Papers*, i. 287–96.

65 M. E. Evans, 'Yorkshire and the Revolution of 1688', *Yorkshire Archaeological Journal*, xxix. (1929), pp. 260 and 262; Arthur Trevor, *The Life and Times of William the Third* (London, 1835–6), i. 249–50; *D'Avaux*, iv. 182, 214–15 and 221–2; BL Add. MSS. 41,805, f. 48, 29 Sept. 1688, William Sandford to Owen Wynne; BL Add. MSS. 28,053, f. 349.

66 BL Add. MSS. 41,805, f. 46, 26 Sept. 1688, Sandford to Wynne; *CSPD 1687–9*, p. 262; Luttrell, *Historical Relation*, i. 461 and 464.

67 Burnet, *History of His Own Time*, iii. 240; A. C. Wood, 'The Revolution of 1688 in the North of England', *Translations of the Thoroton Society of Nottinghamshire*, xliv. (1940), pp. 101–2; *HMC, Buccleuch (Montagu) MSS.*, ii. Part 1, pp. 33–5; L. G. Schwoerer, 'Propaganda in the Revolution of 1688–89', *AHR*, lxxxii. (1977), pp. 851–2; T. C. Nicholson and A. S. Turberville, *Charles Talbot, Duke of Shrewsbury* (Cambridge, 1930), pp. 27–8; *D'Avaux*, iv. 209.

68 *Autobiography of Thomas Raymond and Memoirs of the Family of Guise of Elmore, Gloucestershire*, ed. G. Davies (Camden Society, 1917), pp. 89–91 and 135; *D'Avaux*, iv. 254–5.

69 Rawlinson D.148. Grafton's journey took place in either late September or early October 1688.

70 Dalrymple, *Memoirs of Great Britain and Ireland*, ii. App. Part 1, p. 227, 18 June 1688, anonymous letter to the Prince of Orange; *HMC, Dartmouth MSS.*, i. 170.

VII

The campaign of 1688

The manner [in which] he lost his crown made him appear in so contemptible a light that the Bishop of Rheims, brother to Louvois, said, 'there is a simpleton who for a mass has lost three kingdoms'.[1]

After a severe winter, during which the river Thames had been frozen over, the spring of 1688 was late and dominated by cold easterly winds. In spite of this the harvest was 'abundant' but by October and November the icy grip of the weather was closing in once more. The North Sea and the English Channel were swept by fierce storms, one of which was responsible for driving the Dutch invasion fleet back into port after its first sailing. On 18 November John Evelyn recorded a heavy frost and on the following day there were reports of snow in Oxford and 'a great drift' near Coggleshall in Essex. Accompanying the king from London to the concentration on Salisbury Plain, the Earl of Ailesbury was thoroughly miserable as the cavalcade ploughed through roads deep in mud, and the wet and the cold gave some real point to the endless bickering between the gentlemen of the bedchamber about whose turn it was to ride in the royal carriage. No sooner had the snow stopped than three nights of squalls battered the south of England between 22 and 24 November, bringing with them fears for the safety of the king's ships in the Channel.[2] This was not the weather for serious military campaigning: there was no forage for horses, roads and tracks were practically impassable, and soldiers were forced to camp in leaky tents in near-freezing temperatures. By the gentlemanly standards of the late seventeenth century, even to attempt warfare in such circumstances was verging upon the ridiculous, and neither the Dutch nor the English armies were able to operate at their full potential. These savage conditions probably favoured the invaders, who were more accustomed to campaigning in the field than their enemies, but the advantage was marginal. Both sides struggled in the teeth of the early winter.

This foul weather must be borne in mind when considering both the decisions and the events of the campaign of 1688. The strategy which James adopted in dispersing his troops to meet the Dutch invasion has been variously criticised but it is difficult to discover any one mistake that was sufficiently grave to have cost him his throne. During the operations on land following William's disembarkation at Torbay, James and some of his subordinates were guilty of errors of judgement, but these related more to those nebulous qualities of morale and confidence than to strictly tactical matters. Given the limitations of his intelligence of the Dutch intentions and the advanced season of the year, James's martial policies appear competent if not inspired. In the first place, he had very imprecise information about William's invasion plans: he did not know how many men would be sailing for England and he was most certainly ignorant of where they intended to come ashore. Contradictory reports of the Dutch plans flooded into England during September and October, leaving many Englishmen as confused as their king.

We cannot tell what to think of the invasion. The king said he thought the Prince of Orange would go on board on Monday next, letters last night say on Thursday or Friday. The merchants' letters are wholly silent and all news is from an envoy in Holland, only all agree in great preparations.[3]

One William Leck landed at Tynemouth on 16 October, having left the United Provinces two days before, and the Duke of Newcastle forwarded his information to Westminster. Some of it was surprisingly accurate but much was highly misleading. The Dutch fleet, Leck maintained, consisted of 450 transports guarded by eighty warships, and these were to convey between thirty and forty thousand soldiers. No horses were to be brought over, although the vessels carried stores of 'horse furniture', and the party was to be landed on the Holderness coast of Yorkshire above Spurn Head. Individuals received snippets of news from relatives and contacts across the North Sea but virtually none of this material reached the king and his ministers. Sir William Blakeston was warned by one Thomas Moores at The Hague to 'take care' of himself, 'for you will certainly find an invasion and rupture in England within fifteen days' time for they will set out to sail and go to sea this next week in order to invade England'.[4] Basing his opinion on letters from Holland, Samuel Pepys informed Lord Dartmouth on 27 October 1688 that the Dutch would attempt to land 'somewhere in Essex' but, on the very same day, he was forced to revise his judgement when a new packet of dispatches indicated that Burlington

Bay was the most likely landfall of the invading armada. If the wind was from the south, then the Dutch would sail for the north of England; if it was from the north or the north-east, then they would head for the West Country. This intelligence was more helpful than the report on 7 October which had stated that William was bound to land in the area round Ramsgate and Margate, 'where they have already magazines of provisions', but it was still sufficiently indefinite as to be useless in planning the English military reaction.[5] The author of most of this inconsistent and erroneous information was Ignatius White, Marquis d'Albeville, an ageing adventurer whom James had elevated to be his envoy at The Hague. D'Albeville suffered from the dual disadvantages of being despised by the Dutch government and by his foreign diplomatic colleagues in The Hague, and he consequently found it impossible to penetrate the official camouflage thrown up by the Dutch to cover the aims and extent of their military preparations.[6] To add to his embarrassment, William's soldiers and sailors spread wild stories about destinations in Kent, Sole Bay, Essex, and even Scotland, rumours which d'Albeville religiously reported to James without any really critical caveats. Lord Dartmouth was properly suspicious of the contents of these *communiqúes*:

I cannot from any of [the] Marquis d'Albeville's advices make any judgement as to what part of our isle they will make their descent as believing . . . [that] the Prince would not trust the knowledge of a secret of that importance to his designs to above two or three of his private council.[7]

Upon information of this nature the drafting of a definite English strategy was impossible. However, unless the royal troops were to be expected to hurry about England in forced marches during the depths of winter, some anticipation had to be made of William's probable intentions. It was in fact impracticable to move troops at speed. In peacetime in England foot soldiers could only manage an average of eight miles per day during routine marches, and this speed was unlikely to improve over roads deep in mud and snow.[8] This genteel pace was typical of the age; continental armies on campaign regarded a daily journey of ten miles as an exceptional effort and they were generally accustomed to travelling half that distance. The physical state of the roads, the season of the year, and the absence of reliable intelligence meant that James was unable to respond rapidly to William's invasion. He had to make his dispositions prior to the landing and hope that he had guessed correctly. Naturally, this necessarily negative approach resulted in a strategy of compromise which is easy to criticise after the event, but it is hard to see how James could have acted differently during that crisis. There was considerable confusion among the English planners. According to the reports from the United Provinces, William's soldiers might set foot in England anywhere from the Scottish border to Land's End. This did at least rule the whole of the west coast out of contention, but even then the major posts on that side of England – Chester and Carlisle – still had to be provided with sizeable garrisons. Chester was the main port through which supplies and reinforcements could be received from Ireland, whilst Carlisle guarded the vital road into Scotland. All the fortresses in England had to be maintained. Berwick, Hull, and York were responsible for protecting the northern counties and Landguard Fort, Sheerness, Tilbury, Gravesend, and the Medway towns covered the estuary of the Thames and London and ensured that the Dutch could not repeat their tactics of 1667. The south coast was controlled by Dover, the Isle of Wight, Portsmouth, and Plymouth. As well as having to maintain all these regular stations at a reasonable level, James was worried about London. Throughout the seventeenth century, and particularly during his own lifetime, London had been closely associated with all movements against the monarchy: the Civil Wars and their aftermath, the business of Exclusion, and Monmouth's Rebellion. Given suitable encouragement from William, there was every possibility that the capital would erupt once the Dutch had landed and form a severe threat to the rear of the royal field army. London contained a considerable number of catholic chapels and religious institutions which would require close protection, and the presence of the queen and the sacred person of the little Prince of Wales at Whitehall also made it imperative for James to leave a good force of soldiers in and around the twin cities.

James's plan was to man the garrisons, secure London, and then concentrate the remainder of his forces into a mobile field army which would assemble within a twenty-five-mile radius of London, ready to respond in the direction of William's invasion. This rearward concentration around London was the only practical decision which could have been taken. The army would be close to all the major roads to the south, the west, and the north, and it was a densely populated region offering plentiful billets for the troops. There was also no need for James to take up a forward concentration. When William landed he would need time to organise his troops, secure a bridgehead, and collect supplies, a period which James would be able to use to advance from London and attack the invaders before they were well balanced. The severe and unpredictable weather meant that William would have to land in a well sheltered harbour which was remote from one of the principal royal fortresses; amphibious operations were risky enough without attempting to land on an open coast in winter with the threat of opposition on the shore. The estuaries of the Wear or the Tees were possibilities, but the indented coast of south-west England presented more choice and a greater protection from northerly and easterly winds. It is noticeable that although James did not know of William's selected spot his northern garrisons were substantially weaker than those around the mouth of the Thames and the Channel coast. Another factor in James's favour was the physical condition of the troops. In quarters around London, the royal soldiers would be well rested, whilst the Dutchmen would probably be jaded and seasick after being cramped on board transport for four or five days. Men in such a weakened condition would need some time ashore in order to regain their fitness, time which could be well used by James and his army to approach the bridgehead 'by easy marches'. More important than the state of the men was the state of the horses. James knew that many had been lost during the first, abortive voyage, whilst those that did survive the journey to England would need a considerable time ashore in order to become acclimatised. William's army would require between a week and a fortnight at a secure base before commencing any offensive operations. Such an interval would give James ample time to march his fresh forces into an appropriate position.

James could have adopted alternative strategies. Lord Delamere, a man not noted for cool or detached thought, suggested that once James knew that the landing would occur in either the north or the south-west then he ought to have divided his army into two corps and sent one into each region. When William landed there would have been a force at hand to throw him back into the sea before he could establish a bridgehead. This might have proved efficacious, especially in view of the poor physical condition of William's soldiers after their voyage, but the unnecessary division of forces is always an unsound military principle and there would have been an acute danger of either corps being defeated in detail whilst its support was at the other end of the country. Once William had declared his hand and come ashore in the south-west, the tactics which had proved successful against Monmouth in 1685 offered themselves. A rapid movement to the west could have confined William to the south-western peninsula, prevented support from coming into him, and restricted his field of manoeuvre. However, forced marches were impossible in the appalling weather and such a tactic would have negated one of James's principal military assets, his heavy superiority in cavalry. If this arm was to be used to maximum effect then a wide, open battlefield was required, hence the obvious choice of Salisbury Plain. Another uncertainty concerned William's objective once he had landed. There was every likelihood that London would constitute the prime target, but he could easily have moved on Bristol and then marched north to link up with possible risings in Cheshire or Yorkshire. Would there be just one landing? William might cover his main effort by a series of raids and feint attacks, possibly on Portsmouth. In the face of all these imponderables and in receipt of intelligence which clouded rather than clarified, a rearward concentration about London was the best first position for the royal army. After the landing at Torbay, a forward assembly on Salisbury Plain offered a safe, flexible stance, a central pivot from which William's manoeuvres could be observed and countered. A blocking line farther to the west would have been a more dramatic and decisive strategy but it could have been fatal to the king. James's strategy may have been conservative but it was probably the safest and most flexible that could have been devised.[9]

William's reasons for invading England in 1688 were very clear even if the location of his first step on English soil was less obvious.

> The Princes's expedition is looked upon as a means to bring England to a better correspondence as likewise the forces of that crown to be employed against France and that by sea from whence the very heart of the French power may be reached. 'And so, consequently, at the same time may be procured such a considerable diversion to the progress of the French arms in the Empire as that it may be sufficiently unburdened to them.[10]

In case the conspiracy within James's army failed to function, William needed to take a sufficient and loyal force of soldiers with him to England. A sizeable corps was also essential if he was to retain his freedom of political manoeuvre and not have to rely on the local partisans who might be raised by Danby and other potential rebels. This earnest wish to be beholden to no English politician or local satrap also dictated the area of England in which William chose to come ashore. If he had made a landfall on the east coast to the north of the Humber it would have been impossible to avoid linking up with Danby at York and with Devonshire at Nottingham, and this would have involved William in obligations to individual politicians that he was anxious to avoid. By invading in the West Country, he was able virtually to ignore the achievements of the northern conspirators and conduct his own campaign and his own negotiations with James. Apart from this basic need for independence, there were other factors which made the west of England a more likely venue than the north. It was unfortunate for the Prince of Orange that the only breathing space that Louis XIV allowed him for the invasion of England fell in the autumn and early winter of 1688, a time when all sensible navies had laid up their ships for the season and all good armies had abandoned serious operations and departed into winter quarters. In the conditions that were known to exist in the North Sea and the English Channel in October and November, it was imperative for the Dutch to disembark in a sheltered harbour in order to protect the vessels and to permit the men, horses, and stores to be put ashore in relative security. The north of England failed to meet any of these requirements. The insistence upon Burlington Bay which emanated from D'Avaux and d'Albeville was almost certainly the fruit of false information put about by the Dutch and the result of Danby's wishful thinking. Devon, Cornwall, and Somerset were known to be ill-disposed towards James on grounds of religion and because of the judicial barbarities which had followed in the wake of Monmouth's Rebellion. The few reports of military intelligence from agents in England to William that have survived suggest that he was very interested in the state of the royal fortifications along the south coast of England, particularly at Plymouth and Pendennis.[11] William wanted to land as far away from the royal field army and the main garrisons as possible, as his soldiers would need rest after the voyage and the conspirators in James's army would require time to organise and begin their vital work.[12] Burlington Bay was too close to the garrisons at York, Hull and Scarborough, but in the south-west the only fortification of note was at Plymouth, a station that was remote and relatively easy to isolate. Moreover, the march from the south-west towards London was unhindered by adverse river lines, a major consideration in a winter campaign. English letters strongly advised William to make his attempt in the West Country and it seems probable that this was always his intention, weather permitting.[13]

Estimates of the size of William's expeditionary force vary between 10,692 and 14,352 private soldiers and non-commissioned officers. The higher figure is derived from a rather unreliable source, whereas the lower one is taken from a list printed on 6 November. 'Le Journal du Voyage d'Angleterre' reaches a happy compromise and states that the invasion force consisted of 11,212 soldiers. All three documents agree on the number of cavalry being 3,660 but it is over the matter of the infantry that the variance occurs. A clue to the cause of this confusion is contained in a note on the Prince of Orange's army which says that there were initially supposed to be 14,352 foot and 3,660 horse but that the infantry companies were not completed in time and, as a consequence, there were no more than 12,000 foot soldiers with the expeditionary force.[14] The historian can do no better than suggest that William's army numbered between 14,000 and 15,000 fighting men. If there is some doubt over the exact size of the invasion force there is more certainty about its composition. Three thousand of the infantry were English, Irish, and Scots from the Anglo-Dutch Brigade and there were more exiles from Great Britain gathered into loose regiments under Sir John Guise, Sir Rowland Gwynn, Sir Richard Buckley, Sir Robert Peyton, Lord Coot, Lord Mordaunt, and the Earl of Macclesfield. There were contingents from Sweden, Brandenburg, 300 soldiers from Switzerland, 200 from Finland, and even 200 'blacks brought from the plantations of the Netherlands in America'.[15] A large portion of the army was composed of French Huguenots who had fled from France both before and after the revocation of the Edict of Nantes. Some fifty-four officers in the Blue Guards were Huguenot and another thirty-four held commissions in the Dutch Life Guards, thus providing William with excellent propaganda, enabling him to invade England with the help of these obvious victims of catholic absolutism.[16] Although the invading army was a typically cosmopolitan mercenary force of the late seventeenth century, William controlled it with a very firm discipline; James's troops were known to be ill-behaved and above the law, so it was vital for the 'deliverers' to make every effort to appear with impeccable manners. Special care was taken to pay for all food and quarters and to make sure that civilians were not abused, horses were bought at their proper market value, and no goods or carts were requisitioned without adequate recompense. On 30 November two soldiers were hanged for stealing a chicken, and many contemporaries remarked upon the extraordinarily good discipline of the Dutch army. The only blemish on their character came when some of the soldiers took an indirect vegeance upon James by killing hundreds of the royal deer in Windsor Great Park, but this was soon stopped by William's personal intervention, presumably wishing to defend his own future possessions.[17]

It was a professional and well trained army but some of William's propagandists made it out to be a force of supermen. 'Some of them were, I am confident, six foot and a quarter, if not six foot and a half, in height . . . all picked men and many of them personally present at the siege of Buda.' This was in marked contrast to the short, deformed Irish soldiers and corrupt papists who were scattered throughout the royal regiments. The same account continued by saying that William possessed a train of artillery of over two hundred pieces as well as a set of pontoons for building bridges, although 'the badness of the roads' conveniently prevented them from marching east from Exeter.[18] Whether this exaggerated rubbish produced any weakening of either civilian or military morale in England it is impossible to say, but arriving with an army full of English exiles and Huguenot refugees which was led on to the shores of England by Hugh Mackay and the six regiments of the Anglo-Dutch Brigade was a master-stroke of Williamite propaganda. Seasick and tired from two winter voyages, the Dutch soldiers were forced to spend two nights in the open in pouring rain until they could reach Exeter and take up quarters in that city and the surrounding villages. The train of twenty-one cannon and various supplies were brought up to Exeter by small boats from the Topsham road, where the fleet's transports unloaded their holds. Gradually William rested his troops and prepared for the long and arduous trek to London. The army's most pressing need was for horses. Many had been lost during the first sailing and there had not been time to fully replenish the stock before the final voyage. Dutch foragers were reported as far afield as Bridgewater on 22 November, buying up all the horses and cattle they could find.[19] Waggons and carts were also vital, as much of the army's future food supplies would have to be provided from the fleet and the magazines around Exeter – as William advanced towards the east and James's army retired, it was anticipated that the royal troops would consume or destroy most of the available fodder and victuals, leaving little for their foes. Moreover, it was a lean season of the sear. As William prepared his army, waited for news that Plymouth was in safe hands, and looked for definite signs that the conspirators in the English army were starting their work, James completed his preparations to meet his nephew in battle on Salisbury Plain.

One sees now what the subject [was] of the voyages the Prince of Orange and Bentinck have made to several protestant princes and without their help he could never have undertaken this invasion . . . I confess it was a very long time before I could believe that my nephew and son-in-law could be capable of so very ill an undertaking and so began too late to provide against it but if it pleases God that the wind do but continue as it is a few days longer I hope to be in a good condition to receive him.[20]

As early as 7 June 1688 Louis XIV had warned James through the medium of Paul Barrillon to be on his guard against the intentions of the Dutch, and he tentatively offered sixteen French men-of-war to strengthen the English fleet. A week later James refused any assistance from the French on the grounds that he could not visualise a Dutch attack taking place during that year. Early in August, Louis told Barrillon to inform James of the exact state of affairs in the United Provinces and to caution him about relying upon the vague and inaccurate dispatches of d'Albeville. Finally, between 23 and 26 August, Barrillon was able to report to his master that James and Sunderland were beginning to realise the gravity of their position and were ordering appropriate military and naval measures to be put in hand. Even then, according to the French ambassador, James wavered in his belief that William would dare to attempt such a hazardous operation and found it almost impossible to comprehend the magnitude of disloyalty to his own uncle and father-in-law that such an action would entail.[21] James has been accused of making too few martial preparations too late, a tardiness that cost him his three thrones. Most of this adverse criticism is unreasonable. He was indeed slow to appreciate the danger from the Netherlands but, as a man with considerable military and naval experience of conventional warfare, he simply did not believe that William would be physically or strategically able to launch an offensive operation within the campaigning season of 1688. That William might invade during the winter does not seem to have entered into James's calculations. In the first place, James thought himself safe behind the shield of his navy, and secondly, the increasing tension in western European politics and the short time available between June and the end of the recognised campaigning season precluded a Dutch assault. James was not helped by his own high notions of duty within the family but he was more seriously misled by applying rational military principles to his interpretation of his nephew's probable strategy. At this distance from the event it is difficult to understand fully the impetuosity and unorthodoxy of William's plans. Winter campaigns were not unknown in the seventeenth century – Turenne, James's military mentor, had fought a highly successful battle at Turckheim on 4 January 1675 after a march which had begun in the previous December – but to execute an amphibious operation was altogether different. William invaded a well defended island in winter, leaving his homeland vulnerable to a heavy attack by the French. It is not surprising that James did not take William's reported aims seriously, for the Dutchman did not enjoy a reputation as an adventurous and exciting general or as a gambler. During the Franco-Dutch war from 1672 to 1678 William had been regarded as a very average commander, uninspired but with a rugged determination. It was this latter characteristic which upset his uncle's smug self-confidence. There would not, in James's mind, be much likelihood of an invasion until the spring of 1689 at the earliest, and then, given the deteriorating international situation in Europe, William would be tied down in the defence of the Spanish Netherlands and would have neither the time, the money, nor the troops to mount an invasion of England. With some justification, James thought himself safe from attack. As a result, his preparations to meet the threat were always less than thorough and were hampered by his basic disbelief in the reality of the build-up against him.

Military improvements in training, drill, and the education of officers and men had been constant throughout the reign. Attention was also given to the more important garrisons with the modernisation and enlarging of the fortifications at Hull and Portsmouth. The decision to fortify the landward side of Portsmouth was taken in July 1686, when the Board of Ordnance was instructed to begin work immediately 'according to the agreed models and costs'. This decision to improve the works at Portsmouth was thus not hurriedly reached after the discovery of Mary Beatrice's pregnancy in the late autumn of 1687 in order to give James and his family 'a secure bolt hole' from which they could make their escape to France in an emergency, as J. R. Western implies.[22] Similarly, the erection of a platform of fifty guns at Sheerness and the construction of some batteries along the Medway in April 1688 were not early responses to premonitions of a Dutch invasion but precautions against any naval conflagration that might have occurred over the dispute between Sweden and Denmark.[23] Another military movement in May 1688 can probably be similarly explained; a regiment of foot was stationed in Rochester and Chatham and additional soldiers were quartered in all the English forts and garrisons. After the fiasco of 1667 the Medway was a tender spot. Hints of any possible naval disturbance in the North Sea or the English Channel were sufficient to lead to a temporary reinforcement of Sheerness, Rochester, Chatham, and Upnor Castle.[24] On 29 May 1688 Sir Charles Littleton, the colonel of Prince George of Denmark's foot, was given the command of all the forces in Kent, which amounted to three full regiments of infantry, with specific orders to concentrate his soldiers upon the Medway towns if a 'foreign fleet' should sail into the estuary of the Thames. These plans were similar to those that had been devised in 1674 and seem to have constituted a standing reaction to any possible English involvement in a naval war.[25] The measures may have been indirectly aimed at the Dutch but only in a sense of a purely maritime war after the manner of the three Anglo-Dutch conflicts. There is no suggestion that the troop movements implied any knowledge or expectation of an invasion.

The precise purpose of the next bout of military preparations is difficult to assess. A report on 9 August announced that the English fleet was being hurriedly fitted out, with work continuing even on Sundays.[26] This frenzied activity was almost certainly intended to counter the Dutch naval build-up but as there were no accompanying preparations in the English army it seems likely that the message of a potential invading armada had still not registered with James and Sunderland. Serious military measures were put into effect on 23 and 24 August, and it must be from this time that James finally began to realise that the Dutch naval concentration was not intended to fight another naval war over trade. All officers and soldiers, lords lieutenant, deputy lieutenants, and governors of garrisons were ordered to report to their commands immediately and army officers were given the additional instruction to bring their troops and companies up to full strength. Another significant measure was the moving of soldiers from inland garrisons to stations on the sea coast. Reresby's soldiers were detailed to march to Hull, 'so that not so much as one company was to remain behind'. The governor protested against this short-sighted policy and was finally allowed to retain three companies at York, although the remainder, some five companies, set off to reinforce Hull. When Captain Charles Hatton received the order to repair to his command he doubted if it had much to do with a threatened Dutch invasion but thought it more likely 'to be a piece of Mr. Blathwayt's policy to get fees for licences to be absent for the rumour of the Dutch invasion is generally ridiculed'. Not until 6 October did Hatton become convinced that the military measures were in deadly earnest.[27] Until 22 August the marching orders issued by the secretary-at-war were routine arrangements for troops returning to their garrisons for the winter after their summer on Hounslow Heath. Suddenly, on 24 and 25 August, the tone of the orders altered dramatically and the army began to be disposed on a strategic basis. As the Scots Guards passed through York on their long march home from Hounslow they were halted at Hull and ordered to reinforce the garrison; on the approach of the 'Dutch fleet' the commander at Sheerness was instructed to alert all the other senior officers in Kent; the commander at Arundel was ordered to concentrate his troops forward at Portsmouth on the first sighting of the Dutch ships; Prince George of Denmark's foot was brought into the Tower Hamlets to keep a watch over the City.[28]

These steps illustrate the partial alarm of James and his ministers. Officers were ordered to their commands, troops were concentrated into coastal stations, and senior officers were placed on the alert, but no new forces were raised. On 20 September the English standing army numbered just over 21,000 men, a wholly inadequate force, as after the essential garrisons had been manned there would have been no more than 15,000 English soldiers left to form a field army. To correct this imbalance, on 21 and 22 September Blathwayt issued instructions for every troop and company in the English army to be increased by ten men and set about raising several new regiments of horse and foot. After this burst of energy the preparations to meet the invasion died away for a month. 'Frequent councils of war' may have been held at Windsor early in September but, apart from the strategic decision to assemble the forces 'about London' in the event of the anticipated invasion, no positive measures were taken.[29] Typical of the half-hearted preparations was the resolution to embark Lord Dartmouth's regiment of fusiliers on board the fleet at the Nore, a decision taken not from military necessity but because too many of the soldiers had deserted from their previous quarters in the Tower of London.[30] By the middle of the last week in September even James had to face the reality of his nephew's intentions; he accordingly ordered troops from Ireland to make all possible haste to sail to Chester or Liverpool, and on 27 September the English troops began to leave the smaller garrisons and outlying billets and concentrate into quarters within easy reach of London. All of the Scottish standing army was ordered to march into England, and the money thus saved by the Scottish Treasury was used to support the Scottish militia and 'other forces'.[31] James publicly acknowledged the danger from Holland in a proclamation of 28 September in which he called upon his subjects to assist him in opposing the Dutch, and on the same day the train of artillery, consisting of twenty-six cannon and four mortars, was ready to move from the Tower of London to Finchley Common, where it was to await further directions.[32] As the reports of rumour and hearsay reached the court from d'Albeville, James began to spread his forces over longer and longer stretches of the east and south coasts, in particular covering Portsmouth, Harwich, and Kent.[33]

Although loyal noblemen came forward to offer their services and their purses to the king, a great sense of uncertainty and confusion descended upon the country. 'We have so many soldiers about us,' wrote Sir John Chicheley, 'that none knows what may happen. All people dispose both of money and plate for fear of the worst.'[34] The young Duke of Ormonde, deep in the conspiracy against James, took no chances.

> Being uncertain when I shall go to Kingston Hall and having several writings in my closet there relating to my estate, lest if any accident of fire or otherwise might happen I send you the key of the closet and I desire you will do me the favour to get the writings and papers in the manner they are tied up and placed in boxes without mixture because they are sorted and in order ready to be found and that you will remove them to some place where you judge they will be safe.[35]

Magistrates and officers were directed to take care that all horses and cattle 'fit for draught' were driven at least twenty miles inland from the place where the Dutch might come ashore, whilst James himself inspected the ground about Blackheath, which he clearly intended to employ as the site of an army camp if he was forced back upon London.[36] By 2 October the defences of the Medway were well advanced and Landguard Fort, the protector of the rivers Stour and Orwell and of the entrance to Harwich harbour, was strengthened by an additional 100 men.[37] As the ordnance stores were ransacked to find arms for the new regiments the ramshackle nature of many of the kingdom's fixed defences began to be revealed. The mutually supporting posts of Tynemouth and Clifford's Fort which governed the mouth of the Tyne were reported to be in a very sad condition: guns were dismounted, Tynemouth Castle was falling down about the heads of the garrison, and the new position at Clifford's Fort had been badly designed and had been built in the wrong place. Fether south, in York, matters were little better. The garrison, reported Sir John Reresby, had virtually no powder or ammunition, 'only some very few balls and some match which is most of it decayed'. It was a blessing that William had no intention of landing so far north.[38] During the first fortnight of October the Irish soldiers began to arrive at Chester and were immediately dispatched south on the road to London.[39] Between 2 and 10 October the militia of Norfolk was put into readiness 'to hinder evil disposed persons from joining with the enemy' in the event of an invasion and up to 6 November this county always had one troop of militia horse mustered and on duty.[40]

The Scottish army reached York on 15 October and after a short rest departed for London four days later to swell the concentration in the Home Counties.[41] James was particularly worried lest William should land several small parties at various points on the east and south coasts to spread alarm and confusion. One method of achieving this end would have been for the Dutch to have lighted the beacons, and James must have had this in mind when he ordered Sir John Lanier, commanding a cavalry brigade in East Anglia, not to fire the beacons if he should sight the Dutch fleet.[42] The king held frequent meetings with his senior officers at the house of Major-General Robert Werden to discuss 'what was necessary to be done', and one of the fruits of these consultations was the revision of the Articles of War.[43] It is tempting to suppose that at one of these conferences the officers who were privy to the conspiracy argued strongly against any plan of dividing the field army into two corps, one to cover the north of England and the other the south coast. The conspiracy would have been emasculated by such a decision, as it could only have operated effectively if the army was grouped into one composite formation. Special emphasis was placed upon the condition and preparedness of Hull, the pivotal point of the east coast defences. One man from every family in the town and from the neighbouring villages was conscripted to work on the fortifications for a minimum period of ten days beginning on 20 October, a mobilisation so efficacious that within one week the governor, Lord Langdale, was able to assure James that Hull was ready to face the Dutch and could withstand a siege. The garrison consisted of two full infantry regiments reinforced by some units of the East Riding militia, sufficient stores had been accumulated, the low-lying land to the west and north had been inundated for a distance of two miles, and all the trees and hedges beyond the glacis had been cut down.[44] In the crucial breathing space between William's first and second sailings James ordered Sir John Lanier to Ipswich to cover Landguard Fort with three cavalry regiments, whilst a further three horse formations rode up to Colchester in support. Sir John was given definite instructions: if William landed in the west he was to retire on London but if the invasion materialised in the north then he was to march to Newark.[45] These orders clearly indicate a total ignorance of William's plans, and as late as 1 November it appears that James was still bemused. On that day the king himself was at Colchester reviewing Lanier's supporting brigade whilst a regiment of foot began to march from London up the Great North Road and Blathwayt instructed the Duke of Newcastle to withdraw his command into Berwick if William should land anywhere to the north of the Humber.[46] The sum total of these manoeuvres suggests that, at the last minute, James was actually thinking of a Dutch landing somewhere on the Lincolnshire or Yorkshire coast.

From 4 November express letters poured into James's hands, giving news of the course of the Dutch fleet and finally announcing the landing at Torbay on the fifth. Immediately, in accordance with the plans which had been finalised at a meeting of general officers on 28 October, Lanier's six cavalry regiments, the main strength of the English mounted arm, marched through London to the west, first heading for Salisbury Plain and then farther towards William in order to throw a defensive screen between the Dutch and the assembling royal army. Lanier was entrusted with the vital task of discerning William's precise strength, the location of his operational base, and the probable route of his advance. As Lanier and Sir John Fenwick hurried towards Warminster and Marlborough, messengers rode post-haste to summon the troops from the north of England back towards the rendezvous on Salisbury Plain. The basic plan was to leave the newly raised forces to police London and man the garrisons, thus freeing the Irish, Scottish, and veteran English troops to form the field army to oppose William directly.[47] To begin with, on 5 November, James was convinced that the Dutch fleet was sailing for Portsmouth and he accordingly ordered a battalion of the First Foot Guards to travel in carts to the threatened port 'so as to make the greater speed ... and to take no more rest than is absolutely necessary'.[48] Once Admiral Herbert had passed Portsmouth, the bulk of the garrison was released for service with the field army. As Lanier led his cavalry screen westwards, the Earl of Feversham, the prosaic commander of the royal army, lumbered up to Salisbury with the bulk of the infantry, heavily encumbered with the train of artillery and a long baggage column. By 15 November he had reached Salisbury with the lead elements but many of his troops straggled down the London road, struggling through ice and mud. The worst of the stragglers were the Irish and Scottish regiments, which were already tired from their long marches to reach the assembly areas about London. With these soldiers in poor physical condition, it is doubtful if all the royal field army ever reached Salisbury; some formations were still marching to the west when the order to retreat was given, and this marching and counter-marching must have been damaging to the troops' morale. Whilst his forces gradually gathered around Salisbury, James gave some brief attention to Scotland. Totally denuded of regular troops and with just the militia to enforce order, serious anti-catholic or pro-Williamite disturbances north of the border were a distinct possibility. True to his belief that the entire issue of 1688 depended upon the outcome of a military confrontation between two opposing armies, James spared no soldiers to guard his position in Scotland during the course of the campaign in England and he was forced into the curious expedient of issuing a proclamation from Edinburgh which naively requested 'no one to believe' the reports that the Prince of Orange had invaded England.[49]

Already, before Feversham had arrived at Salisbury, there had been a number of desertions from the royal army, sufficient for James to order his army commander to bring the advance cavalry closer to the main body, thereby abandoning the few contacts that had been made with the invaders.[50] The conspiracy had begun its operations from the moment the cavalry vanguard had come within range of William's forces, and on the night of 13 November Lord Cornbury and Thomas Langston had defected with some of their officers and troopers. Either by accident or by design many of the principal conspirators served with the horse regiments which formed the cavalry screen: Sir John Lanier, Sir Francis Compton, Hatton Compton, Lord Cornbury, and Thomas Langston. James left London on 17 November and arrived in Salisbury two days later, a very rapid journey in the circumstances. To guard the capital in his absence he had left two regiments of foot, a force which he could well afford, given his huge superiority in numbers. Between 4,000 and 5,000 of the royal army were tied down in garrison duty and 4,400 of the newly raised troops had not completed their training, yet James was still able to call upon the services of 24,000 English soldiers to meet him at Salisbury, with 2,964 Scottish troops and 2,820 Irishmen in addition. Altogether, between 29,000 and 30,000 soldiers were ordered to Salisbury Plain, giving James an advantage over his nephew of two to one. James also enjoyed the luxury of a further 8,000 – 9,000 men who could be recalled from garrison or brought into action as they became fully trained. William, on the other hand, possessed no reserve of troops apart from the few recruits whom he managed to gather from the western counties.

At Salisbury, James found everything in confusion. The desertions that had occurred had already gravely affected the operational capacity of the army. The very real fear of further defections had caused Lanier's cavalry to be ordered back from its advanced positions, and this had immediately deprived the army of all accurate knowledge of the Dutch movements and intentions. Without definite intelligence, Feversham was forced to direct his troops by intuition and guesswork. Although he was Turenne's nephew by blood, Feversham was not related to him in either spirit or ability. Instead of trying to reconnoitre the Dutch cantonments with small parties of horse which would have provided some information even if a few troopers had ridden into the Dutch lines, he was overcome by uncertainty and indecision and did nothing at all. No deserters appeared from William's camp to offer news, and the 'common people' seemed to favour the invaders rather than the cause of the king. It was an inauspicious start to the campaign to save the kingdom.[51]

Charles Burrington, a cornet in George Holman's recently raised regiment of horse, was the first defector from the army to reach William at Exeter. His arrival on 12 November was the prelude to a steady trickle of desertions which gradually expanded into a regular stream. It is most unreasonable to criticise the army conspirators for being tardy in fulfilling their obligations to William. No moves were possible until his precise landfall was known, and it was not until the Dutch had formed a permanent base at Exeter that large-scale desertions became practicable. The conspirators had also to be reasonably close to the Dutch forces. When the orders to march on Salisbury were issued, many of the plotters were with Lanier's cavalry force in East Anglia, Percy Kirke's regiment was in London, and most of the others were quartered in the Home Counties. Lanier's screen was preparing to move to the west of Salisbury by 11 November and, almost immediately, the desertions which had been organised by the Treason Club, the 'Tangerines', and the Association of Protestant Officers began. Lord Colchester, with some of his Life Guards, Thomas Wharton, William Jephson, Charles Godfrey, Sir Scrope Howe, and Captain Henry Wharton of the Earl of Lichfield's foot made their way through the ill-formed royal lines and rode into Exeter on 13 November. This group, composed mainly of members of the Treason Club, had got under way very soon after news of the successful landing had reached them, for they were reported to have passed through Oxford on 8 November. Three days later the Earl of Abingdon was seen leaving Oxford on his way to the west. Bearing in mind the distances that had to be covered, the state of the roads, the omnipresence of the royal troops, and the weather, the active conspirators in the army put their plans into operation almost as soon as the invasion had taken place. The conspiracy seems to have been well prepared and resolute.[52] Lieutenant John Livesey of the Royal Fusiliers was arrested on 11 November on suspicion of plotting to desert, and on that same day Lord Lovelace with seventy 'well appointed men' ran into some Gloucestershire militia near Cirencester and was apprehended after a short, sharp engagement. Two days later the Earls of Shrewsbury and Wiltshire joined the Prince of Orange at Exeter.[53]

These early defections promised well for the total success of the aims of the conspirators but their principal purpose was to persuade others to follow them and thoroughly ruin James's army. It was to be expected that the plotters themselves would desert but, as yet, there was little sign that they were going to fulfil their promises to undermine the bulk of the army. On either 9 or 10 November the first of the major desertions initiated by the Association of Protestant Officers occurred. Lord Cornbury, commanding the Royal Dragoons, Thomas Langston with the Duke of St. Albans' horse, and Sir Francis Compton's Royal Horse Guards set out from Salisbury on an expedition to 'beat up' some of the advanced Dutch quarters around Honiton. This corps of 1,150 cavalrymen did not suspect that they were being deceived by their commanders, as it was their function to make contact with the enemy outposts and to reconnoitre in force. They rode quickly through Blandford and Dorchester but by the time the leaders clattered into Axminster the very speed of the march had broken the cohesion of the force and the three regiments had become separated from each other by some miles. Both the unexplained haste and the failure of Cornbury to observe routine precautions in the presence of the enemy aroused the suspicions of some of his officers. When he ordered out a division of sixty troopers to fall upon the Dutchmen in Honiton, his catholic major, Robert Clifford, demanded to see his orders. At this challenge Cornbury panicked, and he galloped into William's lines, accompanied by a small number of troopers, whilst the remainder of the regiment followed Clifford back towards Salisbury. Langston was more successful in retaining the confidence of his officers and men, and took the whole of his regiment into the Dutch cantonment. The Royal Horse Guards were at the rear of the straggling column and their lieutenant-colonel, Sir Francis Compton, lost his nerve when he was threatened by his major, William Littleton, and tamely led his regiment back to Salisbury.

Although the greatest part of two regiments returned to the royal army and many of Langston's men who found themselves virtually prisoners-of-war in the Dutch camp managed later to escape, the operation had been well planned and conceived. Colonel Thomas Talmash's regiment of the Anglo-Dutch Brigade had been ordered forward to Honiton to receive the deserters, and billets in neighbouring villages had been especially reserved for the incoming soldiers. The trouble with the design was that the three commanding officers had either been unable, or had not dared to try, to convert a majority of their colleagues and their men to the Orange cause. Some officers did desert with Cornbury and Langston – Anthony Heyford and Hatton Compton – but in all three cases the major—arguably the most important officer in a seventeenth century regiment — remained loyal to James and succeeded in returning his charges to the field army. The conspiracy, based as it was upon the self-interest of a small number of officers, was not strong enough to overcome the attachment of the majority of officers and soldiers to their sovereign.

The confusion of the night and Sir Francis Compton's want of head or heart, together with the vigour of some popish officers among them, put all in so much disorder that the greater part, after they had marched above sixty miles to come and join us, wheeled about.[54]

According to a Dutch report the advantage to the invaders from this mass defection amounted to Cornbury, with a number of his officers and 100 troopers, Langston's entire command, and Cornet Hatton Compton and a mere thirty troopers from the Royal Horse Guards. From William's point of view this was a poor return, for although the principal objective of the conspiracy was to demoralise James's army he undoubtedly hoped to gain a considerable number of deserters as recruits for his own outnumbered forces. The quarters which Bentinck had reserved for the three defecting regiments indicate that he was expecting the entire corps to come over: six villages were selected to house the 1,150 soldiers complete with their officers. As a small compensation, the arrival at Honiton of these few deserters coincided with Lieutenant-Colonel John Beaumont's defection to William at Exeter.[55]

The number of officers and men who actually defected may have been disappointingly small but their effect upon the morale of James and on the spirit of his army was out of all proportion. For some time, until Compton's and Cornbury's soldiers began to meander into Salisbury, it looked as though an entire brigade of élite cavalry had crossed the lines, and the real scale of the desertions was not apparent until after the campaign had ended. To an extent, Cornbury's expedition broke the ice for the more timid and cautious conspirators, and the number of desertions substantially increased after 10 November. Cornet Henry Littleton of Richard Hamilton's horse, the son of Sir Charles Littleton, ran from his colours on 15 November, and five days later three troops from Sir John Lanier's regiment of cavalry and the independent company of John Sibley were reported to be 'missing'. The news of these early defections reached James when he was still at Whitehall and put him 'into great disorder'. The only solution seemed to be for him to travel to Salisbury 'as the best means of restraining the army from deserting'. Mentally unprepared for the Dutch invasion, uncertain of his own policies, and surrounded by rumours of desertions in his cherished army, James would have been better employed at Whitehall, for when he reached Salisbury on 19 November his discouragement must have increased substantially. Several officers, both senior and junior, had defected, three crack cavalry regiments had crossed the lines, and Wiliam had been granted a fortnight in which to prepare his soldiers and establish himself at Exeter. Feversham did not know where William's forces were located, whether the main body was still at Exeter or marching to the east, or what road they were using, and he was unable to discover such vital information because he was afraid to order out scouting parties in case they rode straight into the Dutch camp. Cornbury, Langston, and Compton might have achieved little in the numbers that they took with them but their achievement, when added to the fog of war, was immense. After their desertion the camp was in a turmoil, with 'each man suspecting his neighbour', rendering the army useless.[56] A bold and resolute commander might, even then, have put some spirit and heart back into the soldiers by playing upon the national hatred of the Dutch and the humiliation of being invaded, but James was wracked by nosebleeds and seemed thoroughly depressed and deflated. The invasion had occurred after he had convinced himself of the contrary; the army upon which he had utterly relied had let him down; and the loyalty of his subjects could not be regained even by the flood of concessions and reversals of domestic policy. James was beaten.

The council of war on 23 November which persuaded him to retreat from Salisbury towards London was really a formality. With the army in such a state, any thought of standing up to the Dutch had disappeared, which, for James, meant the collapse of the last remaining pillar of his reign. A withdrawal on London could not improve the morale of his soldiers — quite the reverse in fact — but it might have hindered William's advance. On his arrival at Salisbury James was full of positive plans to advance rapidly to the west to confine William to the south-western peninsula but the overall gloom of the camp and the disappearance of Cornbury's force destroyed the development of this decisive approach. The arguments and the strategy which were proposed by the council of war were illogical and negative. By falling back towards London the royal army would indeed place the line of the Thames between itself and its pursuers but unless every effort was made to hold that river line the whole exercise was pointless. No such suggestions appear to have been made. It was agreed that Feversham would remain at Reading with the main force of the cavalry to eat up the available forage and delay the Dutch advance, but what then? If there was to be no decisive battle for the line of the Thames about Reading and Maidenhead then James's forces would be pushed back into a small circle around London, and William, with the assistance of the risings in York, Nottingham, and Cheshire, would be in almost total control of England and Wales. The royal army would have no room for manoeuvre and could easily be blockaded by the Dutch army and the Dutch fleet. In effect, once James had decided not to attack William, thereby assuming the strategic initiative, but to retreat on London instead, the campaign was over as a military entity. James could not possibly win, although he might have staved off defeat long enough to force William to negotiate. That William was in a hurry to conquer England and then return to the war in Europe was well known. Throughout the campaign the Prince of Orange had half expected Marshall d'Humières's army to swing north from Cologne and attack the United Provinces through Maestricht. There were reports in England that the French had advanced as far as Boisleduc by 1 December and were busy burning villages in that region, clear indications that a serious French assault would fall on the Spanish Netherlands in the spring of 1689. After the sad retreat from Salisbury this was James's one remaining hope – to play for time and hope that the winter, his own delaying tactics, and French military pressure would force William to come to a negotiated settlement. Even this negative strategy of hope required patience and resolution in its execution but James, under constant stress and seemingly suffering from some sort of nervous breakdown, was not in a fit state to outmanoeuvre a politician of the calibre of William of Orange.[57] Whilst James ordered Lord Dover, the governor of Portsmouth, to stock his garrison with provisions ready for a sustained siege, the flow of defections from the army increased as it straggled eastwards from Salisbury Plain.[58]

Percy Kirke commanded a combined brigade of infantry and cavalry which was stationed at Warminster, and when he was ordered to retreat towards Devizes he made some 'frivolous excuses' and refused to obey. As well as his own regiment of foot, Kirke's formation included the regiment of his co-conspirator, Charles Trelawney, and a division of the Third Troop of the Life Guard under Lieutenant-Colonel Edmund Maine, another hardened professional who had fought in Portugal and France. Clearly, Kirke and Trelawney were expected by the Dutch to defect with their officers and men, as William sent 800 dragoons and 400 cavalry towards Warminster to assist them in case of difficulty. For once, James reacted with speed and determination. As soon as he refused to comply with his instructions, Kirke was arrested and sent to Andover. Unfortunately the case was dealt with by the feeble Feversham, who, doubtless reluctant to break his record of never acting decisively, released Kirke and allowed him to ride towards William's advancing forces. In spite of this unforeseen event, Trelawney, Lieutenant-Colonel Charles Churchill, all the captains except Major Zachariah Tiffin and Captain Charles Fox, five or six lieutenants and as many ensigns and 200 privates deserted from Warminster, leaving the brigade broken and confused. Trelawney's own regiment fell to pieces and virtually disbanded itself.[59] On the night of 23 November Lord Churchill, the Duke of Grafton, and Lord Berkeley rode out of James's camp and reached the Dutch outposts by daylight on the following morning.[60] This desertion was rapidly followed by those of the Duke of Ormonde, the Duke of Northumberland, Prince George of Denmark, Lord Drumlanrig, Sir Oliver St. George, and numerous lesser personages. The heart and the command structure had been ripped out of the royal army.[61] Even more significant was the way in which counties that found themselves under Dutch occupation began to orientate their loyalties towards William. In Dorset the leading gentlemen and peers associated themselves and organised both the militia and the collection of taxation for the benefit of the Prince of Orange. Somerset also showed distinct signs of reaching an accommodation with the invaders.[62]

As James's position at Salisbury and in the main theatre of action crumbled before his own irresolution and the highly effective desertions which had been organised by the military plotters, the conspiracy also operated with great effect in other parts of the country. Lords Derby and Delamere made certain of Lancashire and Cheshire, whilst Danby and the northern conspirators seized York and Nottingham.[63] Plymouth was the most immediately significant fortress. Having landed at Torbay and then marched north-east to Exeter, William stood with the Plymouth garrison directly in his rear. The number of troops was not large but it could have proved a considerable nuisance to William's plans to advance to the west, and Plymouth harbour was needed as a base for the Dutch fleet. The governor, the Earl of Bath, arrived in Plymouth on 6 November to assume command of the 1,000 foot in the garrison, but he took no action to harass the Dutch bridgehead or to reconnoitre the enemy position. By 16 November Plymouth had been effectively cut off from the royal army by patrols of Dutch cavalry which circled about the surrounding countryside. Within that time, Captain John Tidcomb and Ensign Samuel Bonfoy, one of the returned Anglo-Dutch officers, had slipped away from Plymouth and joined William at Exeter, but otherwise all was quiet. Bath finally committed himself to William on 18 November and wrote to him promising to declare for the Orange interest and to surrender Plymouth into his hands. This letter probably reached William on or before 21 November and enabled him to begin his march to the west on that date, safe in the knowledge that Plymouth was secure. On 24 November Bath converted his paper commitment into action. In company with Lieutenant-Colonel Ferdinando Hastings and Captain Sir John Jacob, he arrested the Earl of Huntingdon and all his catholic officers and immediately declared for the Prince of Orange. Plymouth was safe and the whole of the south-western peninsula was under William's control, with his fleet able to operate from a well protected harbour.[64] The next royal garrison to fall was Scarborough Castle, a somewhat hollow victory for those supporters of Danby who carried out the occupation, as it had lost its 100 soldiers to reinforce the main field army.[65] Apart from Plymouth, the second key position in the south-west was the city of Bristol. Not only was it an important seaport but it controlled the passage of the river Severn and lay naturally on the northern flank of any force trying to move out of the south-western peninsula. If, in the early stages of the campaign, James had marched west in an attempt to trap the invaders the rapid occupation of Bristol would have been vital to both sides. As soon as the main force of royal cavalry had begun to spread out to the westward of Salisbury, Feversham had ordered Sir John Fenwick to advance with his regiment on Keynsham to break down the vital bridge across the Avon in order to prevent

William's horse from gaining an easy access to Bristol. Unfortunately, the desertion of Cornbury and Langston caused Feversham to recall Fenwick from his exposed position before he could put these instructions into effect. Once it became clear to the Dutch that James intended to stand at Salisbury, Bristol lost much of its crucial strategic significance and it was not until 2 December that the Earl of Shrewsbury and Sir John Guise were sent to Bristol with two regiments of foot to secure it for William. This could hardly be claimed as a victory for the invaders, as Bristol was devoid of royal troops, but it formally cleared William's northern flank and provided him with an alternative naval base.[66]

On the night of 15 December Carlisle was quietly delivered into the hands of the pro-Williamite elements in the garrison under the leadership of Captain Jeremiah Bubb, who received the governorship of that garrison in 1689 as a reward for his services. The surrender of the town seems to have had no obvious contacts with the main conspiracy in the army but was a resigned recognition by the officers of the new order in the country. There were pressures in Carlisle and interests were at stake but they were related to the basic political power struggle in the borough between the Musgraves and Sir John Lowther.[67] By 9 December Sir Robert Holmes, the governor of the Isle of Wight, found himself deserted by his lieutenant and most of his soldiers, and even the townspeople of Yarmouth seemed to favour the Orange flag. Deprived of all means of resistance, the ageing Holmes was obliged to capitulate.[68] Further north, Lord Lumley rode into Durham on 5 December accompanied by a motley collection of volunteers and militiamen from Yorkshire and, despite the objections of the cathedral authorities, declared for the Prince.[69] After the elimination of York the only remaining garrison of any real importance to the north of the Humber was Kingston-upon-Hull. As early as September 1688 Danby had written to Lord Chesterfield announcing that there were plans afoot to deliver the town into William's hands upon his invasion. The prime movers were four professional officers led by the lieutenant-colonel of Lord Montgomery's foot, Sir John Hanmer, the Flintshire baronet who received the colonelcy of Montgomery's regiment and the governorship of Cork after the Revolution in recognition of his labours. Hanmer's right-hand man was Captain Lionel Copley, the lieutenant-governor of the garrison. Copley had started his military career in Ireland, where he was a captain in the Irish Foot Guards until 1675, but in the following year he succeeded in transferring into the English First Foot Guards as a captain and was elevated to the lieutenant-governorship of Hull in 1681. Clearly, he was a man who put his own interests above all other considerations. Earlier in 1688 he had been strong in supporting the claims of the army and the king against those of the citizens, but he was fully prepared to abandon this allegiance later in the year. The prize for his desertion to William was an appointment as governor of Maryland in 1691, a post which he held until his death two years later. Assistance to Hanmer and Copley came from two captains in Montgomery's foot who had begun their army careers in 1685 – Humphrey Fitzherbert died in the same rank in the infamous camp at Dundalk in 1689–90, but William Carvell received the lieutenant-colonelcy of Hanmer's own regiment in 1689 and became a brevet colonel of infantry in 1704. These four gentlemen arrested the catholic governor of Hull, Lord Langdale, and then seized the romish Lord Montgomery while he was still in bed. They then declared for the Prince of Orange on 3 December and set about the task of reorganising the garrison.[70] The remainder of the royal outposts and fortresses succumbed after the military issue of the campaign had been decided. Portsmouth, no longer required as a safe harbour from which James and his family could escape to France, meekly surrendered to the Dutch on 20 December; Berwick 'fell' on 15 December; Tilbury Fort was undramatically occupied by the Duke of Grafton, and in the remote Scilly Isles the loyal Captain Francis Godolphin was arrested by his lieutenant, William Paske.[71] The fate of the Tynemouth garrison typified the sad demise of James's army. Ordered to march to the concentration on Salisbury Plain, the two weak companies from Tynemouth Castle and Clifford's Fort left their dilapidated posts and moved south, only to be halted and disarmed by Danby's gang of ruffians and enthusiasts at York.[72]

The campaign of 1688 was not wholly devoid of action and bloodshed. A clash occurred at Wincanton on 20 November between a party of royal cavalry and some Dutch infantry. The horsemen from Janes's army numbered 120 and were under the command of the Irishman, Patrick Sarsfield, whilst a Lieutenant Campbell of the Anglo-Dutch Brigade faced them with just twenty-five foot soldiers. The skirmish took place when Campbell's party was out buying carriage horses for the army at Exeter, and they were about to return when they were intercepted by Sarsfield with his division from the Fourth Troop of the Life Guard. Eight or nine of the Dutch force were killed and six were taken prisoner; Sarsfield lost four men, with two more wounded.[73] A fight could easily have come about in the Forest of

Bears to the north of Portsmouth when the young Prince of Wales set out for London under the protection of Lord and Lady Powis without waiting for their cavalry escort. In the forest they narrowly missed a party of Williamite horse which had been dispatched especially to intercept them. Very shortly afterwards they were met by the cavalry regiments of George Holman and the Earl of Salisbury and ushered into London.[74] As the royal army retired from Salisbury behind the line of the Thames some Irish soldiers were ordered to defend the bridge at Maidenhead but the townspeople, understandably wishing to prevent a major battle in their own streets, 'beat the Dutch march on old kettles' and this proved sufficient to send the Irish scurrying down the road to London.[75] More troops from Ireland, to the number of about fifty, stood to defend the bridges over the Thames at Reading but they were forced out of position through a frontal assault by Dutch cavalry and an infiltration into their rear. During this small affair there were some soldiers from Sir John Lanier's horse and Lord Douglas's Scottish Foot Guards in Reading 'but they never a man drew sword but went civilly to make room for the Prince's forces'. They were, apparently, quite happy to see some of the hated Irishmen killed and the remainder driven away.[76]

The withdrawal from Salisbury over the Thames and into the Home Counties reduced the royal army to a shambles. Officers deserted, regiments became disorganised and demoralised, the king abandoned his post in the field and rode for London, and always the Dutch pressed towards the east, giving Feversham no opportunity to reorganise his forces or prepare defensive positions. Hundreds of soldiers took advantage of the chaos to leave the army for good, and by 13 December the bulk of the royal army was squeezed into an area around Windsor and Uxbridge with its discipline and internal cohesion broken. As a fighting force it had ceased to exist and to William it was no more than an untidy nuisance.[77] However, the majority of the rank and file were still, even at this late stage, loyal to James, as were a good number of their officers. Many, like Edmund Maine of the Life Guards and Peter Shakerley in Chester, must have decided that their future lay in reaching an accommodation with William rather than in continuing with a pointless allegiance to a beaten prince but there were no signs that the army would defect to the Dutch *en masse*.

The loyalty and fidelity I paid to my king will not, I hope, be imputed to me a crime by the victorious Prince of Orange, whose commands I now humbly wait and shall steadfastly obey.[78]

The conspiracy wrecked the army as an operational machine but it could not destroy its basic loyalty to James. Ironically, it was the king himself who finally ruined his own army, just as, indirectly and unwittingly, he had brought about the conspiracy. The day before his first flight he wrote a letter to Feversham which was so vague and full of self-pity as to be almost meaningless. Feversham, however, to complete a thoroughly bad personal campaign, summoned a council of the few general officers whom he could discover in or near Uxbridge and, latching on to the words 'though I do not expect you should expose yourselves by resisting a foreign army and a poisoned nation', decided that James intended the army to be disbanded forthwith. The decision was probably erroneous. The royal epistle was muddled and unclear, but if James did have any definite intention for the army it was probably to prevent it losing blood in the pursuit of a hopeless cause by adopting his own supine attitude. In other words, the king wanted his general to surrender his army to the invader. Feversham's natural lassitude gave him a pyschological inclination towards the easy solution but whatever the point of the letter was – disbandment, thanks for services rendered, a free hand for the commander – his interpretation led to the worst possible decision being reached. With discipline collapsing, the thought of thousands of English, Irish, and Scottish soldiers wandering about the south-east of England with arms but no money was truly horrifying. Luckily, Feversham could only directly order the disbandment of the 4,000 men who were under his command at Uxbridge; all the troops who were either in garrison or stationed in areas remote from London were unaffected by the directive.[79] Some officers took a deliberately limited view of their general's order. The officers commanding the royal troops in London decided that he only intended them to disband the Irish and the catholics in their commands, an attitude that was echoed by the Duke of Newcastle.[80] Francis Turner, the Bishop of Ely, decided that James's letter was really an instruction 'to submit his army and navy to the conqueror', an interpretation with which the Prince of Orange would have concurred wholeheartedly.[81] The most ludicrous aspect of Feversham's order was that the Irish troops were to be disbanded and 'assured of safety to retire separately or otherwise'. This resulted in the hated Irishmen attempting to make their way back to their homeland in small groups without supervision, a situation that soon gave rise to the series of 'Irish Alarms' which spread from London across most of central and north-western England. Lord George Livingstone, the acting commander of the Scottish army, adopted a more sensible approach when he asked the Prince of Orange if he might be allowed to march his troops back into Scotland in formed units. William was happy to agree to this suggestion, as it guaranteed the continuity of the Scottish army and preserved law and order.[82]

Without king or commander and uncertain as to whether it was disbanded or still in existence, the royal army was in total confusion. When the Earl of Ailesbury reached Rochester on his journey to Faversham in Kent to rescue James from the local fishermen and vigilantes, he found Captains James Mohun and Thomas Raleigh of the Earl of Bath's foot without orders and not knowing what to do in the face of hostile mobs in the town.[83] Many officers took advantage of the chaos to remove all roman catholics from their troops and companies, and on 14 December the Assembly of Peers at the Guildhall took the prudent decision to order all disbanded Irish soldiers to return to their original regiments, where they would be paid, although not armed, until suitable arrangements could be made to repatriate them. Irishmen who did not comply with the directive were to be arrested and treated as common vagabonds.[84] Even after they had disbanded all their catholic soldiers and officers, the five Irish regiments which had come over to England to reinforce the royal army were subject to considerable abuse and suspicion. After the removal of the catholics, Lord Forbes's regiment of foot contained 'about 130' protestant soldiers 'besides several captains and subalterns . . . sergeants, corporals, and drums'.

Soon after this [i.e. the disbandment of the catholics] a flying report spread throughout the whole kingdom that the Irish were burning, murdering, and destroying the whole country insomuch that there was not one town or village in the whole nation but had an account that they were committing all those cruelties in the very next town or village to them. Sir John Edgeworth, who was major, commanded our regiment at this time (my Lord Forbes being then with the Prince in London) and was quartered at the Lord Oslington's [Ossulston] house near Colnbrook . . . the country people, hearing that an Irish regiment had got in there, came flocking from all parts to knock us in the head but Sir John bid them on their peril keep off and told them that we were not Irish papists but were all true Church of England men. And, seeing a gentlemanlike man, called to him and desired that he would send for the minister of the parish to read prayers to us and then if the minister did not convince them that we were all of the Church of England that we would submit to their mercy upon which the mob cried out, 'a very fair proposal'. The minister was immediately sent for who soon came and to prayers we went. And whether it was out of pure devotion or fear of the mob we repeated the responses of our liturgy with such devotion and so exactly that the minister declared to the mob that in all his life he never heard the responses of the Church repeated so distinctly and with so much devotion as he had done. Upon which the mob gave a 'huzza' and cried out, 'long live the Prince of Orange', and so returned home.[85]

In Chester the catholic Colonel Henry Gage escaped disguised 'in an old grey coat', and all the catholic officers and soldiers in the garrison were first disbanded and then arrested for good measure. 'The boys in the town, when they met any of the officers in the streets after they have been disbanded, went into their pockets and took what they had and they never resisted.'[86] Central though the question of discipline and the fate of the catholics and the Irish was to the future of the royal army, there were numerous other symptoms of decay. Arms were abandoned; officers neglected their duty; and Sir Henry Shere's train of artillery, which had been dragged through the mud and snow to Salisbury and back, was left unattended on Hounslow Heath, where it was looted by the 'rabble'. William of Orange was furious at the disbandment. One of his principal reasons for intervening in England had been to harness the English army and navy to the protestant alliance in Europe, and he did not want the trouble and expense of having to reform and reorganise the entirety of James's armed forces. The weight of the Dutchman's wrath fell upon Feversham, who was arrested on 18 December when he went to Windsor to invite the Prince to make his formal entry into London.[87] By 19 December the majority of the catholic Irish soldiers who had not succeeded in making their escape to Ireland were quartered in Sussex and, shortly afterwards, they were all transported to the Isle of Wight, which was turned into a vast internment camp. Watches were kept on all the shipping that left the island to make sure that the Irishmen did not slip away, but the guard was not especially rigorous and very few of the 1,500 detainees remained by the end of February 1689. Two shiploads of reluctant Irish soldiers were sent to Hamburg to enter the service of the Imperial armies in the fight against the Turk but many managed to desert and made their way to France and Ireland.[88]

From 11 December onwards Lord Ranelagh, the paymaster-general, looked to William for instructions on how to pay the English army and, three days later, Lord Churchill and the Duke of Grafton were given the unenviable task of bringing some semblance of order into the 'disbanded' royal army. Perhaps it is possible to detect here a trace of contempt by William for those who had so smoothly transferred their allegiance; Churchill and Grafton had been instrumental in causing the confusion in the royal army and they were the officers deputed to rectify the ill effects of their own work. Their charge was enormous. In most regiments the structure of command had been wrecked by desertion and by the removal of the catholics and the Irish, but the filling of these vacancies was no easy matter, as the future loyalties of many of the prospective candidates were very uncertain. The long winter had also played its part by ruining many of the army's horses, much of its field equipment, and the major part of its stores. Captain Cooke's troop of cavalry was probably typical of many in that it was desperately short of mounts, lacking in discipline, possessed little ready cash, and its troopers were billeted over a wide area of Nottinghamshire. William took the only possible action in the circumstances. The English regiments were dispatched into winter quarters to reorganise and re-equip whilst all the guard, garrison, and ceremonial functions were assumed by the Dutch and confederate soldiers in England. The army of James II had been disgraced.[89]

Notes

1 *Tusmore Papers*, p. 36, 'Notes on the Follies of King James II and the causes of his defeat in 1690–2'.
2 T. H. Baker, *Records of the Seasons, Prices of Agricultural Produce, and Phenomena Observed in the British Isles* (London, 1883), pp. 162–3; W. G. Hoskins, 'Harvest Fluctuations and English Economic History, 1620–1759', *Agricultural History Review*, xvi. (1968), p. 16; Evelyn, *Diary*, iv. 607; Brotherton Library, University of Leeds, MSS. 9, Joseph Bufton's Diary, i. f. 83, 19 Nov. 1688; Wood, *Life and Times*, iii. 283; Cardigan, *Bruce*, pp. 133–4; BL Add. MSS. 41,805, ff. 275 and 283; *Ellis Correspondence*, ii. 332.
3 Cumbria County Record Office, Carlisle, Lowther MSS. D/Lons/L/Stray Letters, 29 Sept. 1688, Letter to Sir John Lowther from London.
4 *CSPD 1687–9*, No. 1731; SP 84/220, f. 36, 24 Sept. 1688, The Hague.
5 *HMC, Dartmouth MSS.*, i. 176 and 178; Macpherson, *Original Papers*, i. 269–71.
6 E. S. de Beer, 'The Marquis of Albeville and his Brothers', *EHR*, xlv. (1930), pp. 397–408; Edmund Calamy, *An Historical Account of My Own Life*, ed. John Towill Rutt (London, 1829), i. 147–8.
7 *HMC, Dartmouth MSS.*, iii. 60, 28 Oct. 1688, Dartmouth to Pepys.
8 SP 44/52, p. 100.
9 *Hatton Correspondence*, ii. 91–2; Delamere, *Works*, pp. 57–61; John Whittle, *An Exact Diary of the Late Expedition of His Illustrious Highness, the Prince of Orange* (London, 1689), pp. 40–5; Hosford, *Nottingham, Nobles, and the North*, pp. 80–3; Miller, *James II*, p. 200; *Ellis Correspondence*, ii. 220; BL Add. MSS. 41,805, f. 89; Jones, *Revolution of 1688*, pp. 293 and 298; Clarke, *Life*, ii. 191; Luttrell, *Historical Relation*, i. 469–70.

10   *The Lexington Papers*, ed. H. M. Sutton (London, 1851), p. 328, 14 Nov. 1688, Vienna, 'Journal of Mr. Hopp, Envoy-Extraordinary from the States-General to the Imperial Court at Vienna'.
11   Baxter, *William III*, p. 233; BL Add. MSS. 41,805, f. 63, 17 Oct. 1688, Exeter, John White to Lieutenant David Livingstone of Dumbarton's foot at Gravesend; Portland MSS. PwA 2181–3.
12   *HMC, Dartmouth MSS.*, i. 180.
13   *HMC, 7th Report*, p. 422, 2 and 4 Nov. 1688, d'Albeville to Lord Preston.
14   *Somers Tracts*, ed. Sir Walter Scott (London, 1809–15), ix. 270, 6 Nov. 1688, 'A List of the Foot and Horse that are come with the Prince of Orange, as printed in Holland'; Bohun, *History*, pp. 39–40; BL Add. MSS. 33,970; *HMC, Various Collections*, v. 238 'The Prince of Orange's Army'.
15   BL Add. MSS. 41,822, ff. 230–1; A. F. W. Papillon, *Memoirs of Thomas Papillon of London, Merchant, 1623–1702* (Reading, 1887), p. 343; Gilbert Burnet, *The Expedition of His Highness the Prince of Orange for England* (London, 1688), pp. 5–6.
16   C. E. Lart, 'The Huguenot Regiments', *Proceedings of the Huguenot Society of London*, ix. (1911), pp. 480–1.
17   Bohun, *History*, pp. 64–5; *HMC, Le Fleming MSS.*, pp. 225 and 227; Whittle, *Exact Diary*, pp. 70–1.
18   *Somers Tracts*, ix. 280–1, 'A Further Account of the Prince's Army, in a letter sent from Exeter, dated 24 November'.
19   Burnet, *Expedition*, p. 4; Whittle, *Exact Diary*, pp. 48–51; *Ellis Correspondence*, ii. 312–13; 'Correspondence of Admiral Herbert during the Revolution', ed. E. M. Thompson, *EHR*, i. (1886), p. 530; Dalrymple, *Memoirs of Great Britain and Ireland*, ii. App. Part 1, p. 333.
20   *Memoirs of Mary, Queen of England, 1689–1693*, ed. R. Doebner (London, 1886), pp. 71–2, 28 Sept. 1688, James II to Electress Sophia of Hanover.
21   Dalrymple, *Memoirs of Great Britain and Ireland*, ii. App. Part 1, pp. 282–4; *A Complete Collection of the Works of John Kettlewell*, ed. F. Lees (London, 1719), i. 79.
22   SP 44/164, pp. 344–5; Western, *Monarchy and Revolution*, p. 210.
23   Luttrell, *Historical Relation*, i. 438; Tomlinson, 'Ordnance Office and the King's Forts', p. 7.
24   *HMC, Downshire MSS.*, i. 292–3.
25   WO 5/3, pp. 140–2; WO 26/2, pp. 109–10.
26   *Verney Memoirs*, ii. 460.
27   Luttrell, *Historical Relation*, i. 456–7; *Ellis Correspondence*, ii. 139; *Reresby*, p. 506; *Hatton Correspondence*, ii. 90 and 94; *HMC, Rutland MSS.*, ii. 121.
28   WO 5/3, pp. 224–32; SP 44/165, pp. 63–4.
29   Davies, 'Letters on the Administration of James II's Army', pp. 80–1; *Ellis Correspondence*, ii. 203; *Hatton Correspondence*, ii. 91–2.
30   BL Add. MSS. 34,512, f. 99, 21 Sept. 1688, Van Citters to States-General.
31   *CSPD 1687–9*, No. 1552, 25 Sept. 1688; Wood, *Life and Times*, iii. 278;

RPCS 1686–9, pp. xxv–xxvi.
32 Steele, *Proclamations*, i. No. 3876; *HMC, Portland MSS.*, iii. 417.
33 Luttrell, *Historical Relation*, i. 463.
34 Bohun, *History*, pp. 12–13; Newton, *Lyme Letters*, p. 158.
35 Churchill College, Cambridge, Erle-Drax MSS. 2/44, f. 1, 25 Sept. 1688, Ormonde to Thomas Erle.
36 Lonsdale, *Memoir*, p. 52; Steele, *Proclamations*, i. No. 3886; BL Add. MSS. 34,512, f. 108.
37 *Hatton Correspondence*, ii. 93–4; *HMC, Dartmouth MSS.*, i. 143.
38 *CSPD 1687–9*, Nos. 1606 and 1617; SP 44/164, p. 389; BL Add. MSS. 9,735, ff. 39 and 41, 13 Oct. 1688.
39 *HMC, Hodgkin MSS.*, pp. 73–4; Davies, 'Letters on the Administration of James II's Army', p. 81.
40 *Norfolk Lieutenancy Journal.* pp. 89–90; *HMC, Lothian MSS.*, p. 133; Erle MSS. 4/4, f. 1.
41 *Reresby*, pp. 518–20.
42 *CSPD 1687–9*, No. 1781; WO 4/1, p. 106.
43 *HMC, Leyborne-Popham MSS.*, p. 267, 'Autobiography of Dr. George Clarke'.
44 PC 2/72, f. 165; BL Add. MSS. 41,805, ff. 74 and 89; *CSPD 1687–9*, No. 1823.
45 Clarke, *Life*, ii. 205–6.
46 Foxcroft, *Halifax*, ii. 8; WO 4/1, p. 108; *HMC, Le Fleming MSS.*, p. 218.
47 *HMC, Dartmouth MSS.*, i. 179; *HMC, Le Fleming MSS.*, p. 218; Luttrell, *Historical Relation*, i. 477; Mackintosh, *History of the Revolution*, pp. 527–8; *Hatton Correspondence*, ii. 101.
48 WO 4/1, p. 109; WO 5/3, 6 Nov. 1688.
49 Clarke, *Life*, ii. 209; WO 5/3, unpaginated; *HMC, Dartmouth MSS.*, i. 190; *HMC, Kenyon MSS.*, p. 207; SP 54/1, State Papers Scotland, f.1, 14 Nov. 1688.
50 *HMC, Hamilton MSS. (Supplementary Report)*, p. 111, 14 Nov. 1688.
51 Clarke, *Life*, ii. 220–1; *Bramston*, p. 334; *Ellis Correspondence*, ii. 301; *HMC, Hamilton MSS. (Supplementary Report)*, p. 112; *CSPD 1687–9*, No. 1967; WO 4/1, p. 114; Cavelli, ii. 376–7; *Ailesbury's Memoirs*, i. 190; *CSPD 1687–9*, No. 1983.
52 *Bramston*, pp. 331–2; Trevallyn Jones, *Wharton*, p. 258; *HMC, Kenyon MSS.*, p. 207; Wood, *Life and Times*, iii. 282.
53 Luttrell, *Historical Relation*, i. 475; *HMC, Kenyon MSS.*, p. 207; *Ellis Correspondence*, ii. 294–6; BL Add. MSS. 41,805, f. 194; *HMC, Dartmouth MSS.*, i. 210–11; *Hatton Correspondence*, ii. 103.
54 Rawlinson MSS. D.148; Portland MSS. PwA 2212; 'Correspondence of Admiral Herbert', p. 528.
55 Portland MSS PwA 2230; Clarke, *Life*, ii. 215–17; BL Add. MSS. 41,805, ff. 200 and 211; Cavelli, ii. 322–6.
56 *HMC, Le Fleming MSS.*, p. 200; *Hatton Correspondence*, ii. 103; *HMC, Leyborne-Popham MSS.*, p. 267.

The campaign of 1688

57 Clarke, *Life*, ii. 223–4; WO 4/1, p. 110; BL Add. MSS. 28,053, f. 357; BL Add. MSS. 29,593, f. 283; *HMC, Hamilton MSS. (Supplementary Report)*, p. 112; BL Add. MSS. 41,805, f. 289.
58 PC 2/72, f. 187, 1 Dec. 1688.
59 'Correspondence of Admiral Herbert', pp. 530–1; *Hatton Correspondence*, ii. 113; Portland MSS. PwA 2237; Clarke, *Life*, ii. 224–5; BL Add. MSS. 41,805, ff. 283–4.
60 Clarke, *Life*, ii. 224; *Ailesbury's Memoirs*, i. 170; *CSPD 1687–9*, Nos. 1990 and 1991.
61 'Correspondence of Admiral Herbert', pp. 530–1; Portland MSS. PwA 2231, 2235 and 2240; Cavelli, ii. 344–5; *Ellis Correspondence*, ii. 336–8; Luttrell, *Historical Relation*, i. 479.
62 Erle MSS. 4/4, f. 2; Emanuel Green, *The March of William of Orange through Somerset with a Notice of other Local Events in the time of King James II* (London, 1892), pp. 56–7.
63 *The Farington Papers*, ed. S. M. Ffarington (Chetham Society, 1856), pp. 177–9; *Reresby*, pp. 528–31.
64 BL Add. MSS. 41,805, ff. 122, 127, 129 and 217; *HMC, Hastings MSS.*, ii. 191, 195–6 and 198–9; *Ellis Correspondence*, ii. 324–5; Japikse, iii. 69–70; Erle MSS. 2/44; Kenyon, *Nobility*, pp. 15–17; *Somers Tracts*, ix. 280.
65 Wood, 'Revolution in the North', p. 90.
66 BL Add. MSS. 41,805, f. 196; *Marchmont Papers*, iii. 100; Japikse, ii. 72; Portland MSS. PwA 2231; *Pinney Letters*, p. 60; *Annals of Bristol*, pp. 451–2.
67 *HMC, Lonsdale MSS.*, pp. 97 and 99; Lowther MSS. D/Lons/L/Stray Letters, 10 and 16 Dec. 1688, Letters to Sir John Lowther.
68 *HMC, Dartmouth MSS.*, i. 225.
69 C. E. Whiting, *Nathaniel, Lord Crewe, Bishop of Durham, 1674–1721, and his Diocese* (London, 1940), pp. 185–6.
70 HPT; SP 29/145, ff. 156–7; Dalton, *Irish Army*, pp. 93–4 and 99; Dalton, *Army Lists*, iii. 101; Browning, *Danby*, ii. 135; Cavelli, ii. 352–3; Gent, *Hull*, pp. 189–90; *Reresby*, pp. 535–6; BL Add. MSS. 28,053, f. 369; Bodleian Library, Ballard MSS. 45, f. 20, newsletter.
71 *HMC, Dartmouth MSS.*, i. 210–11 and 237–8; *Ellis Correspondence*, ii. 365–6; Bohun, *History*, pp. 92–3; Wood, 'Revolution in the North', p. 91; Erle MSS. 2/44.
72 H. H. E. Cra'ster, *The Parish of Tynemouth* (Newcastle-upon-Tyne, 1907), p. 203; *HMC, Lindsey MSS.*, p. 450.
73 Green, *March through Somerset*, pp. 62–3; BL Add. MSS. 28,053, ff. 355–6; *Hatton Correspondence*, ii. 110; *Portledge Papers*, p. 50; *Ellis Correspondence*, ii. 329–30; Bohun, *History*. pp. 76–7; Cavelli, ii. 337–8; Whittle, *Exact Diary*, pp. 57–8; *HMC, Le Fleming MSS.*, pp. 222–3; *HMC, 7th Report*, App. p. 408, no date, Edmund Maine to Lord Churchill.
74 Clarke, *Life*, ii. 235–7.
75 Whittle, *Exact Diary*, pp. 69–70.

76 *HMC, Dartmouth MSS.*, i. 228; Whittle, *Exact Diary*, pp. 68–9; Cavelli, ii. 374; *Hatton Correspondence*, ii. 122; *Portledge Papers*, pp. 51–2; Bohun, *History*, pp. 87–8.
77 Cavelli, ii. 361–2; Steele, *Proclamations*, i. No. 3923.
78 BL Add. MSS. 38,695, f. 103, 13 Dec. 1688, Peter Shakerley to Blathwayt; John Sheffield, Earl of Mulgrave and Duke of Buckingham, *Works* (London, 1740), ii. 95–6.
79 *HMC, Hamilton MSS. (Supplementary Report)*, pp. 112–13; Clarke, *Life*, ii. 250n.
80 *HMC, Dartmouth MSS.*, i. 230; *Ellis Correspondence*, ii. 346.
81 Robert Beddard, 'The Loyalist Opposition in the Interregnum: A Letter of Dr. Francis Turner, Bishop of Ely, on the Revolution of 1688', *BIHR*, xl. (1967), pp. 106–7.
82 Japikse, iii. 82–3; *HMC, Dartmouth MSS.*, i. 233. For accounts of the spread of the 'Irish Alarms' see: *Ailesbury's Memoirs*, i. 200; Newton, *Diary*, pp. 96–7; *The Correspondence of Isaac Newton*, ed. A. R. Hall, L. Tilling and H. W. Turnbull (Cambridge, 1959–76), iii. 1; Whiting, *Crewe*, pp. 187–8; P. C. Vellacott, 'The Diary of a Country Gentleman in 1688', *Cambridge Historical Journal*, ii. (1926), p. 57; Thoresby, *Diary*, i. 188–91; *HMC, Portland MSS.*, iii. 420; *Bramston*, p. 339; *Ellis Correspondence*, ii. 350–7; *Pryme's Diary*, pp. 15–16; *HMC, Le Fleming MSS.*, p. 224; Clarke, *Life*, ii. 257–8; *Verney Memoirs*, ii. 470–1.
83 *Ailesbury's Memoirs*, i. 205.
84 Luttrell, *Historical Relation*, i. 487; Steele, *Proclamations*, i. No. 3927.
85 NLI MSS. 4166, 1688.
86 *HMC, Le Fleming MSS.*, p. 229.
87 *HMC, Dartmouth MSS.*, i. 236; *Hatton Correspondence*, ii. 127; Clarke, *Life*, ii. 251.
88 Garland, 'Regiment of Mac Elligott', p. 124; Simms, *Jacobite Ireland*, pp. 47–8.
89 *HMC, Cowper MSS.*, ii. 346–7; *HMC, Le Fleming MSS.*, p. 230; Bohun, *History*, pp. 108–10.

VIII

Reflections

Across western Europe the second half of the seventeenth century witnessed the rise of the standing army. The morass of private contractors and mercenaries which had populated the military world during and before the Thirty Years' War had proved inefficient, hideously expensive and wholly unreliable. One of the principal products of the war was the notion that a regular and permanent force which was maintained by the state and owed its first loyalty to that state offered the only practical solution to the problems of national defence. Simultaneously, the cost and social burden of both civil and international war in the hundred years before 1648 had led to monarchs and ruling princes attempting to centralise their governments in order to make their administrative control more effective. The maintenance of a standing army demanded a reasonably efficient system of government with a special emphasis upon the collection of revenue but an army also provided a prince with an excellent means by which to extend his personal authority within his own frontiers. Armies required a centralised and unified state, and such a state could make great social, political and economic use of a standing army. This absolutist form of government came to dominate the countries of western Europe between 1648 and 1700. It was not a new theory of government – any monarch in history has desired an increase in his own power – but the creation of standing armies presented a new dimension and gave monarchs a greater potential for coercion. As armies became permanent they offered attractive and enduring careers to aristocrats, gentlemen, and even commoners, a factor which resulted in a higher degree of professional skill and made the armies even more indispensable.

Although England's involvement in the Thirty Years' War was minimal and her island position protected her from the mainstream of unpleasant events in Europe, her own civil wars, with the corollaries of an Interregnum and an eventual Restoration, brought about the two necessary conditions for the upkeep of a standing army: instability and a centralised administration. Under Charles II, England escaped the consequence of the establishment of absolutism. A suspicious parliament, an acute shortage of money, and an idle sovereign precluded any attempts at a continental style of government, but in 1685 James II found himself in a very different position. A generous parliament, personal energy and attention to business, and the fortunate occurrence of Monmouth's feeble rebellion allowed James to raise and sustain an army that was four times as large as that of his royal brother. Within a few months of his accession James set about the task of making his officers and soldiers loyal to himself by removing politically suspect gentlemen and replacing them with members of the new breed of professional careerists who depended upon their sword for their livelihood. The victims of this trend were the Anglican gentry, the amateur soldiers, and the courtiers who had held so many of the army commissions in the time of Charles II. This had the effect of weaning the army away from its parent society and it allowed the military to formulate its own identity and to occupy a novel position in relation to the populace. This deliberate development was accelerated by granting the army its own independent legal system and by turning a blind eye to its ill-treatment of some civilians. Having created a 'modern' army, James set about employing it for absolutist ends: whole towns were dragooned into following the approved political line, individuals and minorities were suppressed, and the soldiers were garrisoned across the length and breadth of the country in order to police the provinces at the expense of the militia, the traditional armed force. Through the medium of his standing army James set his sights upon a personal, centralised, and absolutist style of government in England, Ireland, and Scotland.

Because of the brevity of the reign it is only possible for historians to catch a glimpse of James II's real objectives. Within the short time available to him James made very considerable progress in channelling the loyalty of the army and in isolating it from society; creating a force sufficiently anaesthetised to do his bidding regardless of social and political prejudices and pressures. Unfortunately, this was achieved only by the dismissal of individual English officers and the wholesale removal of nearly all the protestant officers in Ireland. Such a radical policy left even the professional officers in England feeling distinctly uneasy. They relied upon their swords for a living, and most of them had fought under many flags apart from that of St. George, yet they regarded the English army as their 'home establishment' and were anxious to continue in that service for as long as possible. James's purges and his refusal to offer monetary compensation to those so deprived caused a degree of suspicion and ill-will among some of his officers, and it was this that drove a select few to risk all in agreeing to help William of Orange invade England by undermining the morale of the royal army. Yet the conspirators were very small in number. The attention that James had paid to insisting upon loyalty and professionalism had reaped an abundant harvest. If England had been involved in a normal foreign war in 1688 instead of a civil war fomented by intervention from overseas, there is no good reason to suppose that the army would have demonstrated any disloyalty to King James. The conditions in the autumn of 1688 were bizarre and entirely unpredictable.

The rebellion in the army was small in scale and in the number of officers engaged but it was crucial to the outcome of the campaign of 1688. The planned desertion of Cornbury and Langston shook James's confidence in his cherished army and reduced the Earl of Feversham to a fumbling incompetent. Their departure for the Williamite camp convinced James that, if the army could not be relied upon, an offensive strategy was thoroughly misguided. The conspirators were thus instrumental in undermining the confidence of both James and his commander-in-chief. Once the one supposedly solid bastion of his reign had been found to be rotten, James surrendered the strategic and tactical initiative to his nephew, retired on London, and fled the country. The military conspirators had ruined him.

Without the invasion of William of Orange, James would probably have proceeded in his domestic absolutism: the army would have continued as the main force and influence in England and would probably have been employed in a more assertive manner. Judging from the evidence of 1688, a sizeable proportion of the officers would have sat in the second parliament of the reign and repealed the Test Acts and the Penal Laws. Would William of Orange have been particularly concerned? Probably not. He invaded England in 1688 to prevent her from being dragged into the circle of alliances drawn by France and to secure her financial, commercial, colonial, naval, and military power for the protestant forces of western Europe in their fight against the imperialism of Louis XIV. William did not gamble with the whole of his political and military future in both the United Provinces and Europe to rescue the protestant religion in England out of philanthropic considerations. Quite the reverse. He may well have envied his uncle's freedom to introduce a 'modern' system of government, as he was known to feel frustrated by his ambiguous position within the federation of the Seven Provinces, with its over-complicated constitution. However, all this is but speculation. William did invade and, in so doing, brought James's effective rule to an abrupt end.

At first sight the reign of James II appears to mark the low-point in the fortunes of the young British army. The standing army, which had been the creation of Charles II, had spent the first twenty-five years of its life as an under-strength force which achieved little, but during the following four years it was transformed into a political machine which was designed to attack English 'liberties'. Finally, a part of its officer corps disgraced the whole by deserting to the invader in 1688. Despite these unimpressive facts, between 1685 and 1688 the army was placed firmly upon the road to becoming thoroughly professional and politically detached. The great reservoir of English, Irish, and Scottish professional soldiers who had been forced into foreign service by the lack of opportunities in the British Isles during the time of Charles II were welcomed back into the three national establishments and the army became a technically competent force with a sufficient number of men to make itself effective. One-third of its officers may have decided to serve James II in Ireland and France, another third may have retired from service life, but the remaining fraction continued in their commissions and provided the backbone of the British forces that fought with such distinction during the War of the Grand Alliance and under Malborough in the War of the Spanish Succession.

APPENDIX A
Officers recommended as MPs in 1688

The following regular army officers were either recommended by the regulators to sit for the named constituencies (†) and/or were instructed by the Earl of Sunderland in September 1688 to stand for election to the named constituencies (††). Four of the officers were holders of temporary commissions in the enlargement of the army in the autumn of 1688(‡) and several had experience as MPs (*).

Sir Richard Mauleverer*	Boroughbridge	†	
Sir John Reresby*	Aldborough	†	
Edward King	Grimsby	†	
Sir Thomas Harrington	Grantham	†	††
Sir Thomas Hussey*	Lincolnshire	†	
Oliver Nicholas* {	Wilton	†	
(counted as two officers) {	Bath	†	††
Henry Chivers	Calne, Wilts.	†	
John Webb*	Calne, Wilts.		††
Sir John Talbot*	Chippenham	†	
‡Thomas Neale	Ludgershall	†	
Archibald Clinkard*	Maidstone	†	
Sir Denny Ashburnham*	**Hastings**	†	††
Richard Leveson*	Lichfield	†	††
Richard Baggott	Lichfield	†	††
William Barlow*	Haverfordwest	†	††
Lewis Billingsley	Great Marlow	†	††
William Blathwayt	Newtown, Isle of Wight	†	††
John Butler (Irish army)	Boston	†	††
George Churchill*	St. Albans	†	††
‡Nicholas Cole	Newcastle-upon-Tyne	†	††
William Barnes	Newcastle-upon-Tyne		††
Thomas Condon	Scarborough	†	††

Ferdinando Hastings	Scarborough	†	††
Robert Crawford	Queenborough	†	††
Thomas Wilford	Queenborough	†	††
William Culliford	Corfe Castle	†	
John Deane*	Marlborough	†	††
Sir John Fenwick*	Northumberland	†	††
William Ogle	Northumberland	†	††
Ferdinand Foster	Berwick-on-Tweed	†	††
Edmund Maine	Berwick-on-Tweed	†	††
‡Sir Gilbert Gerard*	County Durham	†	††
‡James Graham*	Carlisle	†	††
Sir Bevil Grenville*	Fowey	†	
John Grenville*	Launceston	†	
Sir John Hanmer*	Flintshire	†	††
Edward Harris*	Liskard	†	
Chichester Wray	Liskard	†	
Thomas Hawley	King's Lynn	†	
Sir Robert Holmes*	Newport, Isle of Wight	†	††
John Hutchinson	Durham City	†	
Roger Kirkby*	Lancaster	†	††
Sir Simon Leach*	Okehampton	†	††
Sir Charles Littleton*	Bewdley	†	††
James Mohun	Lostwithiel	†	
Thomas Musgrave	Appleby	†	††
Sir Theophilus Oglethorpe	Morpeth	†	††
Sir John Parsons*	Reigate	†	††
Roger Pope*	Bridgenorth	†	††
Henry Slingsby*	Knaresborough	†	††
Charles Trelawney*	Eastlow	†	††
Henry Trelawney*	Westlow	†	††
Sir William Villiers	Leicester	†	††
Edward Vincent	Tregonny	†	
Lionel Walden*	Huntingdon	†	††
Sir Charles Wydham*	Southampton	†	
Sir William Booth	Hampshire	†	
Total 59 officers		56	38

Sources: *CSPD 1687–9*, pp. 273–7; BL Add. MSS. 34,516, ff. 50–4; Duckett, *Penal Laws*, i. and ii.

Appendix B
Officers recommended as deputy lieutenants in 1688

The following table presents the number of serving army officers who were recommended by the regulators in late 1687 and 1688 to serve as deputy lieutenants in the named counties.

ENGLAND

	Protestant	*Catholic*	*Total*
Berkshire		1	1
Buckinghamshire		1	1
Cheshire	4	1	5
Cornwall	2		2
Cumberland and Westmorland		2	2
County Durham	2	2	4
Essex		1	1
Gloucestershire	1		1
Hampshire	1	1	2
Herefordshire		1	1
Hertfordshire		1	1
Kent	5	2	7
Lancashire	1	2	3
Leicestershire	3	1	4
Lincolnshire	1	2	3
Newcastle-upon-Tyne		1	1
Northamptonshire		1	1
Northumberland	2	5	7
Oxfordshire		1	1
Shropshire	3		3
Staffordshire		1	1
Sussex		1	1
Wiltshire	2		2

Worcestershire		2	2
Yorkshire, East Riding		1	1
Yorkshire, North Riding	1		1

WALES

Anglesey	1	1	2
Brecknockshire	2	1	3
Carmarthenshire	1	1	2
Carnarvonshire		1	1
Denbighshire		1	1
Flintshire	2	1	3
Glamorganshire		2	2
Merionethshire		1	1
Monmouthshire	2	1	3
Montgomeryshire	1	1	2
Pembrokeshire		1	1
Radnorshire	2		2
Total	39	43	82

Appendix C
Officers recommended as justices of the peace in 1688

The following table presents the number of serving army officers who were recommended by the regulators in late 1687 and 1688 to serve as justices of the peace in the named counties and boroughs.

ENGLAND

	Protestant	Catholic	Total
Berkshire	2	2	4
Berwick-on-Tweed	3	1	4
Buckinghamshire	2	1	3
Cornwall	5		5
Cumberland and Westmorland		2	2
Derbyshire	2	1	3
Devon		1	1
County Durham	2	1	3
Essex		2	2
Gloucestershire	4	2	6
Hampshire	4		4
Herefordshire	3	2	5
Huntingdonshire	1		1
Isle of Ely		3	3
Kent	11	6	17
Lancashire	2		2
Leicestershire	2		2
Lincolnshire	2	4	6
Middlesex	1		1
Norfolk		2	2
Northamptonshire	1	3	4
Northumberland		6	6
Nottinghamshire	1		1

Oxfordshire	1	1	2
Shropshire	5		5
Somerset	1		1
Staffordshire	4	1	5
Sussex	3	2	5
Westminster	1		1
Wiltshire	1	1	2
Worcestershire	1	6	7
York	2	1	3
Yorkshire, East Riding	3	1	4
Yorkshire, North Riding	5		5
Yorkshire, West Riding	1		1

WALES

Anglesey		1	1
Brecknockshire		2	2
Carmarthenshire	1		1
Carnarvonshire		2	2
Denbighshire	4	2	6
Flintshire	1	2	3
Glamorganshire	3	1	4
Merionethshire		2	2
Monmouthshire	1		1
Montgomeryshire		1	1
Pembrokeshire	1		1
Radnorshire	1	1	2
Total	88	66	154

INDEX

Abercorn, Claudius Hamilton, 4th Earl of, 26
Abingdon, recruitment in, 30
Abingdon, Charles Bertie, 1st Earl of, 149, 185
Absolutism, 83–4
   Charles II, xvii
   in Europe, 83–4
   James II aims at, xvii
   growth of, 203–4
   see also James II; Charles II
Act of Supremacy, Irish, 62
Adderley, Charles, 44
Advocate-General, 91
Agents, Dutch, 174
Ailesbury, Thomas Bruce, 2nd Earl of, 8, 21, 36, 37, 142, 168, 196
Albermarle, Christopher Monck, 2nd Duke of, 45, 123
Albeville, Ignatius White, Marquis d', 133, 161, 169–70, 174, 177, 181
Aldgate, army in, 94–5
Anderson, Henry, 32
Anderson, John, 62
Andros, Sir Edmund, 104
Anglo-Dutch Brigade, 2, 74
   and convention of 1678, 120–1
   command of, 123–4
   desertion from, 129
   discipline in, 126, 129
   and English army, 145–6
   exiles in, 121
   history of, 119–20
   hostility to James II, 124–7, 129–31
   in 1688, 135, 175, 187,
   legal status of, 120–1
   loyalty to James II, 128
   marriages in, 122–3
   and Monmouth's Rebellion, 125–6
   morale in, 122–3
   numbers in, 121
   officers, appointment of, 123–4
   officers, catholic, 127
   officers, Dutch, 121
   officers, Huguenot, 121, 130, 132
   officers, Irish, 130, 132
   proposal to replace, 42–3
   quality of, 121
   recall of, 6, 131–4
   recruitment for, 121–2, 147
   regiments, foot, 122, 145, 147
   and Scottish army, 145–6
   soldiers of, 129, 134
   spies from, 145–6
   unpopularity of, 122–3
Anglo-Dutch relations, 141
Anglo-Spanish Brigade, 42–3, 130
Anne, Princess of Denmark, *see* Denmark, Princess Anne of
Argyl, Archibald Campbell, 9th Earl of, 2
Argyll, Archibald Campbell, 10th Earl of, 161
Armourer, Sir Nicholas, 63
Armstrong, Sir Thomas, 125
Army, British, xiv, xv

career for officers, 27–9
duties of, xvi, 2
legal status of, xvi, xvii
popularity of, 19, 94–9
size of, 10
Army, England
  chaplains, catholic, 24
  contact with society, 98–9; see also Civil–military relations
  cost of, 5–6
  disbandment of, 195–8
  dutch ridicule of, 40
  duties of, see Duties, England
  extends royal control, 9–10
  isolation from society, 84–94; see also Civil–military relations
  loyalty of, 150–4
  purge of officers, 46–50
  regiments of dragoons
    John Berkeley's, 110
    Royal Dragoons, 40, 186–7
    Richard Hamilton's, 143
  regiments of foot
    1st Foot Guards, 2, 18, 39, 183;
    Coldstream Guards, 18, 39;
    Earl of Bath's, 38–9;
    Duke of Berwick's, 90, 99, 151–4;
    John Carne's, 3
    Henry Cornwall's, 22, 87, 90, 110
    Lord Ferrers's, 38
    Henry Gage's, 3, 35
    Sir Edward Hales's, 23, 87, 109
    John Hales's, 3, 133–4
    Holland Regiment, 18, 93, 180
    Earl of Huntingdon's, 38, 146–7
    Percy Kirke's, 40, 190
    Earl of Lichfield's, 150, 158–9
    Duke of Newcastle's, 27
    Royal Fusiliers, 180
    Royal Scots, 2, 99
    Charles Trelawney's, 40, 88, 93, 190
    Marquis of Worcester's, 100
    Duke of York's, 18
  regiments of horse
    Earl of Arran's, 143
    Baron Dover's, 2
    Sir John Fenwick's, 111
    Richard Hamilton's, 111
    George Holman's, 23, 194
    Sir John Lanier's, 143, 188, 194
    Life Guard, 2, 18, 34, 39, 142
    Earl of Peterborough's, 29, 37, 100
    Royal Horse Guards, 18, 39, 186–7
    Duke of St. Albans's, 29, 122, 186–7
    Earl of Salisbury's, 23, 194
    Earl of Shrewsbury's, 142
  religion in, 154–5
  size of, 1, 180, 184
  state of in 1688, 194–5
  troops from Ireland, 180
  troops from Scotland, 180
Army, Ireland
  catholicisation of, 60–5
  chaplains, catholic, 62
  competence of, 67
  conduct of, 76–8
  cost of, 4–5
  equipment of, 56–7
  protestants in (1688), 196–7
  purge of, 49, 57–60, 61–6
  regiments of dragoons
    Richard Hamilton's, 4, 22, 61, 67
  regiments of foot
    Lord Forbes's, 196–7
    Irish Foot Guards, 64, 72
    Justin Macarty's, 67
    Roger MacElligott's, 3, 133–4, 153
    Dennis MacGillicuddy's, 99
    Earl of Ardglass's, 64
  regiments of horse
    Duke of Ormonde's, 64
  regimentation, 56
  size of, 1–2, 4–5
  soldiers at Portsmouth, 151
  troops sent to England (1688), 4, 180–1
Army, Scotland
  cost of, 4
  regiments of foot
    Cameronians, 146
    Scottish Foot Guards, 29, 93, 180, 194
    John Wachop's, 3, 133–4, 145–6
  size of, 1–2, 4
  troops sent to England (1688), 4, 180, 182, 195–6
Arran, James Hamilton, 1st Earl of, 31
Articles of War, revised, 182
Artillery, train of, 180
Arundel, 180
Ashby, John, 145
Assembly of Peers, 196

Assizes, 93
Association of Protestant Officers, 143, 185–8
Atcherley, Peter, 42
Aungier, Ambrose, 65
Avaux, Claude de Mesmes, Comte d', 160, 174
Aylmer, Mathew, 145, 156
Axminster, 186

Babbington, Arthur, 120
Babbington, Philip, 120, 125
Baggott, Richard, 207
Balcarres, Colin Lindsay, 3rd Earl of, 146
Barlow, William, 207
Barnes, William, 208
Barnet, quarters in, 88
Barracks, 86, 88–9
Barrett, James, 36
Barrillon, Paul, 131, 177
  and James II, 106
Barry, Edmund, 36
Bath, John Grenville, 1st Earl of, 31, 107, 143, 147–8
  seizes Plymouth, 191
Beaufort, Henry Somerset, 1st Duke of, 30–1, 45
Beaumont, John, 27, 120, 143, 151–4, 187
Bentinck, William, 187
Bere, Forest of, see Forest of Bears
Bellasise, Sir Henry, 122, 147
Bellasise, Thomas, 41
Bellingham, Allan, 44, 47, 48
Berkeley, John, 31, 149
Berkeley, John, 3rd Baron, 145, 190
Bertie, Charles, 47, 149
Bertie, Henry, 47
Bertie, Peregrine, 47
Bertie, Richard, 47, 48
Berwick Address, 110
Berwick, James Fitzjames, 1st Duke of, 41, 48, 151, 153
Berwick-on-Tweed, 9, 183
  civil–military relations in, 89, 99, 108
  curfew in, 92
  fall of (1688), 193
  garrison of, 171
  officers as M.P.s in, 107
Beverley, Robert, 48

Bideford, civil–military relations in, 99
Billingsley, Lewis, 207
Bingham, John, 63
Blackader, William, 146
Blakeston, Sir William, 169
Blackheath, 181
Blathwayt, William, 9, 38, 84, 86, 90, 91, 94, 180, 183, 207
  fees of, 179
Blessington, Murragh Boyle, Viscount, 63–4
Bludworth, Sir Thomas, 47
Blunt, Sir Thomas Pope, 110
Bohun, Edmund, 104
Boisleduc, 189
Bonfoy, Samuel, 146–7, 191
Booth, Sir William, 208
Bothwell Bridge, Battle of (1679), 121
Boyle, Henry, 74
Brandenburg–Prussia, army of, 83, 175
Bradshaw, Dering, 39
Brandling, Ralph, 27
Brandon, Charles Gerard, Lord, 33
Brathwayt, George, 26
Brent, Robert, 107
Brentwood, civil–military relations in, 99
Bridgeman, William, 61
Bridgewater, 176
Bristol
  civil–military relations in, 88, 99
  garrison of, 24
  riots in, 101
  and 1688, 173, 191–2
  treatment by James II, 110
Brooke, George, 72–3
Brown, Ambrose, 47
Brown, Thomas, 42
Brudenall, Lord Francis, 45–6
Bubb, Jeremiah, 192
Buckley, Sir Richard, 175
Buda, Siege of (1686)
  British officers at, 41–2
  re-enacted, 78, 96
Bulstrode, Sir Richard, 133–4
Burke, Ulick, 71
Burlington Bay, 169–70, 174
Burlington, Richard Boyle, 1st Earl of, 74
Burnet, Gilbert, 21, 140, 148
Burrage, Captain, 126
Burrington, Charles, 185

Burton, Richard, 41
Butler, George, 40, 45
Butler, John, 207
Butler, Lieutenant, 72
Butler, Walter, 63
Byng, George, 145, 156

Cambridge, 106
Camden, Baptist Noel Wriothesley, Viscount, 13
Carew, Thomas, 39
Campaign of 1688, 183–98
Campbell, Lieutenant, 193
Cannon, Alexander, 127
Cappagh, Laird of, 112
Carlingford, William Taafe, 2nd Earl of, 124
Carlisle, 111
   army pressure in, 111
   fall of (1688), 192
   garrison of, 9, 171
   loyal celebrations in, 106
   officers as M.P.s of, 107
   remarks about, 39
Carlos II, King of Spain, 42
Carne, John, 27, 33
Carnes, Réné de, 62
Carney, Charles, 29
Carruthers, James, 98
Cartwright, Thomas, Bishop of Chester, 100
Carvell, William, 193
Castanaga, Marquis de, 42
Catholics, removed from army (1688), 195; *see* Officers, catholic
Cavalry, 173
Chappell, John, 24
Charles, Landgrave of Hesse-Cassel, 5
Charles I, King of England, 83
Charles II, King of England, 10
   and Anglo-Dutch Brigade, 123–4
   and absolutism, xv, 84, 204
   death of, 1
Chatham, 178
Chelsea, 88
Chelsea Hospital, *see* Royal Hospital, Chelsea
Cheshire, 191
   rising in (1688), 173
   treatment by James II, 110
Chester, 100, 180, 181
   garrison of, 7, 9, 24, 171
   meeting of James II and Tyrconnell at, 59, 131
   quarters in, 89
Chesterfield, Philip Stanhope, 2nd Earl of, 192
Chicheley, Sir John, 181
Chivers, Henry, 207
Christian V, King of Denmark, 5
Churchill, Arabella, 149
Churchill, Charles, 190
Churchill, George, 145, 148, 207
Churchill, John, 1st Baron, 27, 45, 110, 138, 140, 142–3, 148, 163
   and John Beaumont, 154
   and conspiracy, 148, 159
   defection of, 190
   and James II, 157
   and Hugh Mackay, 147
   reorganises army (1688–89), 197
Churchill, Sarah, Lady, 148
Churchill, Sir Winston, 12
Civil–military relations, 85–95, 98–101; *see also under individual towns*
   in Scotland, 95
Cirencester, 186
Clarendon, Henry Hyde, 2nd Earl of, 61, 63, 100
   complains to Sunderland, 64–5
   observations on Irish recruits, 66
   weak position of, 64
Clarges, Sir Walter, 48
Clark, Edward, 41
Clarke, George, 91–2
Clavering, William, 27
Cleland, William, 146
Clifford, Robert, 186
Clifford's Fort, 181
   garrison captured (1688), 193
Clifton, Sir William, 31
Clothing contractors, 69–70
Clinkard, Archibald, 44, 207
Coggleshall, 168
Coke, John, 47
Coke, Thomas, 13
Colchester, 182
Colchester, Richard Savage, Viscount, 155, 163, 185
Cole, Nicholas, 207
Colnbrook, 88
Colombine, Ventris, 122

Index

Commissariat, 98
Commissions, England
  cost of, 37, 46
  purchase of, 27–8
Commissions, Ireland
  cost of, 72–3
  compensation for loss of, 72–3
Common law, 93–4
Compton, Sir Francis, 184, 186–7
Compton, Hatton, 159, 184, 187
Compton, Henry, Bishop of London, 100, 149
Condon, Thomas, 38, 208
Coningsby, Thomas, 13
Conspiracy, 173, 184–8, 205
  aim of, 138–9
  history of, 148–50
  knowledge of, 141–4
  plans, 159
  success of, 139, 162–3, 187–8
Conspirators, 159
  channels of communication, 159–62
  connections with Monmouth, 163
Constable, William, 47
Constable, Sir William, 119
Cooke, Captain, 198
Cooke, Richard, 44
Cooke, William, 151, 153
Coote, Richard, 2nd Baron, 62, 75, 175
Copley, Lionel, 192–3
Cornbury, Edward Hyde, Viscount, 40, 139, 149, 184
  defection of, 159, 186–7
  wealth of, 157
Cornwall, 174
  civil–military relations in, 99
Cornwall, Henry, 27, 31, 45
Cornwall, Wolfran, 145
Corporations, officers serving on, 108
Councils of war, 180, 188–9
Court-martial, 46, 91–4
  at Hounslow Camp, 92
  of Portsmouth Captains, 153
Courtney, James, 98
Coventry, 111
Crawford, David, 38
Crawford, Robert, 208
Culpepper, John, 44
Cunningham, John, 75
Cunningham, Henry, 75
Curragh, Irish army camp on the, 65, 78

Cutts, John, 42, 130, 156

Dalyell, Thomas, 28
Dalton, Captain, 35
Danby, Thomas Osborne, 1st Earl of, 142–3, 147, 163, 173–4, 191
  and conspiracy, 148, 159–61
Darcy, John, 47, 142, 149
Darcy, Nicholas, 64
Dartmouth, George Legge, 1st Baron, 31, 145, 158, 162, 169–70
Declaration of William of Orange, 161
Deane, John, 208
Defections to William of Orange, 159, 184–8
Delamere, Henry Booth, 2nd Baron, 104, 149, 163, 172, 191
Delaval, William, 44
Dempsey, James, 71
Dempsey, Lawrence, 64, 71, 78
Denmark
  relations with Sweden, 178
  standing army of, 5
Denmark, Prince George of, 140, 142, 190
Denmark, Princess Anne of, 89, 148
Deputy Lieutenants, 109
Derby, William Stanley, 18th Earl of, 191
Desertion, 92–4, 180
  and Anglo-Dutch Brigade, 129
  a felony, 93
  in 1688, 194
  at Portsmouth (1688), 153–4
  Scotland, 92–3
Devon, 174
Devonshire, William Cavendish, 4th Earl of, 142, 147–9, 163, 173
Discipline, 91–6
  Anglo-Dutch Brigade, 126, 129, 175
  Scotland, 99
Dissenters, 88–9
Dongan, Thomas, 70
Dongan, Lord Walter, 42
Dorrington, William, 64, 66, 71
Dorset, 190
Dorset, Charles Sackville, 6th Earl of, 149, 158
Douglas, Archibald, 33
Douglas, James, 28
Dover, 171

Huguenot church at, 100–1
Dover, Henry Jermyn, 1st Baron, 2, 31, 40, 189–90
  malpractices of, 34
Dragonades, 110–12
  Scotland, 111–12
Drumlanrig, James Douglas, Earl of, 149, 190
Drummond, William, 28
Dryden, John, 8–9
Dumbarton, George Douglas, 1st Earl of, 28–9, 37
Dumblane, Peregrine Osborne, Lord, 141, 160
Durham, 192
  recruitment in, 31
Dutch invasion fleet, 168
Dutch invasion force, 169–70, 173–6, 183–4, *see* United Provinces, army of
Duties, England, 99–112
Duties, Scotland, 101, 110–12
Dyckveldt, Everard van Weede, Heer van, 141

East Claydon, Bucks., 99
East India Company, army of, 42
Ecclesiastical Commission, 100
Edgeworth, Sir John, 196
Edict of Nantes, revocation of, 175
Edinburgh, 98, 101
Education, military, 40–2
Edwardes, Sir Francis, 48
Egerton, Sir John, 48
England, population of, 103
Errington, John, 25
Errington, Thomas, 25
Etherege, George, 158
Evelyn, John, 37, 99, 129, 143, 168
Exclusion Crisis, xvi, xvii, 1
Exeter, 99, 147, 176

Fairfax, Charles, 48
Fairfax, Thomas, 63
Fairfax, Thomas, 5th Baron of Cameron, 149
False musters, 45
  in Ireland, 70
  in Portsmouth, 153
Fenwick, Sir John, 27, 120, 183, 191–2, 208

Ferrall, Gerald, 70–1
Ferrers, Robert Shirley, 1st Baron, 31
Feversham, Louis de Duras, 1st Earl of, 45, 142, 183–4, 189–90
  arrest of, 197
  competence of, 185, 188
  disbands army, 195
Fife, Frederick, 41
Finchley Common, 180
Finland, troops from, 175
Fitzgerald, Fr. Ambrose, 76
Fitzgerald, Sir John, 64
Fitzgerald, Robert, 62
Fitzherbert, Humphrey, 193
Fitzwilliam, Charles, 47
Flood, Ralph, 38, 40
Flower, Thomas, 74
Foliott, Richard, 42
Forage, shortage of in 1688, 168
Forbes, Arthur, Lord, 65, 196–7
Forbes, Sir Robert, 42, 65
Forest of Bears, 193–4
Fortifications, England, 57, 100, 178
Fortifications, Ireland, 57
Foster, Ferdinand, 208
Foster, Mr., 162
Foubert, Henri de, 26
Foubert, Solomon de, 26
Foulkes, John, 125
Fox, Charles, 47, 190
Fox, James, 125
France, army of, 3, 5, 83, 103, 120; *see* Louis XIV, King of France
France, British troops in (1672–78), 18
Frankland, Sir William, 98
Frederick II, King of Prussia, 150
Freeman, Ralph, 44
Freeman, William, 44

Gage, Henry, 24, 33, 197
Gainsborough, Edward Noel, 1st Earl of, 48
Games, William, 45
Garrisons, *see under individual towns*
Garrison governors, 107, 111
Gasshion, Henry, 44
George, Prince of Denmark, *see* Denmark, Prince George of
Gerard, Sir Gilbert, 208
Gibson, John, 123, 124–5
Gifford, John, 109

Index

Glorious Revolution, xiii, xiv, 139
Gloucester, 110
Godden v. Hales, 20
Godfrey, Charles, 149, 155, 158, 163, 185
Godolphin, Francis, 193
Godolphin, Sidney, 131
Godolphin, Sir William, 143
Goodricke, Sir Henry, 149
Gordon, George, 1st Duke of, 29
Governors, see Garrison governors
Grafton, Henry Fitzroy, 1st Duke of, 43, 138, 140, 142, 148–9, 156, 161–2, 190, 193, 197
Graham, James, 208
Graham of Claverhouse, John, 28
Graham, Ronald, 62
Granard, Arthur Forbes, 1st Earl of, 63, 65
Gravesend, 99, 171
Great Yarmouth, 7, 98, 99
Greenwood, Mr., 162
Grenville, Sir Bevil, 208
Grenville, John, 208
Grey de Ruthin, Henry Yelverton, 15th Baron, 149
Griffin, James, 40
Grimston, Sir Samuel, 110
Guernsey, 98, 99, 144
Guildhall, the, 196
Guillims, John, 25
Guise, Sir John, 44, 161, 175, 192
Gwynn, Sir Roland, 175

Haggerston, Sir Thomas, 94
Hales, Sir Edward, 31
Halifax, George Savile, 1st Earl of, 143, 148
Hamburg, 197
Hamilton, Anthony, 76, 78
Hamilton, Charles, Lord, 42
Hamilton, James, 64
Hamilton, Richard, 27, 48, 78
Hampden, Richard, 163
Hanmer, Sir John, 111, 192, 208
Harrington, Sir Thomas, 207
Harris, Edward, 208
Harwich, 181
Hastings, Ferdinando, 147, 191, 208
Hatton, Charles, 38, 140–1, 143–4, 157, 179
Hawley, Thomas, 208

Head, Sir Richard, 21
Henderson, James, 29
Henry, Philip, 7
Herbert, Arthur, 148, 156, 160, 183
Herbert, William, see Montgomery, William Herbert, Viscount
Hesse-Cassel, 5, 120
Heyford, Anthony, 187
Hill, Thomas, 99, 106
Hire of troops, 120–1
Hodges, Robert, 95
Holman, George, 33
Holmes, George, 91
Holmes, Sir Robert, 192, 208
Holt, Sir John, 93
Holy Island, 88
Honiton, 99, 186
Hope, John, 159
Hôtel des Invalides, L', 84
Hounslow Heath, 24, 29, 40
  army camps on, 37, 87, 92, 96–8, 163–4, 158–9, 179
Howard, Bernard, 111, 118 n. 99
Howard, Francis, 111
Howe, (Jack) John Grubham, 155
Howe, Sir Scrope, 147, 185
Huguenots, 130, 132
  officers, 121, 175
Humble and Hearty Address to all the English Protestants in this Present Army, 154
Hume, Patrick, 127
Hume, Sir Patrick, 127
Humières, Marshal d', 189
Huntingdon, 111
Huntingdon, Theophilus Hastings, 7th Earl of, 31, 38, 143–4, 191
Hull, 87, 108, 110–11
  fortifications of, 41, 178
  garrison of, 9, 86, 90, 171
  in 1688, 174, 179, 182, 192–3
Humber, the, 173
Hussey, Sir Thomas, 88, wp8,'
Hutchinson, John, 208
Hyde Park, 96

Intelligence in 1688, 169–70
Invasion, attitudes towards the, 141
Invitation, the, 139, 140, 160; see also 'Seven', the
Ipswich, 143, 182
Irish, hatred of, 184

'Irish Alarms', 195–6
Isle of Wight, 171, 192, 197

Jacob, Sir John, 38, 147, 191
James II, King of England
  and absolutism, 84, 204
  accession of, 1
  aims of, xiv, 104
  and Anglo-Dutch Brigade, 123–4, 126–7, 129
  and army discipline, 43–6
  and Bristol, 110
  closeting, 47–8
  and conspiracy, 139, 142–3, 161–2
  and defections (1688), 188
  and disbandment of army, 195
  and dissenters, 88–9
  and Hounslow Camp, 96–7
  and Huguenots, 100–1
  intelligence of Dutch plans, 169–70
  interest in military, 40–1
  and Irish army, 57–60
  and Lichfield's foot, 158–9
  and London, 88–9
  mental state of (1688), 188
  and militia, 6–8
  and Parliament, 10–14
  patronage of, 163
  plans (1688), 169–70
  policy of, 84 *et passim*
  political use of army, 85–91, 100–12, 204
  preparations (1688), 177–83
  and Portsmouth Episode, 153–4
  and officers, 46–50, 107–10, 163
  retreat by (1688), 189
  relies on army, 102
  revenue of, 5, 19
  at Salisbury Plain (1688), 140, 184–5
  and Scotland (1688), 184
  strategy (1688), 169–73, 176, 182–4, 189–90
  and William of Orange, 177–8
James, Prince of Wales, *see* Stuart, James Francis Edward, Prince of Wales
Jeaffreson, Christopher, 99, 106
Jeffreys, George, 1st Baron of Wem, 94
Jennison, William, 27
Jephson, William, 155, 158, 163, 185
Johnson, Samuel, 154
Johnston, James, 148

Jones, Ambrose, 72
Jones, David, 104–6
Jones, Henry, 72
Journal du Voyage d'Angleterre, Le, 174–5
Justices of the Peace, 109

Keynsham, 191
Kilmainham Hospital, 68
King, Edward, 42, 207
Kirkby, Roger, 208
Kirke, Percy, 27, 86, 91, 138, 142, 143, 145, 156, 163–4, 190

Lacey, Robert, 64
Lancashire, 110, 191
Landguard Fort, 143, 171, 181, 182
Langdale, Marmaduke, 2nd Baron, 160, 182, 193
Langston, Thomas, 27, 40, 139, 155, 156, 159, 163, 184, 186–7
Lanier, Sir John, 27, 31, 143, 157, 163, 182, 183, 184
Lascelles, Talbot, 39
Lauderdale, John Maitland, 1st Duke of, 121
Law and the army, 91–4; *see also* Common law; Court-martial; Desertion; Discipline; Martial law
Lawson, Henry, 48
Lawson, Sir John, 26
Lawson, Philip, 26
Leach, Sir Simon, 208
Leck, William, 169
Leeds, 89
Legard, Thomas, 42
Leicester
  quarters in, 88, 90
  recruitment in, 32
Leicester, Robert Dudley, 1st Earl of, 119
Letter to the English Army, 154
Leveson, Richard, 207
Levy Money, 33
Lillingstone, Henry, 120
Lillingstone, Luke, 120
Littleton, Sir Charles, 27, 87, 178, 208
Littleton, Henry, 188
Littleton, Walter, 27, 44, 186–7
Liverpool, 110, 180
Livesey, John, 186

Livingstone, Lord George, 195–6
Lloyd, William, Bishop of St. Asaph, 148
London, 173
   civil–military relations in, 98, 171
   defence of (1688), 171
   garrison, 1, 9, 88–9
Lords Justices of Ireland, 62, 72
Loughborough, 94, 99
Lovelace, John, 3rd Baron of Hurley, 160, 186
Louis XIV, King of France, xvi, 5, 6, 10
   and Anglo-Dutch Brigade, 131
   and army, 83
   attacks Spanish Netherlands (1688–89), 189
   and James II, 177
   and William of Orange, 174
   see also France, army of
Louvois, François Michel le Tellier, Marquis de, 150
Lowestoft, 160
Lowick, Robert, 26
Lowther, Sir John, 148, 192
Lumley, Richard, 1st Baron, 31, 47–8, 142, 192

Macarty, Charles, 24–5, 91
Macarty, Justin, 63, 78
Macclesfield, Charles Gerard, 1st Earl of, 175
MacDonnell, Alexander, 65
McGennis, Murtagh, 68
Mackay, Aeneas, 145–6
Mackay, Hugh, 123–4, 129, 145, 176
   and John Churchill, 147
Magdalen College, Oxford, 100, 153
Maidenhead, 189, 194
Maine, Edmund, 190, 194, 208
Man, Captain, 162
Manchester, Charles Montague, 4th Earl of, 149, 161
Marches, speed of, 170
Margate, 170
Marlborough, 183
Marriage of soldiers, 122–3
Martial law, 92, 93
Martin, John, 8
Mary of Modena, Queen of England, 106
Mary Stuart, Princess of Orange, *see* Orange, Mary Stuart, Princess of
Mathews, Edward, 125, 126

Mauleverer, Sir Richard, 207
Maulle, Thomas, 158
Medway, the, 171, 178, 181
Meeting houses, 88–9
Meldrum, Sir John, 119
Melfort, John Drummond, 1st Earl of, 28
Melton, Gregory, 89
Members of Parliament, 107–8
Mercenaries, 120–1
Mews, the Royal, 105–6
Middleton, Charles, 2nd Earl of, 12
Middleton, William, 120, 128
Military discipline, 77
Miremont, Armand de Bourbon, Marquis de, 33
Militia, xvi, 1, 6–13, 32, 60, 181–2, 186
Mockerhide, Dutch camp at, 78
Mohun, James, 196, 208
Monmouth, James Scott, Duke of, 155–6
   rebellion of, 2, 6, 172, 174
Montgomery, William Herbert, Viscount, 42, 48, 109, 193
Moody, John, 134
Moore, Rev. William, 8
Moores, Thomas, 169
Mordaunt, Charles, Viscount, 175
Morea, the, 42
Morgan, Charles, 44
Morgan, Henry, 40
Morgan, Sir John, 27, 48
Mountjoy, William Steward, 1st Viscount, 41, 66
Moxon, Robert, 44
Musgrave, Sir Christopher, 107
Musgrave, family of, 192
Musgrave, Thomas, 208
Mutlowe, John, 64

Nangle, Robert, 77
Navy, Royal, 144–5, 148, 177, 179
Neale, Thomas, 207
Negus, Francis, 41
Newark, 182
Newcastle, Henry Cavendish, 1st Duke of, 33, 36–7, 169, 183, 195
Newcome, Henry, 100
Newcommen, Sir Thomas, 70
New England, Dominion of, 104
New York, 104
Nicholas, Oliver, 207
Nimmo, James, 98

Norfolk, 32
Norfolk, Henry Howard, 7th Duke of, 30, 31, 32, 45–6
Nore, Buoy of the, 145
Norton, Ambrose, 40, 167 n. 64
Northampton, 90
Northampton, George Compton, 12th Earl of, 149
Northumberland, George Fitzroy, 1st Duke of, 190
Nottingham, 173, 191
  civil–military relations in, 89, 98
Nottingham, Daniel Finch, 2nd Earl of, 142, 148
Nugent, Christopher, 65
Nugent, Thomas, 63

Oath of Fidelity, Ireland, 62
Oaths of Supremacy and Allegiance, 62
O'Brien, Terence, 36, 71
O'Connor, Hugh, 29, 37
Officers, 19–20
  ages of, 39
  catholic, 10–14, 195
  discipline, 43–6
  leave, 39
  loyalty of, 140–1
  numbers of, 22–3
  professionalism of, 140–1; see also Professionalism
  religion of, 43–4
  see also Commissions
Officers, Anglo-Dutch Brigade, 145–7, 160
  appointment of, 123–4
  catholic, 127
  numbers returning (1688), 133
  spies from (1688), 145–6; see also Mackay, Aeneas; Bonfoy, Samuel
Officers, Dutch, 121
Officers, England
  appointment of, 101–2
  catholic, 18–27, 109
  in corporations, 108
  dismissal of, 46–50, 142
  expenses of, 36–7
  as J.P.s, 109–10
  loyalty, 84–5, 102, 157; see also Portsmouth Episode
  as M.P.s, 107–8
  politics of, 101–3

purge of, 46–50, 84–5, 102–3
support James II, 107–8
wealth of, 36–7
Officers, Ireland
  in Anglo-Dutch Brigade, 130, 132
  catholic, 68–72
  in Hungary, 65–6
  protestant, 56, 72–5
  purge of, 49
  and William of Orange, 73–4
Officers, Scotland, 28–9
Ogle, William, 208
Oglethorpe, Sir Theophilus, 27, 35, 208
Old Bailey, 93
Oliphant, Lawrence, 29
Oliphant, William, 29
Orange, Mary Stuart, Princess of, 149
Orange, William, Prince of, xiv, 143
  aims (1688), 140
  and Anglo-Dutch Brigade, 120–1, 123–4
  boldness (1688), 174
  and conspiracy, 13–14, 140, 159, 163–4
  and Danby, 150
  Declaration of, 161
  and disbandment of English army, 197
  and discipline (1688), 175
  and France, 189
  as a general, 177–8
  haste of (1688–89), 189–90
  and international affairs (1688), 174
  intervention of (1688), 173
  invasion plans, 143, 173–4
  and Louis XIV, 174
  objectives (1688), 205–6
  outnumbered (1688), 184
  and Plymouth, 191
  problems (1688), 141, 171–2
  and propaganda, 175–6
  reorganises English army, 197–8
  strategy (1688), 173–4, 182
  and Treason Club, 159
  unorthodoxy of (1688), 177–8
Ordnance, Board of, 178
Orme, Thomas, 151–3
Ormonde, James Butler, 1st Duke of, 6, 60
Ormonde, James Butler, 2nd Duke of, 142, 145, 148, 149, 163, 181, 190
Ormskirk, 110

Orwell, the, 181
Ossory, Thomas Butler, Earl of, 120–1
Oxford, 168
   civil–military relations in, 95, 99
   recruitment in, 30
Oxford, Aubrey de Vere, 20th Earl of, 48, 119
Oxford Parliament (1681), xvi, 105, 155

Pack, Simon, 44, 151–2
Palatine, destruction of the, 150
Pargiter, Henry, 72
Parker, John, 94
Parker, Robert, 61, 65
Parliament, xvi
   of 1685, xvii, 10–14
Parsons, Sir John, 208
Parsons, Robert, 122, 127
Paske, William, 193
Paston, Thomas, 151–2
Paz, Samuel de, 141
Pembroke, Thomas Herbert, 8th Earl of, 8, 123–4
Pendennis, 99, 174
Penn, William, 162
Pensions, 35–6
Pepys, Samuel, 158, 169
Perth, James Drummond, 5th Earl of, 28–9
Peterborough, Henry Mordaunt, 2nd Earl of, 31
Petre, Fr. Edward, 26
Petty, Charles, 97
'Peyton Affair', the, 128
Peyton, Sir Robert, 128, 175
Phillips, John, 73
Pinney, Jane, 98
Pinney, John, 98
Plantte, Jean Martin de, 133
Plymouth, 87
   fortification of, 174
   garrison of, 9, 24, 144, 171
   in 1688, 143, 146–7, 174, 191
Plymouth, Thomas Windsor, 1st Earl of, 31
Pope, Roger, 208
Port, John, 151, 153
Porter, James, 42–3, 130
Portsmouth, 87, 173, 183
   civil–military relations in, 99
   fortifications of, 178
   garrison of, 9, 86, 151, 171
   garrison officers, 108
   in 1688, 180, 193
   Irish soldiers in, 99
   quarters in, 86, 90
Portsmouth Episode, 143, 151–4
Power, Richard, 77
Powis, Elizabeth Herbert, Marchioness of, 194
Powis, William Herbert, 1st Marquis of, 194
Preston, 110
Preston, Richard Graham, 1st Viscount, 12
Professionalism, 27–8, 39–42, 84–5, 102, 140–1, 150–4, 157, 204
Propaganda, 175–6
Purcell, James, 101

Queenborough, 107, 118 n. 99
Quarters, 85–91
   abuse of, 85–91
   free, 87–9, 90
   location, 39
   payment for, 86–7, 90
   registration of, 9
Quarter Sessions, 93

Radcliffe, William, 27
Rade, Henri de Caumont, Marquis de, 133, 134
Raleigh, Thomas, 196
Ramsgate, 170
Ranelagh, Richard Jones, 1st Earl of, 12, 197
Reading, 189, 194
Recruitment, 30–3
   of Anglo-Dutch Brigade, 121–2, 147
   in Ireland, 66–7
Regan, Tege, 71
Regimental agents, 69
Regulators, the, 107
Religion, 154–5
Reresby, Frances, 97
Reresby, Sir John, 21, 38, 40, 45, 89, 94, 107, 179, 181, 207
Richards, Jacob, 41
Richards, Solomon, 33, 41
Richards, William, 158
Riddell, Mark, 27
Roads, state of (1688), 168

Rochester, 178
Roscommon, Wentworth Dillon, 5th Earl of, 61
Rose Tavern, 149, 155–6, 158, 164
Royal Hospital, Chelsea, 36, 84
Rupert, Edward, 41
Russell, Bartholomew, 25
Russell, Edward, 160, 161
Rycaut, Sir Paul, 70
Rye House Plot, 1

St. Albans, 110
St. Albans, Charles Beauclerk, 1st Duke of, 48
St. George, Sir Oliver, 41, 62, 74, 190
Salisbury, 4, 99, 183
Salisbury, James Cecil, 4th Earl of, 33
Salisbury Plain, 140, 144, 168, 173, 183–4, 190
Sanderson, Thomas, 27
Sarsfield, Patrick, 40, 78, 193
Saxony, 120
Scarborough, 107, 174, 191
Scarsdale, Robert Leke, 3rd Earl of, 31, 40, 48
Schomberg, Frederick Herman von, 1st Duke of, 40
Scilly Isles, 193
Scotland, 138, 160, 184
Scott, John, 44
Sedgemoor, Battle of, 2, 96
Sedley, Sir Charles, 158
Sellicock, John, 110
Serch, Edmund, 35
'Seven', the, 140
Seven Bishops, the, 150
Seymour, Sir Edward, 12
Shadwell, Thomas, 158
Shakerley, Peter, 38, 89, 107, 194
Shales, John, 98
Sheerness, 87, 171, 178, 180
Sheldon, Dominic, 62, 64, 72
Sheldon, Ralph, 72, 109
Sherborne, 98
Shere, Sir Henry, 197
Sheridan, Thomas, 73
Shrewsbury, Charles Talbot, 12th Earl of, 31, 47–8, 141, 161, 186, 192
Sibley, John, 188
Sidney, Henry, 123–4, 140–2, 147–8
Skelton, Bevil, 33, 125–6, 128

Slater, Solomon, 128
Slingsby, Henry, 33, 208
Soldiers, Anglo-Dutch Brigade
  escape of (1688), 134
  marriage of, 122–3
  morale of, 122–3
  quality of, 121, 129
Soldiers, Dutch, 172, 174, 176
Soldiers, England
  catholic, 29–30
  condition of (1688), 172, 183–4
  duties of, 100
  and Irish soldiers, 194
  loyalty of, 150–1, 194
  politics, 150–1
  quality of, 30–1, 34–6
Soldiers, Ireland
  duties of, 56
  escape from Isle of Wight, 197
  numbers dismissed, 68
  popularity of, 99–100, 194
  at Portsmouth, 151
  re-regimented, 196
Somerset, 174, 190
Somerset, Charles Seymour, 6th Duke of, 31
Spanish Netherlands, 42–3
Spies, 145–6, 160
Statutes of Parliament
  Disbanding Act (1679), 85
  Militia Act (1661), xvi, 7
  Mutiny Act (1689), xvi, 87
  Penal Laws, 141
  Test Acts, 141
Stafford, Henry, 1st Earl of, 33
Stamford, Thomas Grey, 2nd Earl of, 149
Standing armies, development of, 83–4, 203
Stearne, Robert, 61
Steward, William, 41
Stour, the, 181
Strangways, Thomas, 32
Strode, Bernard, 39
Stuart, James Francis Edward, Prince of Wales, 106
Studd, Joseph, 129
Sunderland, Robert Spencer, 2nd Earl of, 1, 107, 177, 179
Sussex, 197
Sweden, 175, 178

Switzerland, 175

Taafe, John, 63–4
Talbot, Jack, 43
Talbot, Sir John, 27, 48, 207
Talbot, Mark, 42
Talmash, Thomas, 130, 156, 187
'Tangerines', the, 156–7, 185
Tangier, 10, 18, 156, 158
Tankard, Christopher, 149
Tees, the, 172
Tempest, Nicholas, 27
Temple, Sir Richard, 12, 48
Tenison, Thomas, 143
Tern, Henry, 44
Thanet, Thomas Tufton, 6th Earl of, 31
Thirty Years' War, 203–4
Thompson, James, 126
Thornton, Hamond, 35
Three Questions, the, 151
Tidcomb, John, 38, 147, 191
Tiffin, Zachariah, 190
Tilbury Fort, 38, 171, 193
Tollemache, Thomas, see Talmash, Thomas
Topsham road, 176
Torbay, 140, 173, 183
Tower Hamlets, 180
Tower of London, 180
Townley, Anthony, 73
Trant, Dominic, 25
Trant, Sir Patrick, 25
Trapps, Nicholas, 24
Treason Club, 149, 155–9, 164, 185
Trelawney, Charles, 27, 138, 142–3, 148, 156, 163–4, 190, 208
Trelawney, Henry, 208
Trelawney, Sir Jonathan, 148
Trevanion, John, 26
Tufton, Sackville, 27, 38–9
Turckheim, Battle of, 177
Turenne, Henri de la Tour d'Auvergne, Vicomte de, 177
Turner, Francis, Bishop of Ely, 195
Twist, Charles, 93
Tyne, the, 181
Tynemouth Castle, 169, 181
  capture of garrison, 193
Tyrconnell, Richard Talbot, 1st Earl of
  and Anglo-Dutch Brigade, 131
  assumes control in Ireland, 60–1
  behaviour of, 61, 64–5
  caution of, 62–3
  and Ormonde, 63
  policy in Ireland, 57–67

United Provinces, the, 2
  army of, 74, 120, 121, 175; see Dutch invasion force
  attitudes towards, 141
Upnor Castle, 178
Uxbridge, 88, 195

Vaudrey, Edward, 41
Venice, 42
Vere, Aubrey de, see Oxford, Aubrey de Vere, 20th Earl of
Verney, Edmund, 99
Villiers, Sir William, 208
Vincent, Edward, 208
Visconti, Fr., 134

Wachop, John, 132
Walden, Lionel, 208
Walker, Obadiah, 101
War
  of the Grand Alliance, xvi
  in Hungary, 19, 40–2, 65–6
  projected with France, xvii
  see Thirty Years' War
Wars, Anglo-Dutch, xvii
Warcup, Lenthall, 37
Ward, William, 93
Warminster, 183
Warrington, 110
Warwick, 94, 111
Wear, the, 172
Weather, 98, 168, 172, 173, 174
Webb, Edmund, 47
Webb, John, 207
Weimar, 120
Wentworth, Sir Michael, 48
Werden, Robert, 182
Westbourne, John, 160
Wharton, Henry, 44, 150, 185
Wharton, Philip, 4th Baron, 149
Wharton, Thomas, 13, 149, 155, 158, 185
White, Jacob, 94
Whitehall, as a military base, 105
Wicksteed, Mr., 162
Widdrington, Edward, 27
Widdrington, Ralph, 38

Wigan, 99, 110
Wilford, Thomas, 208
William of Orange, see Orange, William, Prince of
Willoughby d'Eresby, Robert Bertie, Baron, 47, 149
Will's Coffee House, 158
Wilson, Edmund, 47
Wiltshire, Charles, Paulet, Earl of, 186
Wincanton, 193
Winchendon, 149
Winchester, 111, 118 n. 99
Winchester, Charles Paulet, 6th Marquis of, 147
Windsor, civil–military relations in, 99
Windsor Castle, 105
Windsor Great Park, 175
Winraham, George, 146
Wooburn, 149
Wood, Anthony, 99
Worcester, Charles Somerset, 4th Marquis of, 48, 148
Wray, Chichester, 208
Wray, Sir Edward Baptiste, 26
Wren, Sir Christopher, 105–6
Wrexham, 110
Württemberg, 120
Wycherley, William, 158
Wycke, Colonel, 21
Wyndham, Sir Charles, 208

Yarmouth, Isle of Wight, 192
Yarner, Abraham, 62
Yeates, Samuel, 44
Yonge, James, 87
York
  civil–military relations in, 95, 99, 101
  garrison of, 1, 9, 171
  quarters in, 89
  in 1688, 148, 173–4, 179, 181, 191
Young, Sir Walter, 88